The 1986
Price Guide
to Goss China

William Henry Goss in his smoking chair, taken by Adolphus around 1880

The 1986 Price Guide to Goss China

Nicholas Pine

Milestone Publications

Published by
Milestone Publications
Goss & Crested China Ltd.,
62 Murray Road,
Horndean, Hampshire PO8 9JL

Design Brian Iles
Photography Michael Edwards Studio, Havant

Typeset by Inforum Ltd., Portsmouth
Printed and bound in Great Britain by
R.J. Acford, Industrial Estate, Chichester, Sussex

British Library Cataloguing in Publication Data

Pine, Nicholas J.
  The 1986 price guide to Goss china.
  1. Goss porcelain——Prices
  338.4′3738′27   NK4399.G6

ISBN 0-903852-74-8

Contents

Acknowledgements

I wish to thank all those who have been kind enough to notify me of new pieces in order that this catalogue might be updated. In particular Alan Aldrich, Ted Bond, June and David Brown, Joan Dodds, Sheila and Alan Donnelly, Stephen Godley, Len Harris, Tony Munday, Maurice Regnard, Pat Tillbrook, Peter Tranter, Graham Walder, Celia Waller and John Varley. Michael J. Willis-Fear, M.A. has been very helpful and supportive, for which I am most grateful.

I also with to thank the following members of the Goss family for their assistance. In particular, Major W.R. Goss and also Dorothy and Harold Goss, Clara Goss and Valentine Taggart.

Alex Shaw has been researching diligently and carefully for many years and his work and photographs have been of great value.

Ever faithful, John Galpin has once again allowed us unhindered access to his collection and many of the illustrations in this book are of his pieces.

Norman Pratten has advised on and edited the manuscript in a most professional manner for which I thank him sincerely.

Without the invaluable knowledge and support of my wife, Lynda, this book would be incomplete. I thank her together with my fellow directors and staff of Goss & Crested China Ltd who constantly record new models and suggest improvements, in particular Vanessa Amis, Alison Tanner and Christine Hogben.

John Magee will always merit a credit in any book about Goss China. He set Goss China on its present popular course and even now in his retirement from the world of Goss, his wisdom and advice are still as positive as ever.

Introduction

This fourth edition of *The Price Guide to Goss China* includes details of more than fifty new pieces and variations which have been discovered since publication of the 1984 guide. Numerous detail corrections and improvements have been made and the height or other main dimensions of virtually every piece has been stated.

The wares produced by the Goss factory can be divided into three periods as follows:

The First Period	1858–1887
The Second Period	1881–1934
The Third Period	1930–1939

The first period covers ware manufactured by William Henry Goss whilst he owned and ran the factory. The second period spans the stewardship of his sons Adolphus, Victor and William Huntley. The third period embraces wares made by other factories but which carry the Goss mark.

The guide has been re-structured to divide the products of The House of Goss into these three periods. The first period covers ware produced from the start of the firm in 1858 to 1887 and includes the early Victorian unglazed figurines, together with the series of famous portrait busts and terracotta wares.

The earliest crested models were made towards the end of the first period and the reader's attention is drawn to the introductory comments in each chapter in order to be able to differentiate the wares of one period from another. In particular, the first period ornamental ware chapter introduction establishes the distinguishing features of the early crested wares which will enable such pieces to be accurately identified.

The second period is from 1881–1934 and encompasses the introduction of heraldic china, the bulk of which was mass produced and comprises named models and special shapes, ornamental and domestic wares. Those pieces that were also produced during the first period have the following symbol [1] after their respective entries, but as the models and shapes were also made for many years during the second period, and it would be confusing to have chapters on both named models and special shapes in two periods, they are all catalogued in one chapter in the second period. Also included are dolls, miniatures, cottages, crosses, fonts and animals, all under separate headings due to their importance.

Also re-structured are the sections on domestic, utility, and ornamental wares, to assist the reader to locate pieces more easily. The tiny domestic items

The Goss factory in Sturgess Street, Stoke-on-Trent. Note the Goshawk carved in stone and set in the gable wall

The Goss ovens pictured in 1984. Since this photograph was taken, all the original outbuldings have been cleared and a large warehouse now abuts the rear of the ovens

not made for daily use have been classified as ornamental and are re-named fairy shapes as this is how they were originally known. Each piece is catalogued as per its reference in The Goss Records. There are page references in parentheses where items are listed in The Goss Record Eighth, Ninth and War Editions. These books were published originally between 1913 and 1921. They have been reprinted by Milestone and give the flavour of Goss collecting at the time as well as having a full description of the history and origin of most of the originals from which the Goss models were made.

Although the last member of the Goss family to own the pottery sold out in 1929, the crested souvenir china continued to be made in the same way until 1934. Therefore the date given for the end of the period is 1934 when the firm went into receivership.

The third period, from 1930–1939 covers the heavier and more colourful ranges of pottery, introduced to revitalise flagging sales. Although the coats of arms still continued to appear on a range of vases, utility shapes, comical animals and buildings, they are very different from those of the previous period and values are generally lower. Not all of these have the mark 'Goss England' but the heavier, duller quality and more garish colours used in the decoration are easily distinguished. Also in this section are the brightly coloured toby jugs, flower girls, the beige pottery 'Royal Buff' tea sets and the 'Cottage Pottery' domestic ware attractively shaped as thatched cottages. This beige pottery is comparatively fine and has a good 'ring' to it.

Information on The Goss Records, Postcards, the League of Goss Collectors, Cabinets and Leaflets are contained in earlier chapters thereby providing the reader with as much information as possible.

The Goss pottery was ahead of its time and a market leader. The difficult times shared by the pottery industry in England in the last century led the three hundred or so other local potbanks to copy its successful heraldic lines before the turn of the century, and they capitalised on the serious flavour of Goss models by producing generally more light-hearted and amusing shapes. All known crested china made by these other firms is contained, along with their values in *The Price Guide to Crested China* by Sandy Andrews and Nicholas Pine, published in 1985.

Please note that the values indicated in this guide are for shapes only and do not take into account the value of any arms or decorations. Exceptions to this are the League models and the named models bearing matching arms. Prices are given for both matching and non-matching where both exist, and the correct matching arms are listed. Elsewhere, where there are matching arms the additional premium is given. For all other additional crest and decoration values please refer to this guide's sister volume *Goss China Arms, Decorations and Their Values* by Nicholas Pine which was revised in 1982 and lists and values some 7,000 different decorations to be found on Goss porcelain.

Thus, to find the value of any given piece, firstly look it up in the Price Guide, then add any premium for the motif from *Goss China, Arms Decorations and Their Values*.

This 1986 edition of the guide contains many more photographs, especially of first period wares, most of which are now over 100 years old. I shall be continuing to improve and update my listings and will be very pleased to hear about any item of Goss which has not yet been catalogued.

Prices quoted in this guide are for pieces in perfect condition. Worn gilding, faded coats of arms, chips, cracks and bad firing flaws will all affect values substantially. A small crack could easily halve the value, whilst a cottage worth £100 would probably only be worth £25 with a chimney missing.

Although it is always possible to get a damaged piece restored, it is easy to detect restoration. Where the value of a restored item would be greater than that of the same piece in a damaged state, then restoration would be worthwhile. However, inexpensive, sub-standard pieces have always been popular and make it possible for those with limited resources to obtain the rarest specimens. Indeed, damaged Goss has risen in value proportionately more than perfect Goss in recent years.

Over the last few years, the majority of prices have increased steadily. The cheaper ranges have enjoyed higher percentage rises than pieces over, say, £70–£100. The last guide saw certain brown crosses and higher priced models come down in value, but these have now begun to rise again. Matching arms have risen sharply, averaging some 100% in two years.

When the first edition of this guide was published in 1978, the name Goss was still relatively unknown in the antique world. Now nearly all collecting authorities are aware of Goss china and are slowly appreciating its quality, which places it on the same level as the products of many of the more well-known manufacturers.

Prices within are drawn from seventeen years of experience in buying and selling Goss china, and for the majority of that period making an orderly market in this ware and researching the subject. Auctions have never been a good source of price information as such outlets often tend to be used as clearing houses for sub-standard and inferior wares. No auction house as yet really understands or cares about Goss china and this often results in as many bargains as 'rogue' pieces being knocked down. Auction houses are, in my experience, potential minefields for the unwary and there really can be no substitute for knowledge.

Value Added Tax has always been a problem in that it is included as part of the normal retail selling price by Goss & Crested China Ltd, the leading dealers, but not apparently by many others. Indeed, it has often been found that minor unregistered dealers have been charging the same prices as this company and in so doing have in effect been overcharging by some 15%.

In order therefore that prices in this guide should be directly comparable with those quoted elsewhere, VAT has not been included in the value of items under 100 years old which attract this tax.

The leading forum for buying and selling is *Goss & Crested China*, a 28 page illustrated monthly catalogue published by Goss & Crested China Ltd.

Each edition contains examples of pieces from every section of the factory and is available by annual subscription.

There are two clubs for collectors of Goss china. The Goss Collectors Club (Secretary Mrs M Latham, 3 Carr Hall Gardens, Barrowford, Nelson, Lancashire BB9 6PU) publishes a monthly magazine, holds regular regional meetings, and occasional Goss fairs. The Crested Circle (Editor Robert Southall, 42 Douglas Road, Tolworth, Surbiton, Surrey KT6 7SA) publishes a bi-monthly magazine which includes Goss and other crested china items. The Circle also holds specialist crested china fairs.

A photograph of the factory and Ashfield Lodge taken by M.J. Willis-Fear in the 1960's. The spoil heap can be seen in front of the Lodge.

1 · A History of the Goss Factory

The production of porcelain at the firm of W H Goss of Stoke on Trent spanned four reigns and nearly a century from 1858 to 1929. The family-run firm was headed by William Henry Goss, who had learned his trade and gained essential knowledge of chemistry under the personal guidance of Alderman Copeland of the Copeland Works, also in Stoke. It was a small business in the early days when the founder's children were all young and the total work force numbered less than twenty. The Falcon Works was one of 120 potteries, struggling to survive in the smoke, dirt and grime of the area known as 'The Potteries' in Staffordshire. The pottery towns included Burslem, Hanley, Lane End, Shelton, Fenton and Longport (Longton) as well as Stoke. These towns had sprung up along the same turnpike road in an area where coal, water power, canals, lime-stone and raw clay were all available or easily accessible.

In a line of business where masters notoriously ill-treated their work force and used child labour (children down the mines at this time fared better), William Henry Goss, along with other enlightened potters including Minton, Copeland and Wedgwood, campaigned for better working conditions and treated his own staff generously.

When Goss was an impressionable young man of thirteen (he married at sixteen!) the first parian was produced at the Copeland Works by John Mountford in 1846. This was quickly followed by a similar material at Minton's, and very soon all the major factories were using this medium to produce elegant classically styled figures, portrait busts of politicians, notable dignitaries of the day, royalty, poets, authors and musicians. As eventual chief artist and designer at Copeland, William Goss continued to produce similar lines when he became his own boss. These were difficult and costly to produce, and the larger part of his substantial income was derived from the sale of coloured enamels, made up to his own special recipes, to other potteries for decorating china.

He also produced a small range of terracotta ware, using the local marl or clay. In 1867 he had a brief partnership with a Mr Peake, and a few pieces exist marked 'Goss and Peake', mainly terracotta. Mr Peake had financial difficulties as a result of his own activities, and William Goss dissolved the partnership after one year.

Goss's other specialities included jewelled scent bottles and vases, which were produced from pierced and fretted parian, with inset cut glass jewels in the Sèvres style, but more successful than that firm in the setting and firing of the stones. This method was patented in 1872, but jewelled ware ceased to be made after 1885. The noted perfumier Eugene Rimmel was one of the factory's

Adolphus Goss, 1887

customers, having perfumeries in Rome, Paris and London.

Other lines during this first period of Goss china production included intricate flower baskets for table decoration, brooches, spill holders (one in the shape of Dr Kenealy, the then Member of Parliament for Stoke whom Goss loathed) and a bullock and sheep group – a special order from America.

The second period of Goss production is marked by the entry of his eldest son, Adolphus, into the management and the introduction of heraldic ware. This was to completely supersede the previous ware due to its popularity and ability to be mass produced (though not in the way things are today!) More importantly, Goss became a household name and collecting Goss china a national hobby.

It was Adolphus who realised there was a growing market in providing for the day tripper, because of the introduction by law of holidays for workers, the expanding network of railways across Britain, and the increasing popularity of the seaside, approved of by Queen Victoria herself.

It was his idea that visitors to seaside resorts and other places might like to take home a miniature china ornament as a souvenir. To give it local interest he proposed that it should bear the town's coat of arms. The shape would be the reproduction of some vase, jar or urn of antiquarian interest, such as those found in the local museum. He and his father shared a love of heraldry and archaeology and Adolphus hoped to use these porcelain models to create an interest amongst the middle and working classes in these subjects whilst at the same time enticing the public to buy Goss china as an artistic memento of a visit or holiday.

He enthusiastically explained his idea to his father and expected him to be delighted, but instead was immediately turned down and told that the scheme was not a viable proposition. Adolphus was naturally very disappointed but being the strong minded person he was (his motto was 'Make up your mind and let no one alter it'), he made up a few prototype glazed parian models, applied coats of arms in the form of transfers hand painted with enamels, and managed to get William to agree. 'Crested china' as it is now popularly known started from there. It was not long before this heraldic ware entirely replaced the factory's previous output of figures and busts. This led to a five year building plan to treble the floor space in order to cope with the incredible demand.

Throughout this period of production, only one selected agent was appointed in each town or city. These agencies were only allowed to sell their own town's coat of arms or transfer printed view, but after 1883 they could order any shape instead of being restricted to their own local shapes. For instance, the Gloucester agent could only sell Gloucester Jugs up until that date; thereafter he stocked a wide variety of models, but they all bore the Gloucester crest. In those days, if you wanted a Land's End crest, you had to go to Land's End to purchase it. There was no other way!

It fell to Adolphus, with his business drive and enthusiasm, to be the firm's travelling salesman, spending more and more time away from home visiting

Victor Goss, 1887

suitable places to obtain permission to use the local arms, sketch new models to reproduce, secure agencies and take orders. He was so thorough and successful that he ceased to have anything more to do with the daily running of the firm. By 1900 he had organised 481 agencies inland. He considered he was the mainstay of the business and called himself 'Goss Boss', which irritated William intensely. Letters that passed between father and son reveal a strained relationship and, as our research has shown, life in the Goss household was not easy with such a stern Victorian father as William.

In 1893 Adolphus introduced a new range of coloured miniature cottages. The first three were Ann Hathaway's, Shakespeare's Birthplace, and Burns' Cottage, Ayrshire. This new line proved immensely popular and it was gradually extended to 42 buildings in various sizes. In the latter half of the firm's life, some cottages were glazed which tends to intensify the colouring. This was a good line for improving sales at a time which was particularly poor for British exports, and when the china trade was suffering a depression.

It is hardly surprising therefore, that most of the other pot banks turned their hand to producing crested china, though not one ever reproduced the Goss quality in glaze, parian body, gilding or enamel colour. These were all the secret recipes of William Goss, though they were leaked to the Irish firm Belleek, in 1863 when eleven Goss workers were persuaded to leave in order to save the factory at Belleek in Co Fermanagh. Belleek china using Goss recipes was produced from 1863 onwards, and even today's pieces are similar to Goss. Far sighted firms such as Arcadian, Carlton, Shelley, and Willow Art found a viable trade in modelling animals, especially in amusing and comical poses, buildings, the originals of which were to be found throughout Britain, household objects, military and other items. In this way they catered for the lower end of the market. True Goss enthusiasts, however, would accept no imitations.

J. J. Jarvis, a keen collector, began producing a series of booklets entitled *The Goss Record*, the purpose of which was to provide a catalogue of agents' names, addresses and opening hours. Agencies ranged from restaurants, bazaars, hotels, chemists, and Station bookstalls to local libraries. The first edition was in 1900, and a supplement in 1902 includes 601 British agents and the first foreign agent in Bermuda. By 1921 in the ninth edition there were 1,378 British agencies and 186 overseas in 24 countries.

The range of arms and models was fabulous, all made with care and hand painted to ensure perfection with an exactness one can only admire. The modern souvenir of today formed from plaster of Paris is a sad reminder of how standards have fallen.

The death of the head of the firm in 1906, and Adolphus's exclusion from a share of the firm in his father's will did not affect the boom years of 1900–1914. The third son Victor, who took over the firm (second son Godfrey had also fallen from favour) was killed in a riding accident in 1913. He was a good businessman, but not so Huntley, who was the last son and left in sole charge of the firm. In an attempt to survive the Great War, a range of battleship and

(Richard) John, son of Huntley, designer of the Goss animals and some cottages

Huntley and daughter Margaret Goss, 1920

An original Goss recipe book detailing ingredients for parian

regimental arms was introduced, as were a couple of dozen copyright models, but they were not enough to save the pottery from the decline in trade after the war and Huntley Goss sold the firm and the rights to its trademark in 1929 to Cauldon Potteries, having paid every bill and every wage due.

The new owners continued producing heraldic ware for another four years, but began to specialise in good quality earthenware and pottery similar to that of their other factories which included Arcadian. All of this new ware was marked Goss, Goss England, or Made in England. A new company formed in 1931 by Harold Taylor Robinson known as 'W H Goss Ltd' traded with himself as director, using the Goss mark on shapes made from moulds from other factories. He was declared bankrupt in 1932, having been personally responsible for the takeover of 32 companies, including firms which supplied his potteries with fuel and clay in order to produce more cheaply. He had had to weather the Great War, the 1921 coal strike, the loss of foreign trade with international markets unsettled, Britain going off the gold standard in 1924 and the worldwide depression of the 30's. He said, 'When I saw the depression was developing to the extent it was, I left my country house and came to live practically next door to the works and I have been working 50 weeks out of 52 to try to circumvent the terrible effects of the depression. When you get down to the basic facts you will realise that as the largest potter in Staffordshire, I have been the largest victim.'

The range produced during this third period of the factory was very colourful and distinctive. William Henry Goss would certainly not have approved, but it suited the changing tastes and moods of the roaring 20's. A popular line was the beige pottery tea sets called 'Cottage Pottery' decorated with pictures of cottages with hollyhocks and full beds of flowers.

Commemorative mugs and beakers were issued for the Silver Jubilee of King George V and Queen Mary in 1935, the Coronation of Edward VIII in 1937 and King George VI and Queen Elizabeth in 1937. The last commemoratives were for the 1938 Glasgow Exhibition and were decorated with green trim instead of the usual gilding.

Production ended mid 1940 and all lines stopped, including the coloured flower girls in the style of modern Doulton ladies. The Falcon works were used by a number of different companies after 1940, with uses including the manufacture of parachutes during the Second World War but today they are occupied by a clothing manufacturer. The Goss ovens still stand, in a state of disrepair but deservedly the subject of a preservation order.

2 · Factory Marks on W H Goss Porcelain

The wares of this factory are easy to recognise because virtually every piece was marked, usually on the base. W H Goss himself said that the black printed Goshawk with wings outstretched and the firm's name in capitals underneath, was in continuous use from 1862 onwards. This distinctive factory mark gave rise to the name of the Falcon Works, by which the pottery was known locally.

Before this, the earliest products from the beginning of the firm in 1858 were impressed during manufacture whilst the clay was still damp. They were impressed **W H GOSS** with serif type-face, that is, with cross-lines to the end of a stroke in a letter. This mark was used up until 1887 when the W H GOSS mark was used sans serif, i.e. plain lettering. This seems to have been applied to some shapes and not others right up until 1916 at least, usually with the Goshawk as well.

I have come across many examples of poorly placed impressed factory marks. Often just W H G is visible, or even perhaps the last few letters of GOSS. When inspecting an unmarked piece, check the base and sides, and in the case of busts, the shoulders and back most carefully for even a hint of part of the magic mark. Positive Goss identification will certainly add to the value of anything apparently unmarked at first sight.

Many of the first period busts and figures were incised or printed in longhand with details such as the following:–

> Published as the Act directs (See 54.Geo.III.C 56.)
> W. H. Goss.
> Stoke-on-Trent.
> 1 Dec 1073.
> Copyright

Minor variations in this wording occur.

This identification became standard when used on the majority of the Parian busts, figures and groups produced during the mid-1870's through to 1911. It was either stamped into the still-wet porcelain or transfer-printed onto the finished piece in black, and reads:

> Copyright as Act directs
> W. H. GOSS.
> Stoke-on-Trent.
> 1 November 1881.

Gold, red or puce mark without words. Approx. 1858

Incised inscription on large bust in W.H. Goss's own hand

Black detailed printed mark on Figurine

Black printed mark, 1867

Incised inscription with impressed W H Goss

Black printed mark on terracotta

Serif impressed mark 1858–1887 approximately

Impressed Serif Copyright Mark on a Bust, 1876

Sans-serif impressed mark 1887—1916 approximately

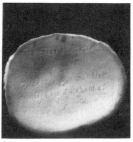

Incised mark on Dr. Kenealy Spill holder in W H Goss's own hand

Impressed Serif Copyright Mark on a Bust, 1881

Incised inscription on a Bust in W H Goss's own hand

Incised mark on Dr. Kenealy Match and Spill Holder

Serif impressed mark 1858–1887 approximately

Incised mark on The Bootblack, 1873

Written mark on Pepper Pot 1895–1925

The normal Goshawk 1862–1927

Black printed mark on a bust

Black printed mark on Bust

Black printed mark on Bust of Queen Victoria

Serif impressed mark 1887—1918 approximately Stamped mark with registration date

Scarborough Flags Plate special mark

Goshawk showing Registration mark

Goshawk and date on Churchill Toby Jug

or, more fully:

Copyright
Pub. as Act Directs
(See 54. Geo III. C 56)
W. H. GOSS.
Stoke-on-Trent.
22 Jany 1893.

These are particularly useful as they incorporate the publication date, which is not necessarily, of course, the date of manufacture of that particular piece.

Identification details varied and this style of marking, usually on the reverse, was in use from the early 1870s until 1911. The dates used in this way are the publication dates of the respective shapes, and not necessarily the date of manufacture. Often only one of a pair of figures, vases or ewers was marked.

The earliest Goshawk was coloured red, gold or puce and appears without the firm's name printed beneath it. Pieces marked in this way are rare and possibly unique such as the cross in the form of a pendant, or the Alhambra Vase.

Terracotta wares were marked with a black printed w h goss or goss and peake, during a brief period of financial partnership with a Mr Peake. See TERRACOTTA, Chapter 9D for full details.

Some first period figures also carry a GOSS AND PEAKE printed mark, usually the four or six line transfer printed copyright mark.

The common black Goshawk was used up until 1934 on heraldic ware and after 1935 the mark was distinctively blacker and thicker, and often applied over the glazed bases of the late colourful pottery, usually accompanied by the word ENGLAND under the firm's name. The printed titles on the base of beige pottery include 'Cottage Pottery', 'Royal Buff' and 'Hand-painted'. These were third period and date between 1930 and 1939. Margaret (Peggy) Goss is said by her family to have introduced the Little Brown Jug as a new line. As her father, Huntley, sold the works in 1929, quite possibly some of the beige ware made afterwards could have been planned by Peggy and Huntley Goss.

Another late line was delicately coloured lustre which was applied to named models as well as domestic ivory porcelain. No arms were applied to these pieces, and handles were thickly coated with gold as well as having gilded rims. It is generally believed these date from 1925 and were rubber stamped with an enlarged Goshawk some 16mm square.

The tiny coloured brush strokes on the bases of most armorial Goss are the signatures of the paintresses. W H Goss was particularly concerned to keep up his high standards, and in order to be able to detect any shoddy workmanship or incorrect colouring of the arms, each paintress had her own symbol which she painted on the base of each of her pieces, in whatever colour she happened to be using at the time. Offenders were given three warnings before being sacked, so in all probability this clever system kept them all on their toes!

Impressed mark G5 on a Goss doll

Goshawk, registration number and agents name

League model inscription. Note the artists mark

Goss England mark on a Flower Girl. Note also the Artists Mark.

Very late Goshawk mark. Probably Post 1930

Post 1930 late mark

Large rubber stamp Goshawk 1925 and after

Royal Cauldon mark over-printed by a Goshawk Post 1925

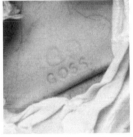

Impressed mark on a Goss doll 1920–1930 approximately

W.H. Goss England Cottage Pottery mark

W.H. Goss England Royal Buff mark

W.H. Goss England hand painted late mark

One only has to compare the products with those of other manufacturers to appreciate their skill. Occasionally, a gilder's mark in gold can also be seen.

A blue Goshawk was used on an experimental range of models decorated with underglaze blue designs which are also marked SECONDS or REJECTS.

Many pieces are marked COPYRIGHT, others have registration numbers on their bases. For a detailed explanation of these see REGISTRATION NUMBERS and COPYRIGHT MARKS Chapter.

3 · Notes for the Collector

MINOR VARIATIONS IN SIZE

Where the dimensions of items are given, these have been obtained from actual specimens and refer to the height unless otherwise stated. Where an approximate measurement is quoted, no immediate specimen has been to hand, and the best available information source has been used.

Where no dimension is given, it has not proved possible to gain access to information other than to confirm the existence of that model.

With regard to slight fluctuations in size in the same model, it must be borne in mind that variations in firing temperatures may give rise to these and, in any case, shrinkage in firing can be as high as ten per cent. In early Goss items this figure is said to be higher, and certainly first period wares have a tendency to firing-cracks and flaws which the factory overcame around 1890. Examples of items particularly prone to having many minor differences in size are Loving Cups, Wall Pockets and Busts. These pieces do have a certain charm, if not importance and should not be disregarded because they lack the excellence of the second period wares.

FORGERIES

Very few forgeries of Goss china have appeared. Those that have usually take the form of a forged Goshawk on a piece that clearly did not originate from the Goss factory. These Goshawks are either crudely rubber stamped or drawn in Indian Ink. The giveaway must always be the quality of the piece the mark appears on. If it is not the fine perfect parian body that is consistent with Goss then look very closely at the mark. Compare a possible forgery with a correct normal mark, and also look at the quality of the porcelain.

In the end however, recognition of forgeries rests with the experience and the knowledge of the collector and there can be no substitute for handling Goss as often as possible in order to familiarize oneself with the ware.

Occasionally forged cottages appear. All Goss cottages produced are listed in the appropriate chapter in this book. Any other cottage which purports to be Goss is most definitely not so if it does not feature in the exhaustive list given. Shakespeare's Cottage is a particular exception as so many sizes were produced by both Goss and other crested manufacturers. A forged example has been found of the half-sized, solid base model as well as the 105mm full length size. The latter cottage is well made and is only prevented from being condemned as a true forgery by carrying the inscription *Reproduction of Model of Shakespeare's House*. It carries the correct registration number and the usual Goshawk so look for the words *Reproduction of* in this case.

THE BLACKPOOL COAT OF ARMS

Presumably at the request of the then Blackpool Agent, the Blackpool coat of arms was placed on a number of items which would not normally carry a coat of arms. Collectors may find it a little distracting to be faced with Blackpool on, for instance, a Manx Cottage, a Lincoln Imp, a St. Columb Major Cross, a Lucerne Lion, a Goss Oven, or even a Cornish Stile, and these are only a few of the examples that may be found.

Another feature of Mr. Naylor, the Blackpool Agent after 1913 was the sale of named models from which the descriptive matter had been omitted. This, together with an over generous use of gilding (e.g. on the ears of the Lincoln Imp) has tended to give some collectors the impression that Blackpool wares are second-rate, and should be generally avoided. Almost all, however, that was sold through the Blackpool Agency, which changed hands at least four times between the years 1901 and 1921, was perfectly normal and correct.

No collection can be considered really complete without an example of these oddities – while the more staunch Blackpudlians may even consider trying to specialize in these wares.

Price-wise, it is felt that items which should not be carrying arms, but are found to have the Blackpool coat of arms tend to detract, reducing the value of the item by, say, between one-third and two-thirds.

However, many items which would otherwise have been factory rejects (by virtue of firing flaws, distortions, etc.,) have been sold through the Blackpool agency and therefore carry the Blackpool arms. Such pieces would be worth around one-third of the normal perfect model and every Blackpool crested item should therefore be closely inspected in order to determine whether or not it was a factory second.

REGISTRATION NUMBERS

No piece of Goss is worth any more or less whether it carries a registration number or not. There is no reason why some pieces carry their number and some not. The production of Goss china was never an exact science and the only reason for putting the registration number on a piece was to prevent other firms from using the design.

Two different aspects were registered. Firstly, the shape or model and, secondly, the decoration. Some pieces have one number which could refer to either and some carry two numbers indicating that both the model and decoration were designed and registered by the Goss factory.

Registration numbers were used from 1884 until they were discontinued in 1914. The following tables give the dates of first registration of numbers between 1 and 630174. It should be noted that the dates given here indicate only the first registration of a design and not the exact year of manufacture. From the time patents began in 1883, registered designs could only run for four years, but were renewable, with a maximum life of 15 years.

Registration numbers were not used by the factory after July 1914, but it should also be remembered that a number tells us only when the registration took place, not when the piece was made which might well be years afterwards.

Rd No   1 registered in Jan. 1884
Rd No   19754 registered in Jan. 1885
Rd No   40480 registered in Jan. 1886
Rd No   64520 registered in Jan. 1887
Rd No   90483 registered in Jan. 1888
Rd No 116648 registered in Jan. 1889
Rd No 141273 registered in Jan. 1890
Rd No 163767 registered in Jan. 1891
Rd No 185713 registered in Jan. 1892
Rd No 205240 registered in Jan. 1893
Rd No 224720 registered in Jan. 1894
Rd No 246975 registered in Jan. 1895
Rd No 268392 registered in Jan. 1896
Rd No 291241 registered in Jan. 1897
Rd No 311658 registered in Jan. 1898
Rd No 331707 registered in Jan. 1899
Rd No 351202 registered in Jan. 1900
Rd No 368154 registered in Jan. 1901

First Registration No. for 1902   385088
First Registration No. for 1903   402913
First Registration No. for 1904   424017
First Registration No. for 1905   447548
First Registration No. for 1906   471486
First Registration No. for 1907   493487
First Registration No. for 1908   518415
First Registration No. for 1909   534963
First Registration No. for 1910   554801
First Registration No. for 1911   575787
First Registration No. for 1912   594182
First Registration No. for 1913   612382
First Registration No. for 1914   630174

COPYRIGHT MARKS

After the Great War the firm brought out a new range of models including the Egyptian numbered and many other foreign shapes. Most of these had the word COPYRIGHT printed underneath in an attempt to stop other factories copying them. This does not add or detract in the value of the piece but it does indicate it was produced in the latter stages of the second period or early part of the third.

When the factory could not obtain a local authority's permission to use their coat of arms, or if a town did not possess arms, it became necessary to design them. These home made arms were like seal crests, within a consistent circular pattern, using some local symbol usually lifted from the town's arms, for the centre, such as a fish for Newquay to denote a fishing port. The registration number for these seals was 77966 and this was printed on the base of every piece bearing such arms. See *Goss China Arms, Decorations and Their Values* Chapter A.

NON-PRODUCTION WARE

Fragments of pieces that did not go into production have been found in the factory spoil heap. Models seen have been listed below and should perfect examples come to light, the author will be pleased to receive details. Some items are, of course, known with different colouring and glazing and will be found elsewhere in this guide.

White Glazed:
Abbots Kitchen – Glastonbury
Stratford Toby jug and basin
Churchill Toby jug
Bust of Lady Godiva
Ripon Hornblower and verse (Third Period)
Monmouth Mask, The Knight
Crucific Pendants, varying floral designs
Cigarett Holders –
    numerous with occasional examples in coloured lustres
Single Ear –
    on flat base with pierced hole for hanging. Not made as part of a head.
    70mm
Pixie on toadstool

White Unglazed:
Shakespeare standing, leaning on a lectern
    Very large size. Estimated at 330mm

Coloured:
Massachusetts Hall
Sandbach Crosses, brown
    As listed in *The 1978 Price Guide to Goss China* but not seen in one piece
St. Tudno's Church Font. Pale yellow
Thistle Preserve Pot and lid, with thistle knop
Tortoise (Third Period)
Brooches, black
Preserve Pot and lid. Multicoloured, Geometric Art Deco decoration.

4 · The Goss Records

Around 1900, it became obvious to the many collectors all over Great Britain that some sort of catalogue of agents' names and addresses was necessary to enable enthusiasts to plan their excursions. It could prove daunting to make a long, difficult trip to a far away town in search of a Goss agency which may or may not exist. Also, the agent for any area could be a shopkeeper, hotel owner, pharmacist, librarian or the owner of the local fancy stores or bazaar who often kept irregular hours.

J. J. Jarvis, an enterprising collector, approached William Henry Goss and put forward his idea of producing such a listing of agencies. William told him that he had been asked many times before, but he was a busy man, and thought it would be too time-consuming to continually keep updating such a publication with additions and changes of addresses. The thought of constant revision had deterred him. Eventually, mainly through Huntley Goss's help, Mr Jarvis won William's confidence and gained the vital permission required to publish the first *Goss Record* towards the end of 1900, for a shilling a copy. Mr Jarvis, who lived at Riversdale, Enfield, Middlesex, did not have any financial interest in the Record's production, and the proceeds were donated entirely to a fund promoted by the Misses Evans of 58 Holly Road, Handsworth, Birmingham, for giving a Christmas tea and entertainment to some of the poor slum children in their area.

The first Record produced in 1900 was a hand-duplicated sheet, not even stapled or bound. It listed the authorised agent in each town the factory produced arms for, the address, the models and coats of arms stocked together with details of opening hours. Jarvis was limited in the number of copies he could produce by duplication, and the few that he did produce sold out immediately. He was by now receiving letters from all over the country requesting further copies still and he became determined to write a further edition with all the latest information about new models being made, to bind it properly and make a book of it. By having the Record printed and bound professionally, he could have a large quantity produced. Huntley Goss checked the rough draft and made any corrections and additions. In the interests of accuracy, Mr Jarvis wrote to every known agent and asked them to reply confirming the particulars he had of them. Most complied with this request, but some were too lazy or too busy to reply and so providing he thought their addresses were correct, Jarvis kept them in his listing but printed their entries in italics. He was quite happy to send collectors details of any later changes on a free list that he was continually adding to, upon receipt of the stamps for postage.

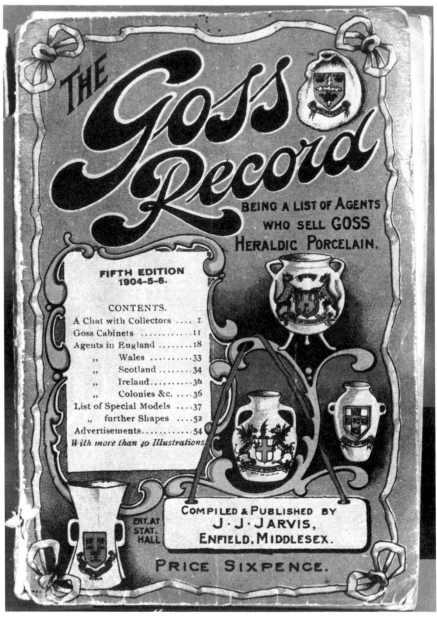

The Goss Record Fifth Edition 1904—5—6

Goss &
Crested China
Limited

Incorporating Milestone Publications

62 Murray Road Horndean Hants PO8 9JL
Telephone Horndean (0705) 597440
Facsimile Horndean (0705) 591975

with compliments

Certain statements had to be made in the *Goss Record* in order to satisfy the Goss factory management. One was: 'I am not personally acquainted with Mr Goss, or in any way financially interested in his business, but I take this opportunity of thanking him most sincerely for the trouble he has taken and the assistance he has given me in compiling this book. J. J. Jarvis.' Another statement was, 'Mr Goss will not supply any of his porcelain except through individual agents; arms of one town where an agency exists cannot be obtained off an agent in another town.' Also contained in *The Goss Record* was the warning, 'Collectors are warned against many inferior imitations of Goss porcelain, mostly of foreign manufacture, that are being sold.'

The agents themselves were very pleased with Jarvis as he increased their trade. In April, 1902, he published an 8-page supplement giving the latest corrections and amendments. In August of that year he produced the second 'Goss Record'. By the time of the third edition, it was not just a list of agencies but contained snippets and hints to collectors and details of the latest shapes being made together with their historical background. With this edition there were also asterisks against certain agencies in the list which signified which particular shopkeepers would be prepared to open after hours to sell Goss to those collectors unfortunate enough to arrive after the close of business for that day. It also contained photographs of the latest Goss models, which were numbered. For example, the Salisbury Gill was No. 127. This was to facilitate pieces ordered from agents by post. Agents also advertised their wares in *The Record* and other adverts included were for such ingenious inventions as the 'Doylesava', a circular glass pane for protecting lace doilies from cakes and the 'Dursley Pederson' cycle which looked remarkably uncomfortable and was supposed to be the 'featherweight of featherweights' in cycling. The 4th edition was a supplement to the 3rd.

The 5th edition in 1905 had a shiny grey cover decorated with artistic sketches of various matching Goss models which, incidentally, Jarvis collected. He related a tale in which he admitted he was responsible for Mr Goss's office being bombarded with requests for an agency list in 1900 from all over Great Britain. This had led to Mr Goss sending the requests to his home in Enfield together with permission to produce the first *Goss Record*.

By now his printing bills were in pounds, not shillings, and his postage bill was £50 a year alone – a terrific sum in those days when one considers that small Goss models were retailing for 9d each! The Record could be obtained directly from him or through most Goss agencies. This fifth edition was 68 pages long and very much larger, thus reflecting the growing popularity of the porcelain and increased output of the factory. Also announced was the League of Goss Collectors. Jarvis formed this in 1904 and was advertising for members in the 5th edition. All readers were eligible for membership.

A few years earlier he had formed a small exclusive club for his own friends but now decided to make it national as its usefulness might be extended if it had a wide following. Leaflets were enclosed advertising the arms of the League, and a form for joining. Cabinets were also advertised from this edition onwards.

The 6th *Goss Record* appeared in 1906. Those copies produced before W H Goss's death on January 4th 1906 were encased in a red binding, those produced after his death had a purple binding and contained an obituary, extending the book to 96 pages. This was a very interesting booklet, full of information.

Three years elapsed before the 7th edition appeared in October 1909. Jarvis announced that a total of 70,000 of the various editions had been sold to date and that the 8th would be printed in 1912. In fact, there was a short supplement to the 7th in 1911, and the 8th did not appear until 1913, not long before the outbreak of war. Jarvis had by that time handed publication over to Evans Bros, the London publishers, who produced a 104 page book. It may be said that Goss collecting reached its peak that year and that this edition was the best of them all.

The War Edition was a supplement to the 8th and was produced in 1916 as a concise booklet due to the shortage of paper, and sold for only 3d. Earlier Records cost 6d, and the 9th and last edition in 1921 was one shilling. The War Edition announced the 'International League of Goss Collectors' and the regimental and naval badges and war shapes available.

The 9th edition was 80 pages in length and in it Jarvis regretted that the Goss cabinets were no longer available due to difficulties in the furniture trade and the heavy demand for essential articles. Nine years after the last Goss Record the Goss family sold the pottery. The editor became Sir Joseph John Jarvis who kept his Goss collection until he died in Godalming in 1950.

A List of Every Edition with Present Value:–

Value

Goss Record		£ p
1900	1st edition. Duplicated leaflet with 4 subsequent pamphlets.	50.00
1901	1st edition. Printed booklet	60.00
1902–3	2nd edition (supplement to 1st)	60.00
1903	3rd edition	60.00
1903	4th edition (supplement to 3rd)	60.00
1904–6	5th edition	25.00
1906–7	6th edition Red binding (no obituary)	30.00
	Purple binding containing an obituary of W H Goss	25.00
1909–11	7th edition	25.00
1911	Supplement to 7th edition	25.00
1913–14	8th edition	20.00
1916–18	War Edition (supplement to 8th). Published by Evans Bros.	35.00
1921	9th edition. Published by Evans Bros	15.00

5 · Postcards

'Goss' postcards were published with the permission of W H Goss by S A Oates & Co. of Halifax who printed on them: 'None genuine without the name "Goss" '.

These cards were published in the latter half of the Edwardian era, postmarks ranging from 1905 to 1912.

They carry the word 'Goss' in gold on a dark blue circular motif in the top left-hand corner, and the description of the particular model at the bottom. (Similarly in gold and on a blue background.) The cards are basically photographs of selected models without coats of arms. It was then for the local agent or stationer to order cards with their own particular town's coat of arms on them. These arms were then over-printed, a process which gives certain combinations of arms and models a peculiar 'flat/round' appearance.

Originally, six cards were produced and sold, if required, in sets, in special envelopes. Later, two further cards were added to the range, and it is these two which are the rarities. The cards are numbered in gold in the top right-hand corner, and are as follows:

Card No.	Model	Value
		£ p
1	Abbot's Cup, Fountains Abbey	4.00
2	Aberdeen Bronze Pot	4.00
3	Ancient Welsh Bronze Crochon	4.00
4	Roman Ewer from York	4.00
5	Loving Cup	4.00
6	Roman Vase from Chester	4.00
7	Bronze Ewer from Bath	8.50
8	Irish Mather	8.50

Prices quoted are for cards in good condition.

No. 1 Fountains Abbey Cup

No. 2 Aberdeen Bronze Pot

No. 3 Ancient Welsh Crochon

No. 4 York Roman Ewer

No. 5 Loving Cup

No. 6 Chester Roman Vase

No. 7 Bath Bronze Ewer

No. 8 Irish Mather

Royal Buff Advertising Ashtray

Late Goss Agents Sign

Goss Agents Change Tray

Third Period Advertising Sign

6 · Goss Cabinets

These were introduced by J. J. Jarvis, Editor of *The Goss Record* and were available from 1905 until 1919.

They were manufactured in six basic types by the firm who made the bookcases for the Encyclopaedia Britannica Company. The following details are taken from the Seventh Edition of the *Goss Record*:–

> These cabinets have been specially designed to hold Collections of Heraldic Porcelain, although equally suitable for other varieties of China, Bric-a-brac, etc. Made by one of the leading wholesale Cabinet Makers in the country to the personal instructions of the compiler of the *Goss Record*, no expense has been spared to produce the most suitable Cabinets to display to advantage the varied shapes of Goss Porcelain obtainable, and the Arms emblazoned thereon.
>
> Every Cabinet is substantially made and well finished. The shelves are lined with green cloth, and the doors fitted with lock and key. They may be had in either Chippendale or Fumed Oak as stated, whilst some are made in both, and each style is priced at the lowest possible figure consistent with the finest workmanship.
>
> A fully illustrated list of Cabinets will be sent on application to the Goss Record Office.
>
> The Cabinets will be sent from the makers direct on receipt of remittance, the carriage being paid by purchasers on delivery; 5s. will be charged for cases and packing unless these are returned carriage paid within 7 days.
>
> The amount paid will be returned in full for any Cabinet not approved of and returned carriage paid upon receipt.
>
> Cabinets may be obtained on the 'Times' system of monthly instalments, particulars of which may be had on application.
>
> All Cabinets bear the 'Goss Arms' on a specially designed porcelain shield, without which none are genuine.

Goss Wall Cabinet, design B

	There are seven types of Cabinets as under:	Current Value £ p
Design A.	A small revolving cabinet in Chippendale to stand on a pedestal or table. 18-ins. square. Holding capacity, 50 average sized pieces inside and 25 outside. Step-shaped shelves from the bottom. Glass sides and top. **Price £2 2 0**	300.00
Design B.	Wall Cabinet 3-ft. 3-ins. wide by 3-ft. 8-ins. high. Holding capacity, 85 pieces. Made in Fumed Oak. A very artistic and pleasing case. **Price £2 18 6**	300.00
Design BB.	The same as B, but with an additional shelf. This will hold 100 pieces. **Price £3 3 0**	300.00
Design C.	A revolving case in Chippendale, somewhat similar to A, but 3-ft. 4-ins. high and 1-ft. 5-ins. wide. This will hold 120 pieces, and where space is a consideration, is an excellent Cabinet. **Price £3 7 6**	300.00
Design D.	As illustration. 4-ft. 6-ins. long by 3-ft. high. Made both in Chippendale and Fumed Oak. The centre door is hinged at the bottom enabling the entire contents to be displayed at once. By a unique mechanical contrivance this door is quite firm when opened. Holding capacity, 125 pieces. **Price £4 4 0**	400.00
Design E.	A handsome Cabinet on legs to stand on the ground, and sliding doors 3-ft. wide and 4-ft. high, will hold 160 pieces. Made in Chippendale or Fumed Oak. **Price £5 5 0**	500.00
Design F.	5-ft. 2-ins. high by 4-ft. wide. Also made in both woods. A very fine Cabinet to hold nearly 200 pieces. The centre is recessed and enclosed by two doors below and one folding door above (as Cabinet D.), whilst the sides are glazed as well as the front. **Price £7 7 0**	700.00

See Goss Record. 8th Edition: Page 109 for illustration of cabinet D in fumed oak.

The porcelain shield alone it worth £75.00 and this is included in the values given above.

Cabinets A and C were of the revolving variety, Cabinets B and D were for attaching to the wall, whilst E and F were free-standing.

Goss Cabinet, design E

7 · The League of Goss Collectors

The League of Goss Collectors was formed in 1904. The initial subscription was 2/6d which entitled the member to a certificate of membership, a copy of *Goss Record* as and when published and a special piece of porcelain bearing the Goss Arms. These Goss Arms were surrounded by the wording 'The League of Goss Collectors', and each model, except the first-issued, bore beneath it the statement *This model is issued to Members of the League and cannot be bought.*

Towards the end of the 1914–18 War, the League spread its wings to become 'The International League of Goss Collectors', and a new model was issued for each year until 1932. These models, together with re-issues of all but the first model, bore a new motif, indicative of the 'International' aspect of the League.

These are the League Models issued:

On joining the League	The Portland Vase.
For members of two years' standing	Ancient Costril or Pilgrim's Bottle.
For members of four years' standing	Staffordshire Tyg.
For members of six years' standing	King's Newton Anglo-Saxon Cinerary Urn.

1918	Cirencester Roman Ewer.
1919	Contact Mine.
1920	Gnossus Vase.
1921	Greek Amphora Vase.
1922	Italian Krater.
1923	Egyptian Lotus Vase.
1924	Wilderspool Roman Tetinae or Feeding Bottle.
1925	Cyprus Mycenaean Vase.
1926	Staffordshire Drinking Cup.
1927	Colchester Roman Lamp.
1928	Fimber Cinerary Urn.
1929	Irish Cruisken.
1930	Northwich Sepulchral Urn.
1931	Chester Roman Altar.
1932	Cheshire Roman Urn.

These pieces are listed and valued in second period E Named Models and Special Shapes chapter.

8 · Advertising Ware and Leaflets

William Henry Goss disliked all forms of advertising and considered that if a product was good enough it would sell itself. Therefore the monthly Pottery Gazette, the trade magazine for pottery and glass manufacturers, did not carry advertisements for Goss until February 1906 – a month after his death!

It is not surprising that other potteries competed with the firm of Goss – W H Goss had left the field so wide open. Toward the end of his life he did accept that china dealers solely engaged in legitimate trade, advertised in order to bring their wares prominently to the notice of their potential customers. Goss agents bought space in *The Goss Record* and probably elsewhere as well.

The advertising material below dates from 1905 with the exception of the shield shaped Goss agents enamel sign which was earlier.

ADVERTISING WARE

		£ p
An unusual Oval Plaque distributed to Goss Agents after 1931 stating 'AGENT FOR W.H. GOSS ART – POTTERY' in red between two Goshawks [3]	Length 220mm	250.00
The Shield from a Goss Cabinet. [2] The shield shape carrying the Goss family arms	70mm	75.00
A Goss Agent's Change Tray [2] One was given to each Agent and bore the arms of his particular town. Examples without arms may also be found	Dia. 140mm	150.00
Plaque shaped with Goshawk in relief at the top and some decoration *GENUINE GOSS COTTAGE POTTERY* [3]	100mm	100.00
Plaque shaped to form Ann Hathaway's Cottage, coloured [3]		65.00
Plaque featuring a toby jug in colour. [3]		65.00
Goss Agents' enamel shop-front sign. Shield shaped	Height 300mm	85.00

LEAFLETS

Queen Victoria's Slipper	10.00
George & Mary Coronation 1911	15.00
Keystones of the Kingdom	25.00
The Loving Cup	15.00
Durham Sanctuary Knocker	10.00

HER MAJESTY'S FIRST LITTLE SHOES.

THE exquisite taste displayed by Mr. William Henry Goss, of Stoke-on-Trent, in his parian and porcelain wares, whether classic and ornamental, or adapted for ordinary domestic use, both in design and material, has been endorsed by prize medals at various of the world's great exhibitions. In one report we read:—"Few displays of porcelain are to be seen in the exhibition which excel those made by Mr. Goss. In the parian statuettes, vases, tazzi, &c., and other ceramic materials under notice, the perfection of art manufacture seems certainly to have been reached."

Mr. Goss is a Fellow of the Royal Geological and of several other learned societies, a chemical expert, an accomplished antiquarian, and the author of a number of valuable biographical, scientific, and literary works.

There is always something touching in looking at the shoe of a little child; for who can forecast the rough and often thorny paths the little pilgrim may have to tread!

Mr. Goss, accidently, in the following manner, got to hear of the Queen's first shoe, which he has now copied and reproduced in porcelain—imitating form, material and colour. The story we give, although it is a story, is quite true.

Her Majesty's father, the Duke of Kent, went to live at Sidmouth, in 1819, to get the benefit of the Devonshire climate. While there, a certain local shoemaker received the order for the first pair of shoes for the infant Princess Victoria. But instead of making two only he made three, while he was about it, facsimiles, and kept one as a memorial and curiosity. It has been preserved to this day, and is now in the possession of his daughter, who is the wife of Mr. Goss's porcelain agent at Sidmouth.

Hearing of this, Mr. Goss borrowed the shoe, and made an exact copy in porcelain. The dainty little shoe is four inches in length, has a brown leather sole, white satin upper, is laced and tied in front with a bow of light blue silk ribbon, and bound with the same round the edge, and down the back of the heel.

In 1820 the shoemaker received the Royal Warrant; and that, also, is preserved with the interesting little shoe.

This little porcelain model, so suggestive, will arouse the loyal thrill of love and blessing in thousands of British hearts, simple little Cinderella sort of thing as it is; while to Her Gracious Majesty herself, it must touch a minor chord that vibrates back to the far reach of memory.

A. J. S.

Queen Victoria's First Shoe leaflet

"THE KEY-STONE OF THE KINGDOM.

" WE do not know whether Mr. Goss, to whose exquisite
and masterly works of Art we have more than once called
attention in our pages, intended in the preparation of the
well modelled portrait before us, to pay Lord Beaconsfield
the high compliment contained in the words we have placed
at the head of these few lines, or not—but this we do know,
that the form he has chosen carries out the idea in the most
emphatic and striking manner, and conveys to the mind an
impression that the compliment was as fully intended as it
was deserved.   The design is, literally, a key-stone—the
centre stone of an arch—and from this, standing out in
alto-relievo, is a marvellously powerfully modelled, speaking,
and well-thought-out life-size head of the present Prime
Minister, Lord Beaconsfield, in all the freshness and vigour
of that mental capacity that so eminently distinguishes
him.   Mr. Goss has won a high and deserved reputation for
the excellence and truthfulness of his portrait busts, and
this one is perhaps one of the happiest and best that even
he has produced.   The head is not only a faithful portrait
of the *features* of the man, but is almost an inspired production, that presents a perfect reflex of the mind that animates
those features.   The modelling is faultless.   We ought to
add that, as a companion to this one, Mr. Goss has produced in a similar manner a very striking head of Lord
Derby, which deserves equal praise with that of Lord
Beaconsfield."

Leaflet sold with the Keystones of the Kingdom

"GOSS" Coronation Porcelain.

This special registered Coronation Badge will not be reproduced after December 31st, 1911.

There will therefore be only a limited number of pieces made, which will gradually get scarcer through breakage, etc., and will therefore become more valuable in the future.

The devices on the five Bezants on the "G" each represent one of the great Colonies, viz., the Tiger for India, Beaver for Canada, Kangaroo for Australia, Lion for South Africa, and Apteryx (or Kiwi-Kiwi) for New Zealand.

The four on the "M" represent the United Kingdom, viz., Rose for England, Thistle for Scotland, Shamrock for Ireland, and Leek for Wales; and the May Blossom round the "M" refers to the Queen's pet name, "May."

The George and Mary 1911 Coronation leaflet

THE LOVING CUP.

The late Lord Lyons, British Ambassador at Paris, used to relate the following history of the Loving Cup:

KING HENRY of Navarre, (who was also HENRY IV. of France), whilst hunting, became separated from his companions, and, feeling thirsty, called at a wayside inn for a cup of wine. The serving maid on handing it to him as he sat on horseback, neglected to present the handle. Some wine was spilt over, and his Majesty's white gauntlets were soiled. While riding home, he bethought him that a two-handled cup would prevent a recurrence of this, so his Majesty had a two-handled cup made at the Royal Potteries and sent it to the inn. On his next visit, he called again for wine, when, to his astonishment, the maid, (having received instructions from her mistress to be very careful of the King's cup), presented it to him, holding it herself by each of its handles. At once the happy idea struck the King of a cup with three handles, which was promptly acted upon, as his Majesty quaintly remarked, "Surely out of three handles I shall be able to get one." Hence the Loving Cup.

[P.T.O.]

The Loving Cup leaflet

Period Symbols

Where a shape was known to have been made during more than one period, the number in brackets behind its entry denotes the other period(s) during which it was manufactured.

The First period	[1]	**1858–1887**
The Second period	[2]	**1881–1934**
The Third period	[3]	**1930–1939**

9 · The First Period 1858–1887

A   BUSTS
B   FIGURES
C   ORNAMENTAL
D   TERRACOTTA

A rare bust of The Prince of Wales, later King Edward VII, wearing the Masonic Collar of Grand Master of the Grand Lodge of England. 520mm.

AN INTRODUCTION TO PARIAN WARE

During his training and career as designer and artist with Copeland's of London and Stoke on Trent, William Henry Goss worked with the relatively new medium of parian. Whilst still in London, he made contact with the inventor of parian, John Mountford, and later wrote the history of that discovery. In his *Encyclopaedia of Ceramics*, W. P. Jervis revealed that 'Its origin has been disputed, both Mintons and Copeland claiming to have invented it. Mr W H Goss, who, when all the experiments were being conducted, was a young boy, knew all the parties concerned and afterward wrote the particulars of the discovery for a book published at The Hague in 1864, entitled *Verslag der Wereldtentoonstelling Te London in 1862*, which was an important work on the London Exhibition produced by order of the Government of Holland. Mr Goss states that it was during the year 1845 that experiments were made at the manufactury of Alderman Copeland to obtain a ceramic material that should resemble marble'.

S C Hall, Editor of the Art Journal (and guide and mentor of William Goss), suggested that reductions from stone sculptures of the modern masters be made in a material that could imitate the stone visually. These miniatures could be offered as prizes by the Art Union of London. Following this idea, a reduced model of Gibson's Narcissus was despatched to Copeland's works for the potters to work from, until there was success with John Mountford's invention. These experiments were conducted by several experienced artistic potters at Copeland's but the first parian was produced from Mountford's recipe, in the form of Narcissus, on Christmas Day, 1845.

This new medium was immediately known as porcelain statuary. Mountford's figure was sent to Mr Gibson himself for inspection and he declared it to be the best material next to marble for the reproduction of sculpture. The new porcelain statuary was an instant success in the industry and it firmly established itself in the ceramic world. It was at about this time that Messrs. H. Minton & Co began similar experiments for imitation marble, and it was not long before they discovered their own version which they termed 'parian'. It was noticed that their parian was slightly tinted and approximated freshly chiselled parian marble, but Copeland's efforts were those of marble toned down with age. Each manufacturer obtained his own quality and hue using his own adaptation of the inventions, and William Goss, who conducted his own experiments in the outbuildings in the garden of Ashfield Cottage adjoining his factory, perfected his own recipes in the late 1850's.

Inside a book which once belonged to Llewellyn Jewitt was found a portion of a letter from his best friend Mr Goss, obviously saved for its contents, in which Goss stated his beliefs concerning parian. 'We believe the day will arrive when these cream-colour wares shall again be chosen in preference to the bluish tint. For we certainly think that if the materials were thoroughly magnetted, well lawned, and finely ground so as to leave a clean pure tint, the prevalence of the cream or ivory colour of the Dorsetshire ball clay would form

A fine bust of Samuel Carter Hall, 376mm high on socle plinth.

a much more pleasing ground for decoration in colours and gold than that of the stained ware'.

The term 'parian' for this new porcelain composition was derived from Paros, an island in the Aegean Sea. The marble of Paros was known as parian marble. Only the wealthy could afford marble busts and statues. Now the middle classes would be able to obtain the porcelain equivalent.

W P Jervis concluded that basically parian was a non-plastic body composed of 3 parts china stone to 2 parts felspar. William Goss's ingredients according to his notebook were Norwegian and Swedish felspar, white glass (obtained from grinding up old bottles made of clear glass only), flints and kaolin or china clay. Goss obtained the latter from Messrs Varcoes Sales Co Ltd, High Cross Street, St Austell, Cornwall. Incidentally, the type of felspar used came from certain beds in Norway and Sweden which were almost worked out by the end of the Goss factory's life in 1929, and there was no known similar alternative. It is the felspar which influences the colour, texture and feel of the final result, making each factory's products so different from its rivals. The felspar Goss favoured produced the ivory translucency which was so distinctly his own.

Most pottery was 'thrown' on a wheel and shaped by hand, but parian was mixed and ground into a liquid state and poured into moulds and left only until a sufficient coating had been absorbed into the walls of the moulds, then the excess poured out to be used again. In this way simple hollow shapes were made in two halves, although the more complex figures made used up to twenty moulds. Most of these were for the detailed floral headbands, or intricate fingers etc.

Bust of Llewllyn Jewitt, on socle plinth, 380mm high.

A Busts

The most important parian productions by Goss were busts. Llewellyn Jewitt, in his *Ceramic Art of Great Britain*, described these portrait busts as ranking far above the average, and perfect reproductions of the living originals. 'It is not often that this can be said of portrait-busts, but it has been a particular study of Mr Goss, and in it he has succeeded admirably.' He later described Goss in *The Reliquary* as 'the leading portrait-bust producer of the age'. Vastly underrated by the majority of collectors who 'play safe' with the glazed heraldic ware so much easier to recognise, the busts nearly all date from the last century and mainly bear impressed titles.

The first parian bust to have been made was 'Mr Punch' in 1861. William Goss was on friendly terms with two successive editors of 'Punch' and made this study for the then editor Mark Lemmon.

Other early portrait-busts for retail sale were those of Lord Palmerston whose term of office was 1859 to 1865. The earliest models were marked Copyright and also signed by W H Goss in his own hand on the shoulder. The majority of parian busts were made for 30 years after 1861, with subjects such as eminent musicians, members of the clergy, political and literary figures, royalty and personal friends. A bust was eventually made of the manufacturer himself in 1906, shortly before his death. Contrary to popular belief that he was so conceited that he made one of himself in large numbers, it was not his wish at all to be depicted in this way, and it was only in his old age that enforced feebleness prevented him from standing up to his sons who organised its modelling as a good sales line.

Up until 1881 when he emigrated to America, the chief artist and modeller was W W Gallimore, except for the three years 1863–6 when he was induced to go to Ireland to work for the Belleek factory, taking the highly prized and secret Goss recipes with him, in particular the wafer thin egg-shell method. After losing his right arm in a shooting accident, he returned to Stoke and modelled with his left arm and was said to have modelled even better than before!

After 1881 Joseph Astley became Goss's chief designer, until his death in 1902. Astley had carried on where Gallimore left off with the creation of parian busts, with his boss often putting the finishing touches to his designs. William really valued his work and respected his talent. The two men worked well together for 21 years, with Astley religiously carrying out William's every instruction. It was as though William had two pairs of hands.

The portrait busts were favourably criticized by *The Reliquary* and *Art Journal* (The editors of these journals happened to be William's closest friends of whom he made busts!)

The high quality of the busts, individually made from moulds from the one original, included detail about the eyes which most factories tended to ignore, giving the appearance of the subject being blind. Not so with the Goss versions, for the factory strove to obtain a true likeness. Readers of *The*

A fine Goss & Peake figurine. Ophelia 535mm. Note the gilding and attention to detail.

Reliquary were recommended to purchase a Goss bust of Mr Gladstone because 'it conveys to the eye a far more truthful, and eminently pleasing likeness of the great statesman, than has ever been produced either by painting, engraving or sculpture.' Admirers of Charles Swain were also advised to purchase the Goss version of this well loved poet, because of its truthful and intellectual likeness.

The main series had either a square two-step plinth or a socle base, sometimes mounted on an octagonal plinth. The square based bust would carry the name of its subject impressed on to the lower step, or impressed into the back of the shoulder. Early busts had a circular (or socle) plinth, and tended to be of classical subjects.

Very little unglazed parian was issued after the turn of the century with the exception of the busts of W H Goss, Shakespeare, King Edward VII, Queen Alexandra, The Prince of Wales (1911) and Scott. The 'ivory porcelain' used for the production of heraldic ware was of the same recipe but glazed.

ROYALTY

		£ p
Queen Victoria in Mob-cap, socle/octagonal plinth	236mm	300.00
	201mm	175.00
Queen Victoria in Mob-cap	151mm	140.00
Unglazed	129mm	110.00
Glazed	129mm	110.00
	101mm	90.00

Queen Victoria – wearing Imperial Crown,
the top of which is extremely fragile

Two step plinth	180mm	200.00
Socle/octagonal plinth	245mm	250.00

Note: Should any of the above busts bear reference on the back to Queen Victoria's Diamond Jubilee, it will indicate that they are commemorative items and of higher value, say, £15.00 extra.
Some busts of Queen Victoria have a single frill to the front of the bonnet, others have a double frill. Value unchanged.

		£ p
Prince of Wales later King Edward VII wearing Masonic collar	520mm	1250.00
Prince of Wales later King Edward VII	167mm	165.00
Princess of Wales later Queen Alexandra	176mm	165.00
King Edward VII	163mm	165.00
King Edward VII socle plinth glazed	133mm	145.00
unglazed	133mm	145.00
Queen Alexandra socle plinth	132mm	145.00
Queen Alexandra approx.	175mm	185.00
Prince of Wales, later King Edward VIII, bearing details of Investiture, and mounted on column bearing arms	143mm	170.00
As above but lacking Investiture details [2]	143mm	135.00

OTHER

		£ p
Adonis socle plinth	265mm	500.00
Apollo socle plinth – with some gilding approx.	260mm	550.00
Beaconsfield	104mm	130.00
(a) glazed	154mm	120.00
(b) unglazed	154mm	120.00
(c) bronzed	154mm	90.00
	385mm	750.00

Queen Victoria
Socle/Octagonal Plinth

Queen Victoria wearing Mob
Cap

Queen Victoria Wearing
Crown

Prince of Wales

The Princess of Wales

King Edward VII

King Edward VII, Socle
Plinth

Queen Alexandra, Socle
Plinth

Keystone of the Kingdom,
Lord Beaconsfield

The Prince of Wales

Beaconsfield

Beaconsfield, Socle Plinth

			£ p
Beaconsfield – wearing coronet		181mm	225.00
Beaconsfield socle plinth, glazed		111mm	120.00
Beautiful Duchess, The.	White, on 3-step plinth	242mm	900.00
The Duchess of Devonshire	Coloured, on 3-step plinth	242mm	1250.00

NOTE: This bust stands on a separate highly ornate plinth, always unmarked. Height 132mm. Add the price of this plinth to that of the bust when present 200.00

Beethoven	glazed	116mm	145.00
	unglazed	116mm	145.00
Bright	glazed	165mm	145.00
	unglazed	165mm	145.00
Bunyan	glazed	132mm	145.00
	unglazed	132mm	145.00
Burns socle plinth	glazed	136mm	90.00
	unglazed	136mm	90.00
		155mm	120.00
Burns socle/octagonal plinth	glazed	166mm	135.00
	unglazed	166mm	135.00
Byron		179mm	155.00
Byron socle/octagonal plinth		193mm	175.00

Children A pair of busts, with cartouche affixed to front of socle

plinth	(a) Mirth (Laughing)	218mm	250.00
	(b) Grief (Crying and wearing shawl on head)	210mm	250.00
Christ socle plinth		300mm	500.00

Classical Lady, coloured, with butterfly upon lapel. Socle/ octagonal plinth. A similar bust was made by Belleek, evidently after the Goss original .... 270mm 550.00

Clytie socle plinth, sunflower model	215mm	300.00
Clytie socle plinth		300.00
Clytie square base	approx. 160mm	200.00
Derby socle plinth	105mm	125.00

*Beaconsfield Wearing
Coronet*

Burns Socle Plinth

*Burns, Socle/Octagonal
Plinth*

*The Beautiful Duchess
Coloured*

Beethoven

John Bright

John Bunyan

Byron

*Byron Socle/Octagonal
Plinth*

Child — Grief

Child — Mirth

Clytie, sunflower model

			£ p
Derby square base		105mm	125.00
Derby	glazed 160mm		120.00
	unglazed 160mm		120.00
Dickens socle plinth		256mm	250.00
Dickens socle plinth – Goss & Peake		650mm	1250.00
Gladstone square base	approx. 400mm		700.00
Gladstone		162mm	145.00
Gladstone socle plinth		132mm	125.00

Godiva, Lady
(Goss Record. 9th Edition: Page 29)

(a) White	108mm	85.00
(b) Coloured	108mm	165.00
(c) Socle/octagonal plinth	210mm	325.00

Guiseppe Garibaldi	174mm	375.00

Incised on rear in W H Goss' own hand
Published as the Act directs under the Superintend J.A.P. McBride

Gordon, General		189mm	165.00
Goss, William Henry [2]	glazed 160mm		150.00
	unglazed 160mm		150.00
Granville	glazed 176mm		145.00
	unglazed 176mm		145.00
Gully, W.C.		120mm	210.00
		160mm	250.00
Hall, Samuel Carter, socle plinth		376mm	1000.00
Handel	glazed 116mm		145.00
	unglazed 116mm		145.00
Hartington	glazed 174mm		150.00
	unglazed 174mm		150.00
Hartington socle plinth		130mm	150.00

Hathaway, Ann, on two books
(Goss Record. 9th Edition: Page 30) [2]

(a) White	75mm	70.00
(b) White	100mm	75.00
(c) Coloured	100mm	175.00

Christ

Derby

Derby Socle Plinth

A Massive Bust of Dickens

Charles Dickens, 256mm

Giuseppe Garibaldi

Gladstone

Gladstone, Socle Plinth

W.H. Goss

General Gordon

Granville

W.C. Gully

		£ p
Irving, Washington	325mm	500.00

Jewitt, Georgiana socle/octagonal plinth   198mm   850.00
The inscription on the back of this bust reads: '*Georgiana. The beloved wife of Edwin A. G. Jewitt, and daughter of William H. Goss. She was born in London July 30, 1855, died at Matlock, Nov. 3, 1889 and is buried in Winster Churchyard*'.
The grave may still be seen today in the delightful Derbyshire village of Winster.

Jewitt, Llewellyn socle plinth   380mm   1000.00
The inscription on the back of this bust reads:
This bust of Llewellyn Jewitt F.S.A. is made expressly for presentation to his son Mr. Edwin Augustus George Jewitt on the occasion of his 21st birthday the 13th Oct. 1879 as a mark of the highest esteem for both by their devoted friend William Henry Goss.
This bust was used as the frontispiece for *Ceramic Art in Great Britain*, First Edition, 1878, by Llewellyn Jewitt

Dr. Samuel Johnson socle/octagonal plinth   190mm   350.00

Keystones of the Kingdom, The, being almost life-size heads of
    (a) Lord Derby   325.00
    (b) Lord Beaconsfield   325.00
Mounted on 'Keystone' shaped slabs dated 1880
Dimensions: Height 300mm; Width 175mm reducing to 144mm
See also 9D TERRACOTTA.
An advertising leaflet was issued with these models and is valued at £25.00

For **Lady Godiva** see **Godiva**

Lawson, Sir Wilfrid	163mm	300.00
Longfellow	174mm	200.00
Mars socle plinth	320mm	500.00
Mary, Queen of Scots socle plinth	131mm	165.00

Mendelssohn   glazed 116mm   145.00
                           unglazed 116mm   145.00
                                     125mm   145.00

Milton   glazed 167mm   145.00
                           unglazed 167mm   145.00

Milton socle plinth   210mm   120.00

Samuel Carter Hall

Handel

Hartington

Georgiana Jewitt

Llewellyn Jewitt

Mary Queen of Scots

Ann Hathaway, Coloured

Ann Hathaway

Longfellow

Sir Wilfrid Lawson

Mars

Milton

			£ p
Montefiore, sometimes **Montifiore, Sir Moses** with hat		130mm	150.00
Montefiore, Sir Moses without hat		123mm	155.00
Moore, Thomas		170mm	185.00
Mozart	glazed	118mm	145.00
	unglazed	118mm	145.00
Napoleon	(a) square tapered plinth, unglazed	142mm	70.00
	(b) plinth only glazed	142mm	70.00
	(c) completely glazed	142mm	70.00

NOTE: This bust normally carries the arms of St. Helena, and the above prices are for this model. Rare examples have been found bearing the arms of Napoleon, which would increase the above values by £20.00 [2]

Northcote, Sir S.	glazed	169mm	150.00
	unglazed	169mm	150.00
Ophelia socle plinth		250mm	500.00
Palmerston socle plinth		164mm	150.00
		223mm	125.00
Palmerston socle plinth and fluted column		335mm	150.00

Peeping Tom
(Goss Record. 9th Edition:
  Pages 29 & 30)

	(a) White glazed	114mm	85.00
	(b) White unglazed	114mm	85.00
	(c) Coloured	114mm	145.00

Pitman, Sir Isaac. This bust is an apparent anomaly. Sculpted   281mm   425.00
by T. Brock, R.A. in London in 1887, it has an unusual square
plinth, and carries the GOSS ENGLAND mark. In view of its
early date it is included in this section [3]

Punch, Mr.   295mm   500.00
The three-quarter length figure resting on a base consisting of
four volumes of Punch and backed by two more. Copyright
1861

Salisbury	glazed	163mm	145.00
	unglazed	163mm	145.00
Scott, Sir Walter	glazed	176mm	145.00
	unglazed	176mm	145.00

Milton, Socle Base

Thomas Moore

Sir Moses Montefiore with Hat

Sir Moses Montefiore without Hat

Mozart

Napoleon

Palmerston, Socle Base

Palmerston, Socle Base 223mm

Lord Palmerston on Socle Base and Fluted Column

Lady Godiva, White

Peeping Tom, White

Mr. Punch

		£ p
Scott, Sir Walter socle plinth, and wearing tartan plaid	135mm	40.00
Scott, Sir Walter socle plinth, and wearing jacket, waistcoat and cravat	138mm	90.00
Scott, Sir Walter socle/octagonal plinth, and wearing jacket, waistcoat and cravat	168mm	175.00

Shakespeare from the monument, socle/octagonal plinth. Impressed in manuscript *Shakespeare from the monument at Stratford-On-Avon. 1616.*

(a) Unglazed	165mm	100.00
(b) Coloured	165mm	145.00

Shakespeare from tomb, mounted upon two books (Goss Record. 9th Edition: Page 30) [2]

(a) White	75mm	60.00
(b) White	102mm	45.00
(c) Coloured	102mm	70.00
(d) White	158mm	70.00
(e) Coloured	158mm	100.00
(f) Black	158mm	85.00
(g) White	200mm	100.00
(h) Coloured	200mm	125.00

Shakespeare – The Chandos, socle plinth	133mm	110.00
Shakespeare – The Davenant	117mm	70.00
	165mm	85.00
Shakespeare socle plinth	224mm	75.00

See also THIRD PERIOD R. for late examples of busts of Shakespeare.

Sister Dora	174mm	200.00
Southey	180mm	145.00
Southey socle/octagonal plinth	205mm	170.00
Stanley, H.M. socle/octagonal plinth	212mm	350.00
Swain, Charles socle plinth	283mm	600.00
Veiled Bride, The, after Monti, socle plinth	270mm	500.00
Venus de Milo socle plinth	273mm	500.00

Sir S. Northcote

Lady Godiva, Coloured

Peeping Tom, Coloured

Shakespeare,
Socle/Octagonal Plinth

Salisbury

Sir Walter Scott

Sir Walter Scott Wearing
Jacket and Cravat

Sir Walter Scott, Tartan
Plaid

Sir Isaac Pitman

Shakespeare from
Monument, Coloured

The Chandos
Shakespeare

Shakespeare Socle Plinth

Sister Dora

Southey

Southey,
Socle/Octagonal Plinth

Charles Swain

Sir William Wallace

H.M. Stanley

Wordsworth

The Veiled Bride

Venus de Milo

John Wesley

Virgin Mary

Black Bust of Wesley

		£ p
Virgin Mary socle plinth		400.00
Wallace, Sir William socle plinth	134mm	225.00
Webb, Captain Matthew	230mm	550.00
Wesley	unglazed 168mm	145.00
	glazed 168mm	145.00

NOTE.; Black Basalt busts of Wesley were also made, height 154mm – but these, whilst being perfect, smaller replicas of the above, carry no manufacturer's identification mark. The author definitely believes them to be products of the Goss factory. Half-price.

| **Wordsworth** | 164mm | 125.00 |

B Figures

William Henry Goss's extensive education and instruction in the arts influenced the products of his potbank from the start in 1858. The long reign of Queen Victoria had led to a very peaceful and stable era in fashions and art, and made the nation feel secure in the permanency of its beliefs and tastes, and this was reflected in Staffordshire china. The new parian medium was readily approved of by the Queen and the manufacturer's top ranges were aimed at the middle classes who were emulating the upper classes in the collection of marble statues.

William Goss had a desire to create shapes of beauty, mostly relating to known subjects in order to teach the general public an appreciation of art, history and culture. He felt, as head of his firm, and of better education and intellect than most, that he had a responsibility to educate others.

As a student he had studied art at Somerset House from the age of 16 to 19 years, and his love of art led him to model superb classical figures in the popular fashion at that time of partly clothed mythical beauties in a variety of poses, often taken from classical mythology. A lady holding an asp aloft was 'Cleopatra'. A robed woman, deep in thought with a dagger partly concealed in her dress, was the Shakespearian character 'Tragedy'. A young woman praying is thought to be the 'Virgin Mary'. Not all the figurines were plain; some were coloured or were trimmed with colours, particularly gold, rose and turquoise, William's favourite colours.

In 1862 he won the much desired award of a medal at the Great International Exhibition for his display of parian and figurines. Many laudatory articles and engravings of his exhibits appeared in journals such as the *Illustrated London News* and Cassell's *Illustrated Family Paper*. Cassells wrote on November 15th, 1862, when examining an exhibit belonging to Goss of Stoke, 'It is necessary to glance at our engraving to perceive with what exquisite taste this manufacturer has worked out the several designs he had produced in fictile wares. Here, classic forms blend harmoniously with the more ordinary forms in use in our domestic life . . . With the parian statuettes, the perfection of art manufacture seems certainly to have been reached.'

The two largest and most important figurines are 'Leda and the Swan' and a 'Lady holding a Kid', of which coloured examples are dated 1867 or 1868. Figurines made and sold in pairs were usually only factory marked on one of the pair. Almost all these were first period and production had ceased well before 1900. The only figures listed on sale in the editions of the *Goss Record* were 'St Cuthbert of Durham' and the coloured statues of the 'Trusty Servant' and 'William of Wykeham', the latter two of which could only be obtained from the Winchester Agency during the second period. The same exclusivity applied during the first period when Goss's friend, the first Winchester agent, William Savage, stocked his products.

The Lincoln Imp was available during the first and second periods, in both brown and white, in a variety of sizes.

		£ p
Angel, standing with hands clasped in front	318mm	250.00
Angel, holding shell in left hand	318mm	250.00
Angel, kneeling, holding large shell (stoup). Reputedly St. John's Font, Barmouth	148mm	300.00
Bather, nude, in pensive mood, seated on rock	220mm	300.00
Bather, seated on a draped rock, holding conch shell with fishnet draped over knees and purse on ground.	240mm	350.00
Bather, nude, standing beside pump	410mm	650.00
Blind Highlander and Lass with dog gazing up, on circular base	280mm	600.00

Boys – a pair

(a) Holding paint palette	220mm	300.00
(b) Holding writing tablet	220mm	300.00

Bride of Abydos, The,

Goss & Peake	535mm	1000.00

Two Cherubs

(a) The Captive Cupid, some colouring, feet chained	215mm	300.00
(b) Cherub Standing, holding book	220mm	300.00

Child kneeling on cushion, at prayer

(a) Coloured, the decoration is third period [3]	165mm	400.00
(b) White, glazed or unglazed	165mm	300.00

Children Standing Beside Pillarboxes – a pair

(a) Bootblack	210mm	350.00
(b) Crossing-sweeper	224mm	350.00

NOTE: This pair, originally published in 1873 as unglazed figures were re-issued in the latter days of the firm, but in colour. In the earlier models, the Post Box has a loose top often missing, and more rarely a fixed top, while in the later models it is always fixed.

(a) Bootblack, coloured [3]	210mm	650.00
(b) Crossing-sweeper, coloured [3]	224mm	650.00

See illustration on jacket front

Angel Holding Shell

Angel kneeling holding large shell (St. John's Font)

Bather, Partly Draped, Seated on Rock

Bear and Ragged Staff

The Bride of Abydos

Cherub Standing

Winged Putto, the Captive Cupid

The Boot Black

The Crossing Sweeper

The Chimney Sweep

Classical Figurine, Tragedy

Cleopatra Holding an Asp Aloft

£ p

Children – a pair
(a) Partly draped, standing with foot on stool   200.00
(b) Seated on rock   200.00

Chimney Sweep, Boy
(a) White unglazed   292mm   800.00
(b) Coloured, decoration probably late [3] 292mm   800.00

Classical Figurine, Comedy, lady holding mask away from face
                    (a) White or with some colour   320mm   275.00
                    (b) Earthenware   320mm   250.00

Classical Figurine, Tragedy, lady with dagger.
                    (a) White or with some colour   328mm   275.00
                    (b) Earthenware   328mm   250.00

Classical Ladies. A pair, each reclining on large base
                    (a) observant   length 350mm   600.00
                    (b) in pensive mood   length 350mm   600.00

Cleopatra, seated on draped tree stump holding aloft an asp.
On oval base   240mm   400.00

Cupid, asleep lying on a bed with bow and arrow.   270mm × 140mm   400.00

Cuthbert of Durham, St.   134mm   400.00
(Goss Record. 9th Edition: Page 15) [2]

Devil Looking Over Lincoln, The
                    (a) White   147mm   65.00
                    (b) Brown   147mm   85.00

Figurine, holding trumpet-shaped posy holder   300mm   250.00

Figurine, standing in pensive mood with hand under chin.
Gown edged in gold   345mm   275.00

Figurine, standing, playing lyre. Some colouring   340mm   275.00

Figurines, a pair, each holding a baby.   each 375mm   300.00

Figurines, a pair, 'Seasons' – gowns edged in gold
(a) Holding sheaf of corn on head   345mm   275.00
(b) Holding drape on head   345mm   275.00

Gordon, General. Standing on square base
Not seen by the author   approx. 330mm   500.00

Classical Lady, Observant,
on Large Base

Classical Lady, in Pensive
Mood, on Large Base

Cupid Lying on a Cushion

St. Cuthbert of Durham

The Devil Looking Over
Lincoln

Figurine with lyre

Figurine 'Seasons'

Classical Figurine

Ophelia

Lady Godiva on Horseback,
Coloured

Evangeline Goss Lying on a
Shaped Casket

Evangeline Goss on a Cushion

£   p

Godiva, Lady, on horseback. Sometimes inscribed '*From the figure in Maidstone Museum, Maidstone*' (Goss Record. 9th Edition: Pages 29 & 30)

(a) White	112mm	250.00
(b) White	133mm	250.00
(c) White	165mm	325.00
(d) White	182mm	475.00
(e) Coloured	182mm	600.00

Goss, Evangeline. The child sleeping on a cushion, either forming the lid of a casket, white or coloured, or as a solid-based item (Illustrated in Goss Record. 8th Edition: page 4. Bottom right.) Length of child 130mm

(a) White, on casket	220.00
(b) Coloured, on casket	350.00
(c) White, on cushion	125.00
(d) Coloured, on cushion	225.00

Grecian Water Carrier, holding pitcher aloft, on circular base   250mm   275.00

Happy and Unhappy Children, The. A pair of figures from originals by M. Simonis of Brussels, shown at the Great Exhibition of 1851

| (a) Happy Child, holding toy 'Punch' | approx. 150mm | 300.00 |
| (b) Unhappy Child, having broken drum | 143mm | 300.00 |

Dr. Kenealy. The caricature head entitled **'Dewdrops'**.   130mm   175.00

Dr. Kenealy Caricature Figure Standing and holding top-hat and umbrella, as spill-vase and match-holder   191mm   250.00

Dr. Kenealy, depicted as a lion on circular plinth holding a shield 'Sir Roger Tichborne and Magna Charta Defended' Presumed to have been produced by W. H. Goss.   250.00

Lady, Holding Child, Playing Horn on oval base   275mm   600.00

Classical Figurine, holding a kid

(a) White	435mm	450.00
(b) Coloured	435mm	1250.00

Leda and the Swan

(a) White	430mm	450.00
(b) Coloured	430mm	1250.00

The above two figures are a pair.

Lady, with dove feeding from sea-shell   320mm   450.00

Lincoln Imp. In high relief on beakers.
See L.11 DOMESTIC and UTILITY WARES

The Unhappy Child

The Happy Child

Classical Figurine

*Dr. Kenealy Spill and
Match Holder*

*Dewdrops, Dr. Kenealy
Spillholder*

Classical Figurine

*Child, Partly Draped standing
with Foot on Stool*

Child Seated on Rock

Child Kneeling on a Cushion

Leda and the Swan, coloured

Lady holding a kid, coloured

*Lady Holding a Child
Playing Horn*

£ p

Lincoln Imp. Miniature version on sconce of frilled candle-holder. See L.14 DOMESTIC and UTILITY WARES

Lincoln Imp. (Goss Record. 9th Edition: Page 22)
To hang on wall.

(a) White	38mm	50.00
(b) White	78mm	30.00
(c) Brown	78mm	35.00
(d) White	106mm	35.00
(e) Brown	106mm	40.00
(f) White	120mm	45.00
(g) Brown	120mm	50.00
(h) White	145mm	50.00
(i) Brown	145mm	55.00

These pieces often appear unmarked. Whilst some are from Goss moulds they cannot be properly considered as such and are worth approximately £10.00.
NOTE: Some of the above models are also found glazed, usually with Blackpool Arms for which about £10 should be deducted.

Lincoln Imp seated on column
(a) White unglazed	114mm	60.00
(b) White glazed plinth, usually with matching arms	114mm	85.00
(c) Brown	114mm	150.00

Little Red Riding Hood — 270mm — 600.00

Ophelia — 535mm — 1000.00
Goss and Peake

Putti, a pair of seated cherubs — each 200mm — 275.00

Queen of Light, The. Some colouring — 332mm — 350.00

Shakespeare
Full length figure from monument in Westminster Abbey, — 143mm — 175.00
standing, leaning on a lectern. — 175mm — 235.00

Shepherd Boy. Circular plinth — approx. 300mm — 500.00

Trusty Servant, The [2] — 202mm — 1350.00

William of Wykeham [2] — 202mm — 1350.00
A Winchester pair in full colours. William carries a removable crook with a wire stem without which the figure is incomplete.

Venus, emerging from between two large shells, supported by dolphins. Unglazed or part glazed — 175mm — 350.00

Woman Praying. Standing, possibly the Virgin Mary — 275mm — 300.00

Little Red Riding Hood

The Bride of Abydos

Ophelia?

Lincoln Imp

Lincoln Imp on Pedestal

Shakespeare standing leaning on lectern

The Trusty Servant

William of Wykeham

Virgin Mary

The Alhambra Vase

Bird Resting on Edge of Nest

Bird on Tree Stump

C Ornamental

Apart from the range of busts and figures, the factory, under the management of the founder, produced many other wares.

These included a variety of artistically tasteful vases, scent bottles with pierced sides (the scent was contained in the outer hollow rim of the round pierced bottles), large wall plaques, flagons and flasks, and wall vases with faces in relief. The most costly wares were the jewelled vases and scent bottles, which were made up until 1885. The 'jewels' were, in most cases, paste which had their colours enhanced by being placed into hollows coloured with the Goss enamels. These processes were patented in 1872, and were a successful improvement on the methods used by the Sèvres factory whose enamel jewels frequently rubbed off. Real jewels and pearls were used on certain precious pieces, but the author is unaware of any still in existence.

Pieces in this chapter usually bear impressed marks, sometimes with the addition of a Goshawk.

The first named models appeared around 1881 and were of an uneven, heavy, creamy consistency with mould lines clearly visible down both sides. The gilding had to be fired at exactly the right temperature in order for it to be permanent but the factory was unable to perfect this until approximately 1885–1890. Hence the poor or complete lack of gilding to be found on the majority of first period pieces.

Another characteristic of these important early wares is the somewhat diluted, patchy or pastel-like appearance of the colours used for the coats of arms.

The titles of these models were also printed in large capitals on the bases and the inscriptions were short. Early domestic shapes were also slightly indented on the base and glazed underneath.

From about 1887 onwards production techniques improved dramatically. The porcelain mix became thinner, more delicate and more perfectly formed. The gilding was better, brighter and permanent. Coats of arms were painted with richer colours and were more detailed. The type-size used for the transfer of descriptions to be affixed to the base was smaller and lengthier. Various sizes of shield for the arms were introduced in order to suit the proportions of the shape or model. The first models on the production line were of the larger size, but it soon became evident that the general public appreciated the smaller shapes more, perhaps because they were prettier, or easier to take home, and, as collectors today find, more can be fitted into a china cabinet.

Nothing which one would expect to find in another chapter has been listed in this section in order to save confusion or duplication, but those pieces also produced during the first period have been marked thus [1] in other chapters.

THE BULLOCK AND SHEEP GROUP

Albert Loring Murdock, a native of Boston, Massachusetts, discovered around 1860 that liver, then given only to animals, was the life saving treatment for pernicious anaemia. Murdock perfected a potion which was called 'Murdock's Liquid Food'. He expanded his business, eventually supplying almost every drug store in the USA and many in Europe and the Orient.

Every two years he went to Europe to maintain his agencies. He wanted a statue of a cow, sheep and a pig in white to be manufactured as an advertisement for his medicines. He was told that William Henry Goss's china was the finest so he contacted the factory and asked Goss to design some suitable models.

The chosen group of a bullock and two sheep on an oval plinth, was produced with the printed advertising slogan on the side of the beast 'MURDOCK'S LIQUID FOOD IS CONDENSED BEEF, MUTTON & FRUITS.' It is surprising that William undertook the order, considering he abhorred advertising himself. Murdock and Goss, both eccentrics, became good friends and were regularly in contact with one another.

Murdock was a very generous and charitable man, who built and ran a free 175 bed hospital for the poor women and children of Boston. He also sent free cases of his liquid food to the Civil War wounded. Yet a member of his family can recall him as 'stingy'! He was married with two sons and his unfulfilled ambition was to have a daughter, so he much admired Goss for having four beautiful girls. He particularly liked the youngest, Florence, and asked William if he could 'adopt' her, pay her school fees and bring her up as his own. This offer was, no doubt, firmly rejected.

Murdock remained in contact with Florrie by sending her letters and postcards from his travels all over the world, and when, by chance, he returned to Stoke in 1905, he found a beautiful, mature, composed young woman in her thirties and was amazed to find her still single. She had had many suitors and offers of marriage but had declined them all. Murdock had lost his wife and so proposed to Florrie, who eventually accepted. They married on St. Valentine's Day in 1906, one month after her father's death. Albert Murdock was older than her father! In his wedding photograph he had white hair and long grey whiskers. Life with him looked to be a life of luxury. Their honeymoon was a six month world tour including Paris, New York, California and Japan. But Murdock's real ambition was realised when they had a daughter in 1907.

Murdock died aged 82 years old, when his daughter was still only 5. His headstone holds pride of place in a South Hingham, Massachusetts cemetery, and his home, Maple Hall, still stands nearby.

Examples of the bullock and sheep group often come to light in the USA, but the purported group with pig has yet to be seen.

Bird on Rock, Inkwell

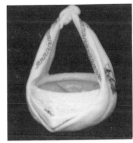

Bird's Nest in a Napkin

Early Jug, Acanthus Leaf Pattern

Bullock and Sheep Group, Reverse

Bullock and Sheep Group

Dolphin Inkwell

Eggshell Cup with twig handle and feet

Eggshell Cream Jug

Eggshell Cup and saucer with raised floral decoration

Early Teapot with Raised Floral Decoration

Elephant with Howdah on oval base

Elephant with Howdah

C Ornamental Wares

The Alhambra Vase – after the Alhambra in Granada, Spain. £ p
William Henry Goss was fascinated with Moorish design and
made a copy of this fabulous multi-coloured winged vase in
earthenware. The vase adorned the mantlepiece of his cottage
in Barthomley, Cheshire and has remained in the family until
recently.
See the colour illustration on front jacket flap.

See also THIRD PERIOD for late examples.

For **Basket.** See Fruit Basket and Posy Basket

Bear and Ragged Staff
(Goss Record, 9th Edition: Page 31)
(a) White unglazed	90mm	95.00
(b) White glazed with shield and arms		
(Add £25.00 for Warwick Arms)	90mm	95.00
(c) White unglazed but coloured harness, chain & base	90mm	185.00
(d) Brown and coloured, glazed	90mm	300.00
(e) Brown unglazed	90mm	225.00

Bird, a wren standing on the edge of a nest, coloured light blue
inside 70mm 200.00

Bird on Tree Stump, as posy vase approx. 100mm 135.00

Bird on a rock, as inkwell 125mm 150.00

Bird's Egg. Apart from the named Guillemot's Egg with a
pointed end, for which see 10E NAMED MODELS, there is
also a similar-sized sea-bird egg with a rounded base. Both
varieties were produced in beige, blue and green speckled
colourings.
(a) Closed	93mm	52.50
(b) Open, to hang as posy vase	83mm	52.50

Bird's Nest in Napkin
(a) White glazed with arms	185mm	185.00
(b) Forget-Me-Nots.	185mm	200.00

Bowl and Lid, circular. The body formed from pink rose petals
trimmed with green leaves. The lid has a rosebud knop Dia. 73mm 40.00

For **Brooches** see Floral Decorations page 85

Bullock and Two Sheep on oval plinth 148mm 750.00
See also the story of this group on page 80

Cockatoo, sitting on perch on rocky base 270mm 450.00

£ p

Comport, with three short legs.
Floral decoration in bas-relief inside bowl.   Dia. 234mm   100.00

Cream Jug and Sugar Bowl sea-urchin design.
   Jug 60mm Bowl diameter 100mm
     (a) White glazed   Each   40.00
     (b) Some turquoise colouring   Each   40.00

Cream Jug. Glazed, having acanthus leaf pattern in low relief.
Many variations of coloured decoration, both to handle and
body can be found, as well as inscriptions in Gothic script, 'A
PRESENT FROM . . .' or 'FROM . . .'   75mm   40.00
See photograph on jacket rear

Dog Bowl. Illuminated lettering in relief around rim.
'Quick at Work, Quick at Meals'   Dia. 210mm   100.00

Dolphin – Tail uppermost on small round hollow plinth,
presumably for use as posy holder or inkwell   98mm   100.00
The example seen has an early puce Goshawk mark without
lettering and the registration mark for 1874. Found either
white or tinted pink glazed, after Belleek.

Eggshell Porcelain
   Tea Service. Cups, saucers, plates and jugs, bearing only the
   impressed W.H. GOSS mark. Cups and saucers are very
   fine wafer-thin glazed parian ware with ivy, fern, violets or
   vine and grape decoration in bas-relief. Belleek later used
   the same design.

   Cup with twig handle and three feet   60mm   125.00

   Cup and saucer Taper glazed   80mm   100.00

   Cup and saucer, begware with gilded cord trim.   Glazed 55mm   75.00

   Cream Jug glazed, blue handle   65mm   100.00

   Milk Jug glazed   70mm   100.00

   Plate. Round, unglazed   approx.dia. 200mm   125.00

   Bread or Cake Plate. Oval, unglazed   Max width 215mm   150.00

   Teapot and Lid. Glazed   130mm   150.00

*Rare Coloured Bowl and Lid
with Floral Decoration*

*Turquoise/white bowl and
lid with floral decoration   B*

*Patterned bowl and lid with
fixed floral spray   C*

*Coloured Powder Bowl with
Floral Decoration*

*Powder Bowl and Lid with
Floral Decoration*

*Bowl and patterned lid with
large floral spray   D*

*Early Lozenge Vase with Oval
Mouth and Floral Decoration*

*Lozenge Vase, Oval Mouth
with Floral Decoration*

Crucifix Pendant

*Lily of the valley Crucifix,
white   I*

*Mixed Floral Crucifix,
White   J*

*Floral cross, black unglazed
H*

Elephant with Howdah on oval base

(a) White glazed	153mm	500.00
(b) Some colouring	153mm	850.00
(c) Earthenware	160mm	500.00

Elephant with Howdah. No base, coloured   140mm   850.00
See also Nautilus Shell

For **Ewer**, early, see **Vases**

FLORAL DECORATIONS

Brooches were a successful line for the factory and these were sometimes affixed to the sides of lozenge and other vases and to the tops of powder bowls and puff boxes. These were often highly decorative with fern and similar patterns in relief and usually multi-coloured in pastel shades, blue, green, pink and yellow predominating.

Floral decorations were used in the third period and are often finished in lustre. Certainly anything with a lustre finish would only have been produced during that period.

Specific items are listed below but generally a floral decoration affixed to a piece would add some £40–£60.

£ p

A   Puff box and lid with a large spray of coloured flowers affixed
     to lid. Several variations   Dia. 82mm   Height 47mm   35.00
B   Circular box and lid with fern and similar pattern in relief
     and criss-cross brooch as a knop.   Dia. 70mm   Height 70mm   250.00
C   Circular box and lid with pattern in relief and floral spray as a
     knop.   Dia. 100mm   Height 75mm   250.00
D   Circular box and lid, patterned in relief and with floral spray
     as knop.   Dia. 110mm   Height 55mm   55.00
E   'Crown Staffordshire' type floral sprays or plants, usually
     planted in bowls. Various types, usually finished in lustre[3].
                                         Approx. 70mm   65.00
F   Pendant, circular white glazed, with roses and speckled buds.
                                          Dia. 56mm   55.00
G   Pendant, in form of a Cross with ivy decoration, unglazed
     brown (red Goshawk).   Dia. 80mm   150.00
H   Pendant, in form of a Cross with roses, forget-me-nots,
     peonies in relief. Unglazed black.   Dia. 90mm   150.00
I   Pendant, in form of a Cross with lily of the valley in relief.
     White glazed.   Dia. 80mm   150.00
J   Pendant, in form of a Cross with roses, daisy, lily of the valley
     and forget-me-nots in relief. White unglazed.   Dia. 80mm   150.00
K   Stick Pin, blue forget-me-nots, pink buds, green leaves.   Dia. 80mm   45.00
L   Earrings, to match above. Priced as a pair.   Dia. 20mm   65.00

BROOCHES

Over twenty-five different designs were made, some white unglazed and others coloured and glazed. As well as being produced during the first period, some of these designs were re-introduced during the 1920's in the Third period.

After manufacture, the brooches were all thrown into boxes and no care was taken to see that they remained perfect. Exceptionally, damage would not affect the values quoted here as all brooches are chipped to some extent.

Brooches, white unglazed

			£ p
A	Petunia, rose and forget-me-nots, oval	47mm	45.00
B	Spray of 3 violets, oval	58mm	45.00
C	Daisy and forget-me-nots, oval	47mm	45.00
D	Rose and speckled buds, oval	50mm	45.00
E	Rose and speckled buds, circular	45mm	45.00
F	Rose and lily of the valley buds, oval	50mm	45.00
G	Forget-me-not spray, oval	50mm	40.00

Brooches, white glazed

A	Scarab	40mm	75.00

Brooches, coloured glazed

A	Petunias and leaves, tied with ribbon, oval	66mm	65.00
B	Forget-me-not circle	42mm	65.00
C	Petunia, rose and forget-me-nots, oval	47mm	65.00
D	Anemone with scarlet pimpernel, circular	45mm	65.00
E	Double daisy, circular	42mm	55.00
F	Two-tone carnation, circular	45mm	65.00
G	Bouquet of roses, tied with ribbon, oval	60mm	65.00
H	Daisy, zinnia and rose circle	60mm	65.00
I	Violet with buds and foliage, oval	58mm	65.00
J	Bunch of red grapes and vine leaves with trailing creepers, oval	46mm	65.00
K	Daisy with buds and leaves, circular	40mm	60.00
L	Roses and forget-me-nots on criss-cross background, circular.	50mm	65.00
M	Wild anemone spray, oval	60mm	65.00
N	Spray of scarlet pimpernel, oval	55mm	65.00
O	Violets with scarlet pimpernel, circular	45mm	65.00
P	Forget-me-not spray, oval	50mm	55.00
Q	Poppy, speedwell and petunia, triangular	47mm	55.00
R	Speedwell, petunia and daisy, circular	50mm	55.00
S	Daisy and forget-me-nots, oval	50mm	65.00
T	Rose and lily of the valley buds, oval	50mm	65.00
U	Rose, forget-me-not and speckled buds, circular	50mm	65.00
V	Rose and speckled buds, circular	45mm	65.00
W	Large initial F on lily of the valley, roses and forget-me-nots on criss-cross background	80mm	150.00
X	Three rosebuds on leaf base, tied with ribbon, oval	70mm	65.00

Daisy and forget-me-nots,
white   C

Petunia, rose and
forget-me-nots, white   A

Rose with speckled buds,
round, white   E

Oval spray of violets,
white   B

Oval spray of rose and buds,
white   F

Rose with speckled buds,
round, coloured   V

Forget-me-not circle,
coloured   B

Daisy, zinnia and rose,
coloured   H

Violet with buds and foliage,
coloured   I

Spray of scarlet pimpernel,
coloured   N

Wild anemone spray,
coloured   M

Forget-me-not spray, oval,
coloured, P

Pink rose pin box lid coloured

Two tone carnation, coloured   F

Daisy with buds and leaves, coloured   K

Speedwell, petunia and daisy, coloured   R

Violets with scarlet pimpernel, coloured   O

Double daisy, coloured   E

Poppy, speedwell and petunia, triangular, coloured   Q

Rose, forget-me-nots and speckled buds, circular   U

Anemone with scarlet pimpernel, coloured   D

Rose with speckled buds, round, coloured   V

Rose and forget-me-nots, circular, coloured   U

Petunia, rose and forget-me-nots, coloured   C

Three Rosebuds, oval,
coloured   X

Petunia, rose and
forget-me-nots, coloured   C

Oval forget-me-not spray,
coloured   P

Roses, a bouquet tied with
ribbon, coloured   G

Daisy and forget-me-nots,
coloured   S

Rose and buds oval spray,
coloured   T

Stick pin and earrings,
forget-me-nots   K

Scarab, white glazed   A

Red Grapes with Green Vine
Leaves, Oval, Coloured   J

Late Floral Decoration Inset
into Lip-salve Pot Base, Lustre

Late Floral Decoration

Roses, forget-me-nots on
criss-cross background,
coloured   L

Fox and its Prey

Small Fluted Basket and Strap

Basket with Acanthus Leaf Decoration and Strap Handle

Game Pie Pin Oval Box and Lid

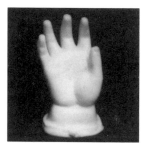

Hand Ring Tree

Hand Holding Bag Vase

Leaf Pattern Cream Jug

Leaf Pattern sugar basin

Lithophane

Sark Milk Churn, Early

Monmouth Mask, The Knight

Monmouth Mask, The Miller

£ p

Fox and Its Prey, a rooster, on oval plinth.
This study may be found in either Parian or Earthenware   90mm   235.00

Fruit Basket. Glazed, with acanthus-leaf pattern and strap
handle   Length 224mm   150.00

Fruit Basket. Glazed, fluted with turquoise strap
handle.   Length 120mm   110.00

For **Fruit Basket**. Glazed, Dutch style with turquoise coral-shaped
handle [2]. See L.11 DOMESTIC AND UTILITY WARES

Game Pie, oval pin box with pheasant and ferns decoration on
lid and ivy around base.   Length 95mm   75.00

Hand. Glazed. A ring tree.   93mm   45.00

Hand. Glazed, holding bag vase.
Some fine gilding and turquoise cord and button.   122mm   75.00

For **Jewelled Ware** see **Vases, Jewelled**

Leaf pattern, folded leaves with handles

			£ p
(a) Cream Jug	Length	80mm	100.00
(b) Sugar Basin	Length	100mm	100.00

Lithopane. A wafer-thin porcelain circle depicting a lady
with a star in her hair   Dia. 89mm   1000.00
Signed and dated *J.A. 1888* (Joseph Astley, chief
modeller at the time).

Milk Can, unglazed, early, with coloured spray of flowers
in bas-relief on both sides. Similar to the First Period
Sark Milk Churn. Marked No. 885X   64mm   150.00

Monmouth Masks. [2]
(Goss Record. 9th Edition: Page 23)
Although there are actually three masks in Geoffrey of Monmouth's study: the Miller, the Knight, and the Angel, only the
former two have so far been found reproduced by Goss:

The Miller	(a) White glazed	81mm	165.00
	(b) White unglazed	81mm	185.00
	(c) Brown	81mm	275.00
	(d) White	95mm	210.00
	(e) Brown	95mm	275.00
	(f) White glazed	120mm	210.00
	(g) White unglazed	120mm	200.00
	(h) Brown	120mm	275.00

			£ p
The Knight (a) White unglazed		80mm	165.00
(b) Brown unglazed		96mm	275.00
(c) White glazed		115mm	275.00
(d) Brown unglazed		115mm	275.00

Mushroom. Brown unglazed, with green grass
around base of stem [2]   60mm   250.00

Picture frame
Rectangular, containing sepia transfer of Romsey Abbey
Crucifix, all made in one piece. [2]   Height 170mm   Width 137mm   140.00

Pierced Bowl.
A latticed window bowl with turned over rim.
(Illustrated Goss Record. 8th Edition: Page 4,   Dia. 140mm   125.00
Middle shelf)

Pierced Dish in imitation basket-work, oval, glazed and having
a coat of arms in base of dish, usually of Boston.   Length 242mm   50.00

Pinbox and lid, oval, cherub lying asleep on lid. Blue dots,
orange diamonds and coloured flowers. Puce mark
                                                        Length 130mm   250.00

Pin-cushion. A round, glazed porcelain base with shell pattern,
to be filled with sawdust and top covered in velvet. Inscribed
in Gothic lettering 'A PRESENT FROM . . .'   Dia. 70mm   25.00

Pin-cushion A round unglazed porcelain bowl with two bands
of turquoise and A PRESENT FROM THE CRYSTAL
PALACE in orange capitals around top, and moulded leaf
pattern to lower half.   95mm   25.00

A Special Plaque. (Illustrated, Goss Record. 8th Edition: Page
4, Top Shelf) measuring 335mm × 275mm was made, possibly specially for the Exhibition at Stoke-on-Trent in 1913 on
the occasion of Their Majesties' visit to the Potteries. Only
one specimen is known and the piece is believed to be unique.
It depicts two bulls fighting, in bas-relief and is unglazed. The
border is perfectly plain. [2]   750.00

Plates. Circular. Various early unglazed plates, measuring
about 345mm in diameter were produced. Some were left
completely white while others had the wording, coats of arms
or other decoration in colour. The most common is the
Winchester College plate, which often bears the inscription:
Published by W. SAVAGE on the back.

Mask from Geoffrey of Monmouth's Study, The Knight

*Large St. Cross Hospice,
Winchester plate*

Large Plate Dia. 345mm

*Large Winchester College
Plate, Dia. 345mm*

*Oval Plate 'Think, Thank
and Thrive'*

*Oval Platter 'Give us this day
Our daily bread'*

*Oval Platter 'Where Reason
Rules The Appetite Obeys'*

*Early Plate with Glazed
Recessed Centre*

*Unglazed Plate with Vine
Pattern in Relief*

*Large Christmas Pudding Plate
with Coloured Holly Decoration*

Pierced Plate Dia. 300mm

*Pierced plate, coloured with
medallions in relief,
225mm dia.*

*Pompeian Vase, Early with
coloured Grecian Scenes*

£ p

Arms of Winchester College centrally, with *Manners Makyth
Man* on surrounding rim:

(a) White		150.00
(b) Coloured		225.00

Arms of St. Cross Hospice, Winchester centrally, with
DOMUS ELEEMOFYNARIA NOBILIS PAUPERTATIS (sic)
around rim:
Translation: YOU ARE AS NOBLE AS YOU LIVE

(a) White unglazed		150.00
(b) White or cream glazed		125.00
(c) Coloured		225.00

Eat Thy Bread with Thankfulness

(a) White		150.00
(b) Coloured		225.00

Think, Thank and Thrive [2]
(Illustrated. Goss Record. 8th Edition: Page 4)

(a) White		150.00
(b) Coloured		225.00

Holly Decoration Round Rim
Hence known as a Christmas Pudding Plate

(a) White	348mm	120.00
(b) Coloured	348mm	165.00

Plate with glazed recessed centre and heavy relief decoration
around wide rim — Dia. 200mm — 75.00

Plate. Nasturtium pattern in relief — Dia. 227mm — 75.00

Plate, circular, wavy edge with vine and grape decoration in
relief, gilded around edges of leaves. — Dia. 210mm — 100.00

Plate, circular, with gilded edge, magneta band, holly and
mistletoe – and inscribed: *A MERRY CHRISTMAS* — Dia. 225mm — 150.00

Plate, pierced although with piercings left in place, with pink
band as decoration. The body is earthenware and a matching
comport was made.
This plate may also be found with an early transfer of a child in
the centre for which add £25.00

Plate Dia.	225mm	80.00
Comport Dia.	170mm	85.00

Plate, square pierced with ring of oval medallions around rim,
coloured — Dia. 225mm — 125.00

£ p

Plate pierced, decorated in relief with linked chain decoration. 'Bournemouth' coat of arms in centre. This is from the same mould as that used for the comport featured in the 1862 International Exhibition.   Dia. 234mm   50.00

Platters, Oval Bread, 310mm × 250mm which appear (a) unglazed, with coloured lettering and (b) glazed with plain or coloured lettering, and with arms or other motif central.
Where Reason Rules, The Appetite Obeys around rim.
Give Us This Day Our Daily Bread around rim.
White or cream glazed.   Prince range: 50.00–125.00

Platters, Almost Oval 328mm × 245mm carrying the *Think, Thank and Thrive* wording around the border are found with two differing types of lettering
    (a) White unglazed   110.00
    (b) White, coloured lettering, glazed or unglazed   135.00

Posy Basket. Glazed. Fluted sides with twisted handle (Illustrated Goss Record. 8th Edition. Page 4, at bottom)   Length 115mm   200.00

Sark Milk Churn, parian with small handle and gilded acanthus decorations in relief and bearing in gilded lettering *Souvenir de Sercq* in gilt script. It has no lid   64mm   175.00

Scent Bottle, circular and pierced, with an openwork twisted stopper. Richly gilded with a wide turquoise band. This item is 'jewelled' with tiny gilt stones set around a central ruby. Originally supplied in a fitted leather case lined with purple velvet.   120mm   1000.00

Scent Bottle with decoration in relief of crown over cipher in orange colour   130mm   200.00

Sheep, lying down, identical to those in the **Bullock and Sheep** group. This same sheep re-appeared some half a century later, this time glazed and on an oval plinth as one of the series of animals produced in the 1920s. [2] Glazed or unglazed   115mm   125.00

SHELLS:
Limpet [2]
An extremely fine glazed limpet shell mounted on a coloured coral tripod base, another example of eggshell porcelain. (Illustrated. Goss Record. 8th Edition: Page 4. Bottom Shelf – front)   66mm   85.00

First Period Scent Bottle with Cipher under Crown

Early Sheep

Delicate Limpet Shell on Coral Tripod

Squirrel beside tree-trunk

Swan

Rare Vase 293mm

Rare jewelled vase

Jewelled scent bottle in original fitted leather case

Rare Jewelled Vase

Jewelled Vase with oviform body and pedestal foot

Three Whelk Shells on Base

Winchester Flagon

		£	p

Nautilus
  (a) large glazed and crested version [2]   155mm   75.00
  (b) a finer smaller, glazed, uncrested version tinted in pink   95mm   275.00
     (Illustrated. Goss Record. 8th Edition: Page 4. Middle
     Shelf). [2]
     This is an example of Goss eggshell porcelain.

Whelk
  (a) a single glazed whelk shell supported on a coral and
     rock base   144mm   75.00
  (b) a group of three glazed whelk shells mounted on a stone
     base and having coloured coral between the shells   137mm   125.00

Squirrel, standing beside a hollow tree-trunk. Trunk glazed
inside for use as a posy vase   117mm   135.00

Swan

(a)	60mm	80.00
(b)	73mm	85.00
(c)	94mm	90.00
(d) Glazed	120mm	120.00
(e) Unglazed	120mm	125.00

Can be either a cream jug or posy holder. Occasionally found
with arms or decorations to rear. Same value.

Vase. Round, flat faced, turquoise or plain leaves on border,
oval base and mouth   120mm   65.00

Vase. Round, flat faced, wreath surround, rectangular base and
round mouth   107mm   65.00

Vase. Oval, flat faced, wreath surround, rectangular base and
oval mouth   170mm   80.00

Vase, decorated with flying cherubs in relief and two gargoyles
on shoulder. Exhibited at International Exhibition 1862.   293mm   750.00

Vases, Jewelled
    These are probably the finest and most beautiful pieces ever
produced by the Goss factory. William H. Goss carried out
hundreds of experiments in order to perfect the parian body,
which the author considers to be among the finest ever
produced. Into this he set stones; some semi-precious, others
glass in the most attractive and decorative way. He patented
this process which was the object of widespread acclaim, for
nobody had yet been able to successfully produce high quality
work of this nature although many, even Sèvres, had tried.
Only a few examples of jewelled ware are known to exist and

Rare Brown Mushroom

Oval plaque 'Oakley Coles'

Oval plaque 'J.S. Crapper'

Oval Plaque 'Robert Garner'

Oval Plaque 'Rev. Lovelace Stamer'

Oval Plaque 'The Prince of Wales'

Pierced Bowl

Oval plaque 'Can't you talk'

Pierced Dish 242mm

Pin Cushion, Acanthus Leaf Pattern

Pin Cushion

A Special Plaque. Bulls fighting

£ p

two are illustrated in this Chapter – and one again in colour on the jacket of *Goss China Arms, Decorations and Their Values* the sequel to this book by the same author.

(a) **Vase** with oviform body, and pedestal foot, having 597 jewels coloured green, red, yellow and magenta set amongst rich and ornate gilding. Goshawk mark 155mm 1000.00

(b) **Vase**, octagonal with two shaped handles. Raised ivy leaf pattern, richly gilded with 740 magenta and green jewels inset 240mm 1000.00

(c) **Vase** with fluted body and two pierced fluted handles. Beautifully decorated on beige ground set with red, yellow and green stones. Glazed interior 170mm 1000.00

(d) **Scent Bottle** See page 96

Vases. A number of early parian vases 70–385mm in height were produced, each unique. Illustrations of these may be found in the engraving of W.H. Goss's exhibit for the International Exhibition of 1862 (see *Goss for Collectors, The Literature*, John Magee. Milestone Publications)

Some specific known examples are given here:

(a) **Vase**. Whorl pattern in relief with lines of alternate blue dots and gilding 70mm 1000.00

(b) **Vase**. Fluted pattern in relief with three horizontal bands of blue dots enclosed by gilded lines. Ivy pattern in relief at neck 70mm 1000.00

(c) **Ewer**. Having horizontal blue lines and raised ivy leaf pattern with two horizontal bands of blue dots enclosed by gilded bands. One shaped handle to side. See photograph on jacket rear 70mm 1000.00

(d) **Vase**. Having vertical flutes with rich multi-coloured floral pattern around bulbous centre 100mm 1000.00

(e) **Vase** of Pompeian slender form and having Grecian scenes in light pastel shades 385mm 1000.00

Wall Plaques, Oval. A number of these were produced with busts in bas-relief centrally. The plaques were normally gold-edged with turquoise ribbon ornamentation at the top. The title for each will be found lightly impressed under the subject.

Oakley Coles	200mm	400.00
J.S. Crapper	200mm	400.00
Robert Garner	200mm	400.00
The Prince of Wales, later King Edward VII	200mm	425.00

One of series of seven oval wall plaques, 200mm high depicting the perfumier Eugene Rimmel in bas-relief. The name is feintly impressed under the bust of the front.

The acanthus leaves are richly gilded with red berries and the ribbon trimmed with turquoise. The figure is raised from a cream ground.

		£	p
Eugene Rimmel	200mm	400.00	
The Rev. Sir Lovelace T. Stamer, Bart.	200mm	400.00	

The above plaques are upright oval; the following is horizontal oval:

Child with Large Dog 'Can't You Talk?'	180mm	400.00	

NOTE: All the above plaques would appear to have been commissioned and published by J.S. Crapper, a colleague of W.H. Goss. All plaques bear the impressed W.H. GOSS mark.

Wall Vases

(a) **Child's Head** with radiating hair and feathers, glazed. Reputedly, the face is that of Florence, William Henry Goss's youngest daughter.

	125mm	175.00
	150mm	175.00
	190mm	225.00

(b) Heads of **Granville, Disraeli, Derby, William Henry Goss, Georgiana Jewitt and Bright** in high relief on front of a glazed or unglazed oval wall-pocket, with plain, blue, or green background and acanthus leaf surround.

White, unglazed	180mm	175.00
Part-coloured, glazed	180mm	275.00

(c) As (b) but without head i.e. a wall-vase decorated with acanthus leaves. Same price.

(d) **A Humming Bird**, taking nectar from a passion flower, and with a nest above containing three eggs in the surrounding foliage. Glazed

257mm	250.00

Winchester Flagons. These are a pair, unglazed, carrying coloured likenesses in bas-relief of:

(a) The Trusty Servant	160mm	125.00
(b) William of Wykeham	160mm	125.00

Many of these appear unmarked and may possibly have been made by the Goss factory. One pair, marked, is reputed to exist but has not been seen by the author. Similar flagons were made by Copeland and other factories for William Savage, the first Winchester Agent. Unmarked varieties would be worth £20.00–£40.00 depending on size and desirability.

Early Vase, Whorl and Blue Dots Decoration

Rare Early Ewer

Rare Early Vase

Rare Early Vase

Humming Bird Wall Vase

Child's Head Wall Vase

Wall Vase, Derby

Wall Vase, Disraeli (Beaconsfield)

Wall Vase, Bright

Wall Vase, Georgiana Jewitt

Wall Vase, Granville

Wall Vase, W. H. Goss

The Nautilus Shell. 95mm eggshell porcelain, tinted pink.

D Terracotta

In 1856 a valuable deposit of red clay was found in the Stoke area giving birth to the red clay tile industry. One manufacturer involved in this trade was a Mr Peake who entered into a brief partnership with W H Goss in 1867. It was short lived due to Peake's own financial difficulties and lasted for less than a year.

The partnership concentrated on the production of terracotta ornamental and utility ware, marked 'GOSS & PEAKE' in fine black lettering. Terracotta manufactured after the partnership dissolved was marked 'W H GOSS'. Few of the utility items such as tobacco jars with lids are to be found perfect today as they were made to be used. Decorations on these heavy wares included transfers of Egyptian and Greek influence in black, red, yellow and green, and amusing cartoons in black silhouette.

Wares marked 'GOSS & PEAKE' are more desirable as they are scarcer in number.

Terracotta was produced between 1867 and 1876 and Goss appeared to be one of the few factories to mark their wares. Probably for this reason much unmarked terracotta is hopefully but incorrectly attributed to Goss.

Terracotta Vase, Cartoons and Patterned

Terracotta Spill Holder, Patterned

Terracotta Vase, Patterned

Terracotta Keystone, Lord Beaconsfield

Terracotta Cambridge Jug, Pewter Lid

Terracotta Bust of Burns

Terracotta comport, Patterned

Terracotta Jug,

Terracotta Tobacco Jar, Patterned

Terracotta Tobacco Jar, Patterned

Terracotta Tobacco Jar Cartoons

Terracotta Tobacco Jar Cartoons

Black Enamelled Terracotta Vase

Terracotta Bag-Vase, Barbados Transfer

Terracotta Vase and Stopper, Cartoons

			£ p
Busts (a) **Robert Burns**, socle/octagonal base		165mm	300.00
(b) **George Dawson**, socle base, dated 1871		305mm	500.00
(c) **Charles Swain**, socle base		280mm	500.00

Cambridge Jug sometimes with hinged pewter lid — 130mm — 85.00

Candle Holders — 75.00

Comports — 85.00

Jardinieres usually found with base plates – often unmarked — 85.00

Jugs — 130mm — 75.00

190mm — 90.00

Spill Holders — 75.00

Tea Pots — 90.00

Tobacco Jars, with lids. These are relatively common — 130mm–150mm — 60.00

A Black-enamelled Terracotta Vase having Classical Figures stencilled around the body. — 180mm — 200.00

Vases of varying heights and shapes — price range 60.00–90.00

Bag Vase with pictorial view of The Cassino, Barbados Aquatic Club, and Arms of Barbados on the reverse. — 50mm — 75.00

'The Keystones of the Kingdom'
being almost life-size heads mounted on Keystone shaped
slabs (dated 1876) of
(a) Lord Derby
(b) Lord Beaconsfield
One example also has impressed on rear in addition to the
W.H. GOSS mark 'WETLEY BRICK AND
POTTERY CO. LIMITED W K.' One wonders
whether they were all made by this firm.
Height 321mm; Width 195mm reducing to 150mm — Each 400.00
See also FIRST PERIOD C. ORNAMENTAL for an unglazed
white variety. An advertising leaflet was issued with these
models and is valued at £25.00.

A rare terracotta bust of Robert Burns on socle/octagonal plinth. Height 165mm

10 · The Second Period 1881–1934

The Rye Cannon Ball and Plinth

PLEASE RETURN THIS CARD with photos

Prices quoted are for ordinary arms, those with supporters &c are extra

NOT LESS than 1/2 dozens under 12/- doz

In ordering please quote distinguishing letters of photograph, size, & price, thus—

(AT) 2 doz 3 inch Bass arms of — 6/-
1 " Ball box Do 7/-
1 " Fairy Wag vase Do 6/

Please do not make any mark on photos.

It is earnestly requested that you will return photos & card at ONCE as they are urgently required elsewhere. If detained they will be charged for

Photos. must not on any account be lent to others.

Explanatory note sent with a set of photographs to agencies by Adolphus Goss to assist them to order stocks of Goss china

Early shapes and decorations. Note the way Adolphus Goss arranged his subjects with the top row balanced on a sheet of glass over the pieces below

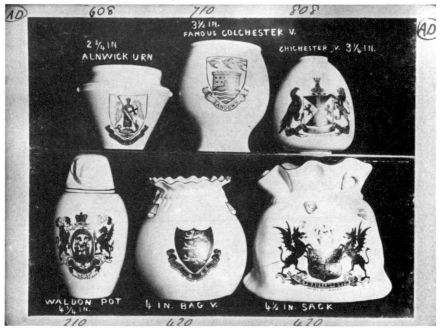

The centre vase in the bottom row did not go into production

E   Named Models and Special Shapes

The majority of models in this section were manufactured during the second period from 1888 to 1929. However, certain shapes, especially the larger versions, were test-marketed during the first period up to seven years earlier, and more popular lines continued for four years into the third period after the sale of the pottery in 1929. Numbers in parentheses throughout the listing indicates other periods where particular models were known to have been in production. It is possible to tell by the thicker feel and slightly gritty texture plus the more yellow hue of the porcelain, if a piece was made pre-1888. Thereafter, the quality of china, enamel and gilt drastically improved and became consistent. Second period named models are very much whiter in appearance and the quality is excellent. The original factory photographs on pages 114/115 show examples of armorial ware made from 1930 to 1934. The named models are the most widely known of all the factory's products and they dominated production for the larger part of its existence. This chapter will probably be the most important to collectors because it contains the six hundred plus models which are most avidly collected. Cottages, Fonts, Animals and Crosses are also models but due to their importance, will be found under their own sub-headings.

Two sets of values are given where applicable, one for any arms and the other for matching arms. For example, an Exeter Vase with the Arms of Exeter will be worth very much more than one with, say, City of Edinburgh arms. No general percentage can be added for matching arms as examples vary so much in rarity. Many collectors prefer to have the correct arms on a model and where possible these are stated. Where there are no arms for a particular model, such as the Ashley Rails Urn, the nearest town or the local agency (New Milton) is considered correct. If a model relates to a specific person rather than a place, such as Dorothy Vernon's Porridge Pot, then the arms of that person is to be preferred. Ethnic shapes such as the Welsh Leek, Welsh Picyn, Welsh Milk Can etc relate to the Principality as a whole and not just to one town. Any Welsh arms can be considering matching although the true correct arms are the Arms of Wales. Foreign models such as the Norwegian Dragon and Horse shaped Beer Bowls and Bucket are matching with the arms of Norway but also with those of any Norwegian town. Matching arms also include the arms of any school, hospital, or nobleman relevant to the respective town of the model concerned. Nearby towns and correct county arms will attract premiums ranging from ten per cent to fifty per cent to be added to the price given with any arms. For the values of the various arms and decorations to be found on any piece of Goss see the Price Guide's sister book – *Goss China Arms, Decorations and their Values* by Nicholas Pine (Milestone Publications).

Some models are listed with only one price. This is where the item is known only with or without matching arms as the case may be. For instance, the Alderney Fish Basket appears only with the matching arms of Alderney so no price is given for a variety with any other arms.

A selection of Second Period Goss models and shapes sold between 1931 and 1934

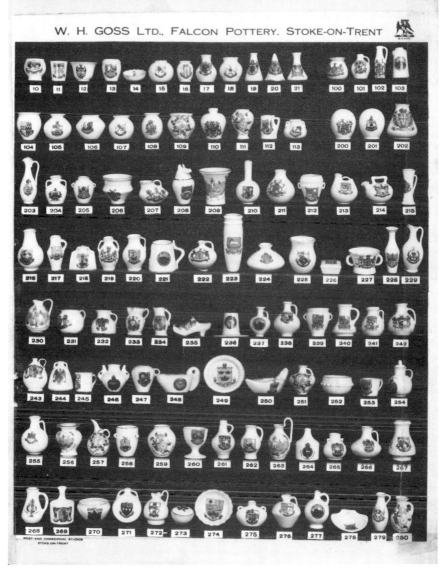

W.H. Goss heraldic ware made between 1929 when the Goss factory was sold, and 1934 when these lines ceased production

Models which bear no arms are included in the first column and are marked thus †.

All dimensions refer to the height unless otherwise stated.

Model		With any Arms £ p	With Matching Arms £ p
for ABBOT BEERE'S JACK see Glastonbury (Abbot Beere's) Jack			
for ABBOT'S CUP, FOUNTAINS ABBEY see Fountains Abbey, Abbot's Cup			
ABERDEEN BRONZE POT (Goss Record. 8th Edition. Page 4) also see POSTCARDS Chapter *Matching Arms: ABERDEEN*	55mm 63mm 89mm 133mm	5.50 5.50 25.75	12.00 25.75 42.50
ABERGAVENNY ANCIENT JAR (Goss Record. 8th Edution. Page 29) *Matching Arms: ABERGAVENNY*	54mm	5.25	12.50
ABINGDON ROMAN VASE (Goss Record. 8th Edition: Page 16) *Matching Arms: ABINGDON*	95mm	17.00	28.00
ACANTHUS ROSE BOWL with wire cage without ware cage (Goss Record. 8th Edition: Page 45) This model was originally sold with a wire cage which is often missing nowadays. *It has no correct arms.*	130mm 130mm	75.00 65.00	
ALDERNEY FISH BASKET (Goss Record. 8th Edition. Page 17) *Matching Arms: ALDERNEY*	40mm 58mm		30.00 35.00
ALDERNEY MILK CAN and lid *Matching Arms: ALDERNEY* This model has a lid without which it is incomplete. Value approximately £8.00	70mm 108mm 140mm		30.00 37.50 43.00
ALNWICK CELTIC SEPULCHRAL URN (Goss Record. 8th Edition. Page 30) *Matching Arms: ALNWICK*	68mm [1]	10.00	19.50

Aberdeen Bronze Pot

Abergavenny Jar

Abingdon Roman Vase

Acanthus Rose Bowl

Alderney Fish Basket

Alderney Milk Can and Lid

Alnwick Celtic Sepulchral Urn

Amersham Leaden Measure

Ancient Costril

Antwerp Oolen Pot

Appleby Elizabethan Bushel Measure

Arundel Roman Ewer

Model		With any Arms £ p	With Matching Arms £ p
AMERSHAM LEADEN MEASURE (Goss Record. 8th Edition. Page 17) *Matching Arms: AMERSHAM*	48mm	10.00	19.50

for AMPHORA VASE
see Greek Amphora Vase or
ORNAMENTAL K chapter

ANCIENT COSTRIL or **PILGRIM'S BOTTLE**   (a) 56mm   34.50
(Goss Record. 9th Edition. Pages 22, 28, 40 and Plate B)   (b) 56mm   37.50
This model was first introduced bearing the League of
Goss Collectors Motif (a) and re-introduced later
bearing the International League of Goss Collectors
Motif (b).

for ANCIENT STONE VESSEL, DOVER CASTLE
see Dover Mortar

for ANCIENT TYG (One Handle)
see Staffordshire One Handled Tyg

for ANCIENT TYG (Two Handles)
see Staffordshire Two Handled Tyg

for ANGLO-SAXON CINERARY URN
see King's Newton Anglo-Saxon Cinerary Urn

ANTWERP OOLEN POT   with 1 coat of arms   70mm   5.50   11.50
                         with 3 coats of arms   70mm   10.50   19.50
(Goss Record. 8th Edition. Page 42)
Matching Arms: ANTWERPEN

APPLEBY ELIZABETHAN BUSHEL MEASURE
(Goss Record. 8th Edition: Page 36)   Dia. 59mm   13.50   28.00
Matching Arms: APPLEBY

ARUNDEL ROMAN EWER   55mm   7.50   19.00
(Goss Record. 8th Edition: Page 34)   102mm   12.00   25.75
Matching Arms: ARUNDEL

ASHBOURNE BUSHEL   Dia. 51mm   9.00   18.50
(Goss Record. 8th Edition: Page 18)
Matching Arms: ASHBOURNE

Ashbourne Bushel

Ashley Rails Roman Urn

Avebury Celtic Urn

(Cup of) Ballafletcher

*Barnet Stone
White and Brown*

Bartlow Ewer

Bath Ancient Roman Cup

Bath Bronze Roman Ewer

Bath Roman Ewer

Bath Roman Jug

Bath Urn

Beachy Head Lighthouse

Model			With any Arms £ p	With Matching Arms £ p
ASHLEY RAILS ROMAN URN		108mm	32.50	46.50
This model is marked COPYRIGHT				
Matching Arms: NEW MILTON				
for ASHMOLEAN VASE, GNOSSUS				
see Gnossus Ashmolean Vase				
for ATWICK VASE				
see Hornsea Roman Vase				
AVEBURY CELTIC URN		105mm[1]	14.50	22.50
(Goss Record. 8th Edition: Page 36)				
Matching Arms: CALNE, MARLBOROUGH or DEVIZES				
for AYSGILL URN				
see Hawes Ancient British Urn				
(CUP OF) BALLAFLETCHER		95mm	25.75	41.50
The Llannan Shee (Peaceful Spirit)				
(Goss Record. 8th Edition: Page 24)				
Matching Arms: DOUGLAS, ISLE OF MAN				
for BARGATE, SOUTHAMPTON				
see Southampton, Bargate				
BARNET STONE	(a) White †	172mm	85.00	
(Goss Record. 8th Edition: Page 24)	(b) Brown †	172mm	125.00	
BARTLOW EWER		104mm[1]	21.75	30.00
(Goss Record. 8th Edition: Page 22)				
Matching Arms: SAFFRON WALDEN				
BATH ANCIENT ROMAN CUP		102mm	82.50	125.00
(Goss Record. 8th Edition: Page 31)				
Matching Arms: BATH				
BATH BRONZE ROMAN EWER		120mm[1]	19.00	26.00
see also POSTCARDS Chapter				
(Goss Record. 8th Edition: Page 31)				
Matching Arms: BATH				
BATH ROMAN EWER		63mm	4.25	10.00 ✓
(Goss Record. 8th Edition: Page 31)		130mm	14.50	23.00
Matching Arms: BATH				

Beccles Ringers Jug

Bettws-y-Coed Ancient Bronze Kettle

Bideford Ancient Mortar

Blackgang Cannon

Blackgang Tower, St. Catherine's Hill

Blackpool Tower

Bognor Regis Lobster Trap

Bolton Abbey Wine Cooler

Boston Ancient Ewer

Boulogne Milk Can & Lid

Boulogne Sedan Chair

Boulogne Wooden Shoe

Model		With any Arms £ p	With Matching Arms £ p
BATH ROMAN JUG (Goss Record. 8th Edition: Page 31) *Matching Arms: BATH*	150mm[1]	28.00	41.50
BATH URN (Goss Record. 8th Edition: Page 31) *Matching Arms: BATH*	75mm[1]	14.50	24.50
for BATTLE OF LARGS MEMORIAL TOWER see Largs Memorial Tower			
BEACHY HEAD LIGHTHOUSE (a) Brown band (Goss Record. 8th Edition: Page 34)(b) Black band *Matching Arms: EASTBOURNE*	125mm 125mm	37.50 37.50	46.50 46.50

This exact model also appears as the extremely rare
DUNGENESS LIGHTHOUSE only one example of
which has been found

BECCLES RINGER'S JUG Very rare, has only been seen bearing matching arms. *Matching Arms: ANCIENT SEAL OF BECCLES*	87mm		285.00
BETTWS-Y-COED ANCIENT BRONZE KETTLE (Goss Record. 8th Edition: Page 38) *Matching Arms: BETTWS-Y-COED*	73mm 114mm	11.00 18.50	19.50 27.50
BIDEFORD ANCIENT MORTAR (Goss Record. 8th Edition: Page 20) *Matching Arms: BIDEFORD*	42mm	8.25	17.00
for BLACK AND BROWN CUP see Newcastle (Staffordshire) Cup			
BLACKGANG CANNON (Goss Record. 8th Edition: Page 26) *Matching Arms: BLACKGANG*	Length 95mm	8.75	15.25
BLACKGANG TOWER, ST. CATHERINE'S HILL (Goss Record. 8th Edition: Page 26) *Matching Arms: BLACKGANG*	112mm	24.50	34.50
BLACKPOOL TOWER (Goss Record. 9th Edition: Page 21 & Plate J) *Matching Arms: BLACKPOOL*	118mm	30.00	40.00

Model		With any Arms £ p	With Matching Arms £ p
BOGNOR LOBSTER TRAP Identical to Lobster Trap but specifically named *Matching Arms: BOGNOR*	51mm		56.50
BOLTON ABBEY WINE COOLER (Goss Record. 8th Edition: Page 38) *Matching Arms: BOLTON ABBEY*	Dia. 68mm	16.00	25.75
BOSTON ANCIENT EWER (Goss Record. 8th Edition: Page 28) *Matching Arms: BOSTON*	70mm	8.00	16.00
BOULOGNE MILK CAN and lid (Goss Record. 8th Edition: Page 42) The model is incomplete without its lid, value £10.00 *Matching Arms: BOULOGNE-SUR-MER*	74mm	14.50	28.00
BOULOGNE SEDAN CHAIR (Goss Record. 8th Edition: Page 42) In the 8th Edition of the Goss Record (Page 1) a version 'specially' decorated in Turquoise Blue is advertised (b). This model has very fragile handles. Even with one of these broken it would be worth only one-quarter of its perfect price *Matching Arms: BOULOGNE-SUR-MER*	(a) 69mm (b) 69mm	40.00 240.00†	70.00
BOULOGNE WOODEN SHOE (Goss Record. 8th Edition: Page 42) *Matching Arms: BOULOGNE-SUR-MER*	Length 118mm	21.50	55.00
BOURNEMOUTH ANCIENT BRONZE MACE HEAD (Goss Record. 8th Edition: Page 22) *Matching Arms: BOURNEMOUTH*	80mm	14.50	21.50
BOURNEMOUTH ANCIENT EGYPTIAN LAMP (Goss Record. 8th Edition: Page 23) *Matching Arms: BOURNEMOUTH* *With Egyptian Arms add £10.00*	Length 105mm	15.25	25.75

Bournemouth Ancient Bronze Mace Head

Bournemouth Ancient Egyptian Lamp

Bournemouth Pilgrim Bottle

Bournemouth Pine Cone

Bournemouth Bronze Urn

Brading Stocks

Brading Roman Ewer

Braunton Lighthouse

(The nose of) Brasenose

Bridlington Elizabethan Quart Measure

Bristol Puzzle Cider Cup

British 6″ Shell

Model		With any Arms £ p	With Matching Arms £ p
BOURNEMOUTH PILGRIM BOTTLE (Goss Record. 8th Edition: Page 23) *Matching Arms: BOURNEMOUTH*	90mm	10.50	19.50
BOURNEMOUTH PINE CONE (Goss Record. 8th Edition: Page 23) *Matching Arms: BOURNEMOUTH*	90mm	10.00	16.00
BOURNEMOUTH BRONZE URN (Goss Record. 8th Edition: Page 23) *Matching Arms: BOURNEMOUTH*	52mm	8.75	15.00
BRADING STOCKS This model is marked COPYRIGHT *Matching Arms: THE KING'S TOWN OF BRADING, SEAL OF BRADING or ANCIENT ARMS OF BRADING*	Length 87mm	160.00	250.00

BRADING ROMAN EWER (a) 70mm 8.25 14.50
(Goss Record. 8th Edition: Page 26) (b) 125mm[1] 11.25 17.50
Also known as the Isle of Wight Roman Ewer by J.J.
Jarvis in the Goss Record. As it is not so named on the
piece itself I prefer to call it the Brading Ewer.
Either THE KING'S TOWN OF BRADING, SEAL OF
BRADING or ANCIENT ARMS OF BRADING and
ISLE OF WIGHT may be considered as Matching Arms.

for 'BRAMPTON WARE' MUG
see Chesterfield 'Brampton Ware' Mug

BRAUNTON LIGHTHOUSE 133mm 400.00 475.00
The third rarest lighthouse, it has a grey roof.
Matching Arms: WESTWARD HO

(THE NOSE OF) BRASENOSE 104mm 17.00 25.75
(Goss Record. 8th Edition: Page 31)
Brasenose is frequently spelt Brazenose.
The Matching Arms are BRAZENOSE or THE CITY
OF OXFORD.

for (OLD) BRAZIER AT TRESCO
see Tresco Old Brazier

British Tank

Brixworth Ancient Cup

Broadway Tower

Burton Beer Barrel

Bury St. Edmunds German Bomb

Bury St. Edmunds Kettle and Lid

Caerhun Roman Burial Urn

Caerleon Lachrymatory or Tear Bottle

Caerleon Lamp

Cambridge Pitcher

Cambridge Roman Jug

Canary Porron

Model			With any Arms £ p	With Matching Arms £ p
BRIDLINGTON ELIZABETHAN QUART MEASURE (Goss Record. 8th Edition: Page 38) *Matching Arms: BRIDLINGTON*		50mm	9.00	17.00
BRISTOL PUZZLE CIDER CUP (Goss Record. 8th Edition: Page 22) *Matching Arms: BRISTOL*		51mm	15.25	24.75

for BRITISH CONTACT MINE or BRITISH SEA MINE
see Contact Mine

Model			With any Arms £ p	With Matching Arms £ p
BRITISH (SIX INCH) SHELL (Goss Record. World War Edition. Pages 5 [illustrated] and 7). This model is marked COPYRIGHT. The value of any military crest is to be added to the price, say £10–£45 depending upon rarity and suitability. *Correct Arms: ANY ARTILLERY REGIMENT*		110mm	16.00	
BRITISH TANK (Goss Record. 9th Edition: Plage L) This model is marked COPYRIGHT. *Matching Arms: (a) LINCOLN* *(b) TANK CORPS*	Length 110mm		34.50	52.50 75.00
BRIXWORTH ANCIENT CUP (Goss Record. 8th Edition: Page 30) *Matching Arms: NORTHAMPTON (SHIRE)*		55mm	6.50	14.50
BROADWAY TOWER (Goss Record. 8th Edition: Page 36) *Matching Arms: BROADWAY*	(a) White (b) Grey† (c) Brown†	75mm 75mm 75mm	110.00 195.00 250.00	185.00
BURTON BEER BARREL (Goss Record. 8th Edition: Page 32) *Matching Arms: BURTON-ON-TRENT*		60mm 73mm	7.00 9.50	16.00 20.00
BURY ST. EDMUNDS GERMAN BOMB (Goss Record. 9th Edition: Page 28) This model is marked COPYRIGHT and has an extremely delicate handle, without which it is of little value. *Matching Arms: BURY ST. EDMUNDS*		75mm	19.50	31.50

Model		With any Arms £ p	With Matching Arms £ p
BURY ST. EDMUNDS KETTLE and lid	76mm	13.00	20.50
(Goss Record. 8th Edition: Page 34)	121mm[1]	19.50	27.50

This model is not complete without its lid, worth £8.00
of the price shown.
Matching Arms: BURY ST. EDMUNDS

for BURY ST. EDMUNDS LIBATION VESSEL
see Bury St. Edmunds Kettle

for CAERHUN BRONZE CROCHON
see Welsh Crochon

CAERHUN ROMAN BURIAL URN	54mm	17.00	30.00

This model is marked COPYRIGHT. It is the rarest of
the smaller urns and is numbered 833
Matching Arms: CONWAY

CAERLEON GLASS LACHRYMATORY			
(or tear bottle)	86mm	6.00	
(Goss Record. 8th Edition: Page 29)			
Matching Arms: (a) CAERLEON			16.00
(b) NEWPORT			14.00

CAERLEON LAMP			
(Goss Record. 8th Edition: Page 29)			
Matching Arms: (a) CAERLEON	Length 88mm	8.00	17.00 ✓
(b) NEWPORT			12.50

for CAERLEON TEAR BOTTLE
see Caerleon Glass Lachrymatory

CAMBRIDGE PITCHER	63mm	4.25	11.25
(Goss Record. 8th Edition: Page 17)	108mm	9.50	17.00
Matching Arms: CAMBRIDGE			

CAMBRIDGE ROMAN JUG	76mm	8.75	17.50
This model is not to be found named in the usual way.	88mm	11.00	17.50
But it is a well-known shape produced by many	94mm	12.50	20.00
factories during Victorian and Edwardian times.	120mm	28.00	35.00
It is also one of the few Goss models not to be named	145mm	31.50	41.50

and the reader is referred to the illustration on page
126 for identification. See also TERRACOTTA
Matching Arms: CAMBRIDGE

Canterbury Jug

Canterbury Leather Bottle

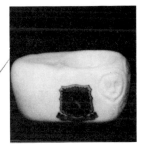
Capel Madoc Stoup

Cardinal Beaufort's Candlestick

Cardinal Beaufort's Salt Cellar

Calisle Old Salt Pot

Carmarthen Coracle

Carnarvon Ewer

Castletown Cinerary Urn

The Cenotaph, Whitehall

Cheddar Cheese

Cherbourg Milk Can and Lid

129

Model		With any Arms £ p	With Matching Arms £ p

for CANARY ANCIENT COVERED JARRA
see Las Palmas Ancient Covered Jarra

for CANARY ANCIENT EARTHEN JAR
see Las Palmas Ancient Earthen Jar

for CANARY ANCIENT JARRA
see Las Palmas Ancient Jarra

CANARY PORRON   68mm   21.00   36.50
(Goss Record. 8th Edition: Page 42)
This model is identical to the Gibraltar Alcaraza – pick
them all up and check the inscription – you may be
lucky.
Matching Arms: LAS PALMAS, GRAND CANARY

for CANNON BALL
see Rye Cannon Ball

CANTERBURY JUG   113mm[1]   9.50   21.50
(Goss Record. 8th Edition: Page 26)
Early models merely state: THE CANTERBURY JUG
Matching Arms: CANTERBURY

CANTERBURY LEATHER BOTTLE   46mm   4.25   8.25
(Goss Record. 8th Edition: Page 26)
Matching Arms: CANTERBURY

CAPEL MADOC STOUP   Length 80mm   17.50   34.50
(Goss Record. 9th Edition: Page 34)
Matching Arms: RHAYADER

CARDINAL BEAUFORT'S CANDLESTICK   152mm[1]   110.00   185.00
(Goss Record. 8th Edition: Page 23)
Matching Arms: CARDINAL BEAUFORT or
  WINCHESTER

CARDINAL BEAUFORT'S SALT CELLAR   70mm[1]   65.00   100.00
(Goss Record. 8th Edition: Page 23)
Matching Arms: CARDINAL BEAUFORT or
  WINCHESTER

CARLISLE OLD SALT POT   46mm   4.25   11.25
(Goss Record. 8th Edition: Page 18)
Matching Arms: CARLISLE

130

Model		With any Arms £ p	With Matching Arms £ p
CARMARTHEN CORACLE (Goss Record. 8th Edition: Page 38) The arms can be found either inside or on the base of this model. *Matching Arms: CARMARTHEN*	Length 133mm[1]	21.75	30.00
CARNARVON EWER (Goss Record. 8th Edition: Page 39) *Matching Arms: CARNARVON*	63mm 89mm[1]	6.00 9.50	14.50 18.50
CASTLETOWN CINERARY URN (Goss Record. 8th Edition: Page 24) *Matching Arms: CASTLETOWN, ISLE OF MAN*	40mm	6.50	11.00
CENOTAPH, WHITEHALL (a) White glazed (b) White unglazed† See also THIRD PERIOD (O) for later varieties. *Matching Arms: CITY OF LONDON*	145mm 145mm	28.00 47.50	34.50
for CHARLOTTE'S (QUEEN) FAVOURITE WINDSOR KETTLE see Windsor Kettle			
CHEDDAR CHEESE (a) Yellow (Goss Record 8th Edition: Page 31) (b) White glazed *Matching Arms: CHEDDAR*	62mm 62mm	24.75† 20.50	24.75 24.50
CHERBOURG MILK CAN and lid (Goss Record. 8th Edition: Page 42) This model is not complete without its lid which is worth £12.00 of the price shown. *Matching Arms: CHERBOURG*	65mm	15.25	30.00
CHESHIRE ROMAN URN International League Model for 1932. *Correct Arms: INTERNATIONAL LEAGUE OF GOSS COLLECTORS*	90mm		300.00
CHESHIRE SALT BLOCK (Goss Record. 9th Edition: Page 11 and Plate K) *Matching Arms: CHESHIRE*	80mm	20.00	30.00
CHESTER ROMAN ALTAR International League Model for 1931 *Correct Arms: INTERNATIONAL LEAGUE OF GOSS COLLECTORS*	117mm		400.00

Cheshire Roman Urn

Cheshire Salt Block

Chester Roman Altar

Chester Roman Vase

Chesterfield 'Brampton Ware' Mug

Chichester Ewer

Chichester Roman Urn

Chicken Rock Lighthouse

Chile Stirrup

Chile Hat

Chile Mate Cup

Chile Spur

Model		With any Arms £ p	With Matching Arms £ p
CHESTER ROMAN VASE	59mm	4.25	11.50
(Goss Record. 8th Edition: Page 17)	89mm[1]	10.50	18.50
see also POSTCARDS Chapter			
Matching Arms: CHESTER			
CHESTERFIELD 'BRAMPTON WARE' MUG	93mm	35.00	62.50
(Goss Record. 9th Edition Page 13)			
This model is marked COPYRIGHT			
Matching Arms: CHESTERFIELD			
for CHESTERFIELD MUG			
see Chesterfield 'Brampton Ware' Mug			
CHICHESTER EWER	63mm	4.75	11.25
(Goss Record. 8th Edition: Page 34)			
Matching Arms: CHICHESTER			
CHICHESTER ROMAN URN	81mm[1]	9.00	17.00
(Goss Record. 8th Edition: Page 34)			
Matching Arms: CHICHESTER			
CHICKEN ROCK LIGHTHOUSE	127mm	24.75	34.50
(Goss Record. 8th Edition: Page 26)			
Matching Arms: ISLE OF MAN			
CHILE HAT	Dia. 86mm	215.00	300.00
(Goss Record. 9th Edition: Page 37 and Plate 0)			
Matching Arms: CHILE			
CHILE MATE CUP	60mm	100.00	175.00
(Goss Record. 9th Edition: Page 37 and Plate 0)			
Matching Arms: CHILE			
CHILE SPUR	Length 114mm	200.00	275.00
(Goss Record. 9th Edition: Page 37 and Plate N)			
Matching Arms: CHILE			
CHILE STIRRUP	50mm	100.00	175.00
(Goss Record. 9th Edition: Page 37 and Plate N)			
Matching Arms: CHILE			

for CHIPPING NORTON FOUR SHIRE STONE
see Four Shire Stone

Christchurch Ancient Bowl

Christchurch Priory Church Norman Tower

Christchurch Romano-British Urn

Cirencester Roman Ewer League Model

Cirencester Roman Ewer

Cirencester Roman Urn

Cirencester Roman Vase

Cliftonville Roman Jug

Cliftonville Roman Vase

Colchester Gigantic Roman Wine Vase

Colchester Native Oyster Shell

Colchester Roman Lamp

Model			With any Arms £ p	With Matching Arms £ p
CHRISTCHURCH ANCIENT BOWL		Dia. 60mm	5.50	12.00
(Goss Record. 8th Edition: Page 23 and also see the advertisement for the Christchurch item on page 64) *Matching Arms: CHRISTCHURCH*				
CHRISTCHURCH PRIORY CHURCH NORMAN TOWER				
(Goss Record. 8th Edition:	(a) White glazed†	123mm	47.50	
Page 23)	(b) White unglazed†	123mm	47.50	
	(c) Grey†	123mm	75.00	
	(d) Brown†	123mm	130.00	
CHRISTCHURCH ROMANO-BRITISH URN		52mm	5.25	12.00
(Goss Record. 8th Edition: Page 23) *Matching Arms: CHRISTCHURCH*				
for CHRIST'S HOSPITAL WINE FLAGON				
see London Christ's Hospital English Wine Flagon				
CIRENCESTER ROMAN EWER	(a) 78mm			35.00
(Goss Record. 9th Edition: Pages 22, 41 and Plate C)	(b) 78mm			56.50
This model was first introduced bearing the LEAGUE OF GOSS COLLECTORS Motif (a) and re-introduced later bearing the INTERNATIONAL LEAGUE OF GOSS COLLECTORS Motif (b).				
CIRENCESTER ROMAN EWER	(a) 2 Crests 115mm[1]		16.00	26.00
(Goss Record. 8th Edition: Page 22)	(b) 3 Crests 115mm[1]		18.50	31.50
Matching Arms: CIRENCESTER				
CIRENCESTER ROMAN URN		165mm	87.00	130.00
This model is marked COPYRIGHT and numbered 784 (see Roman Vase 783 for comparison) *Matching Arms: CIRENCESTER*				
CIRENCESTER ROMAN VASE		80mm	6.50	14.00
(Goss Record. 8th Edition: Page 22 and advertisement Page 66) *Matching Arms: CIRENCESTER*		124mm	12.00	26.00
CLIFTONVILLE ROMAN JUG		180mm	175.00	220.00
Matching Arms: MARGATE				
CLIFTONVILLE ROMAN VASE		70mm	150.00	220.00
Matching Arms: MARGATE		107mm	150.00	175.00

Colchester Vase (Cloaca)

Colchester Vase (Famous)

Contact Mine

Corfe Castle Cup

Cornish Bussa

Cornish Pasty

Cornish Stile

Cuckfield Ancient Bellarmine

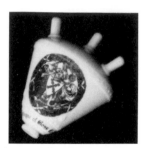

Cumbrae Monument Towtontend

Cyprus Mycenaean Vase

Dartmouth Sack Bottle

Denbigh Brick

Model		With any Arms £ p	With Matching Arms £ p

Colchester enthusiasts should refer to the Goss Record, 8th Edition: Page 63 for a full page advertisement.

COLCHESTER GIGANTIC ROMAN WINE VASE   157mm   34.50   45.00
(Goss Record. 8th Edition: Page 21)
Matching Arms: COLCHESTER

COLCHESTER NATIVE OYSTER SHELL   Width 68mm   7.50   12.50
(Goss Record. 8th Edition: Page 22)
Always appears un-named.
Matching Arms: COLCHESTER

COLCHESTER ROMAN LAMP   Length 100mm   157.50
International League Model for 1927
*Correct Arms: INTERNATIONAL LEAGUE OF GOSS
    COLLECTORS*

COLCHESTER VASE (Cloaca)   Dia. 65mm   5.25   11.25
(Goss Record. 8th Edition: Page 22)
Cloaca refers to the place where the original vase was
found. It is included with the model's name to disting-
uish the piece from the Colchester Vase (Famous).
Correct Arms: COLCHESTER

COLCHESTER ROMAN VASE (Famous)   44mm   4.00   8.75
(Goss Record. 8th Edition: Page 22)   90mm   10.50   17.00
Famous refers to that part of the full name listed in   127mm   12.50   20.00
the Goss Record viz. Famous Roman Colchester Vase. . .
etc. and is quoted to distinguish this model from the
Colchester Cloaca Vase
Matching Arms: COLCHESTER

CONTACT MINE   Length 73mm   110.00
(Goss Record. 9th Edition: Pages 22, 41 and Plate C)
International League Model for 1919.
*Correct Arms: INTERNATIONAL LEAGUE OF GOSS
COLLECTORS*

CORFE CASTLE CUP   62mm[1]   8.25   15.00
(Goss Record. 8th Edition: Page 20)
Matching Arms: CORFE CASTLE

CORNISH BUSSA   55mm   5.50   10.50
(Goss Record. 8th Edition: Page 18)
Matching Arms: CORNWALL

Model				With any Arms £ p	With Matching Arms £ p
CORNISH PASTY			Length		
Matching Arms: CORNWALL	(a) White glazed		82mm	47.50	75.00
	(b) Yellow		82mm	70.00	87.50
	(c) White glazed		110mm	56.50	80.00
	(d) Yellow		110mm	70.00	95.00
CORNISH STILE	(a) White unglazed†		Length	40.00	
	(b) White glazed†		72mm	40.00	
	(c) Brown†			75.00	

Variety (b) can be found with the Blackpool arms, which
could reduce its value by half.

for CORONATION CHAIR IN WESTMINSTER ABBEY
see Westminster Abbey Coronation Chair

for CORONATION CHAIR, PERTH
See Perth Coronation Chair

for COSTREL
see Luton Bottle

for CRICKET STONE, HAMBLEDON
see Hambledon Cricket Stone

for CRONK AUST CINERARY URN
see Ramsey Cronk Aust Cinerary Urn

CUCKFIELD ANCIENT BELLARMINE		75mm	9.00	17.00

(Goss Record. 9th Edition: Page 29)
Matching Arms: CUCKFIELD

CUMBRAE, THE MONUMENT, TOWNONTEND				
(Goss Record. 8th Edition: Page 40)	Brown†	175mm	285.00	

CYPRUS MYCENAEAN VASE	Dia. 90mm		82.50

International League Model for 1925
*Correct Arms: INTERNATIONAL LEAGUE OF GOSS
  COLLECTORS*

for DART SACK BOTTLE
see Dartmouth Sack Bottle

DARTMOUTH SACK BOTTLE	63mm	5.25	12.50
(Goss Record. 8th Edition: Page 20)	92mm[1]	8.25	17.00

Matching Arms: DARTMOUTH

Devizes Celtic Drinking Cup

Devon Cider Barrel

Devon Cooking Pot

Devon Oak Pitcher

Dinant Wooden Shoe

Doncaster Ewer

Doncaster Urn

Doncaster Vase

Dorchester Jug

Dorchester Roman Cup

Dorothy Vernon's Porridge Pot

Dover Stone Vessel or Mortar

Model			With any Arms £ p	With Matching Arms £ p
DENBIGH BRICK	(a) White glazed	82mm[1]	56.50	87.50
(Goss Record. 8th Edition: Page 39)	(b) White unglazed†	82mm	87.50	
Matching Arms: DENBIGH	(c) Brown or red†	82mm	175.00	
DEVIZES CELTIC DRINKING CUP		63mm	5.25	11.25
(Goss Record. 8th Edition: Page 36)		82mm	9.50	19.50
Matching Arms: DEVIZES				
DEVON CIDER BARREL		60mm	9.50	18.50
This model is marked COPYRIGHT. It is identical to the small version of the Burton Beer Barrel but rarer. *Matching Arms: DEVON*				
DEVON COOKING POT		46mm	9.50	18.50
This model is marked COPYRIGHT. It is identical to the Manx Peel Pot but scarcer . . . be sure to look at every apparent Peel Pot more closely. *Matching Arms: DEVON*				

NOTE: These two models are only found with arms of places in Devonshire. The only truly correct arms are those of Devon itself.

Model		With any Arms £ p	With Matching Arms £ p	
DEVON OAK PITCHER	59mm	4.50	10.00	✓
(Goss Record. 8th Edition: Page 20)	114mm[1]	13.50	19.50	✓
Matching Arms: DEVON				
DINANT WOODEN SHOE	Length 74mm	19.50	47.50	✓
(Goss Record. 8th Edition: Page 42)				
Matching Arms: DINANT				
DONCASTER EWER	67mm	10.50	18.50	
This model is marked COPYRIGHT				
Matching Arms: DONCASTER				
DONCASTER URN	39mm	7.50	16.00	
This model is marked COPYRIGHT				
Matching Arms: DONCASTER				
DONCASTER VASE	78mm	9.50	17.00	
This model is marked COPYRIGHT				
Matching Arms: DONCASTER				

Model		With any Arms £ p	With Matching Arms £ p
DORCHESTER JUG	50mm	4.25	12.50

DORCHESTER JUG
(Goss Record. 8th Edition: page 20 and also see full page advertisement on page 60)
Matching Arms: DORCHESTER

| **DORCHESTER ROMAN CUP** | 51mm | 4.75 | 12.50 |
| | 82mm[1] | 11.25 | 17.00 |

DORCHESTER ROMAN CUP
(Goss Record. 8th Edition: Page 21)
Matching Arms: DORCHESTER

| **DOROTHY VERNON'S PORRIDGE POT** | 72mm[1] | 10.00 | 19.00 |

DOROTHY VERNON'S PORRIDGE POT
(Goss Record. 8th Edition: Page 18)
Matching Arms: DOROTHY VERNON

| **DOVER MORTAR (or Stone Vessel)** | 51mm | 5.50 | 11.00 |

DOVER MORTAR (or Stone Vessel)
(Goss Record. 8th Edition: Page 26)
This model is marked on the base *Ancient Stone Vessel found at Dover Castle* but it is listed as DOVER MORTAR in the 8th Edition (page 26) and 9th Edition (page 20) of the Goss Record.
Matching Arms: DOVER

| **DUNGENESS LIGHTHOUSE** | 125mm | | 450.00 |

DUNGENESS LIGHTHOUSE
This model is actually the Beachy Head Lighthouse re-titled, presumably for the local agent. It is the rarest version of this lighthouse, only one example being known.
Matching Arms: THE LORDS OF THE LEVEL OF ROMNEY MARSH

DURHAM SANCTUARY KNOCKER
(Goss Record. 8th Edition: Page 21)

(a) Flower holder, or hair tidy, white glazed	Height 125mm	32.50†	
(b) Flower holder, or hair tidy, white unglazed	Height 125mm	40.00†	
(c) Flower holder, or hair tidy, brown	Height 125mm	40.00†	
(d) Night light with base	83mm	89.50	117.50
(e) Mug or cup	52mm	40.00	65.00
(f) Mug or cup	80mm	56.50	82.50
(g) Mug or cup	118mm	82.50	110.00

A descriptive leaflet can also be found with the above items and is worth £10.00. The brown example is sometimes tinged with green to represent moss or ageing.
Matching Arms: DURHAM (CATHEDRAL)
An illustration of (c) will be found on page 143

Model		With any Arms £ p	With Matching Arms £ p
DUTCH SABOT	Length 82mm	17.00	40.00
(Goss Record. 8th Edition: Page 42)			
Matching Arms: HOLLAND or any Dutch Town			
DUTCH MILK CAN and lid			
(identical to Boulogne Milk Can)	74mm	56.50	82.50
This model is incomplete without its lid, value £10.00			
Matching Arms: HOLLAND or any Dutch Town			
EDDYSTONE LIGHTHOUSE			
Matching Arms: PLYMOUTH	125mm	19.50	30.00

for EDDYSTONE SPANISH JUG
see Plymouth Jug

for EDINBURGH CASTLE, MONS MEG
see Mons Meg, Edinburgh Castle

THE EGYPTIAN MODELS

In order that the Egyptian models may be satisfactorily covered they have been listed in their chronological order of manufacture. According to the 8th Edition of the Goss Record (page 42) models of the Egyptian Water Jar and the Great Pyramid were in the course of preparation at the time of going to press (1913). By the time the 9th Edition was published these two models had been on sale for some time (page 37) and ten other models of ancient shapes were listed as being 'in preparation'.

The production of these models must arouse today's collectors' curiosity, but the discovery of the young King Tutankhamun's Tomb in 1922 was only the climax of many years aggressive investigation of the region by several teams of explorers. Indeed, from a commercial point of view, the Goss factory would have found it much more convenient had the tomb been discovered two or three years later as no sooner had the models made their appearance than interest in Egyptology began to wane.

The models 'in preparation' were given numbers and why 2, 3, 12, 13, 14 and 15 were not used can only be a matter for speculation. The most probable explanation is that around twenty designs were prepared for consideration by the Cairo Agent. He in turn selected the models thought to be most suitable, which he ordered and the rejected designs account for the missing numbers.

An Egyptian Lotus Vase was chosen in 1923 as the model for sale exclusively to members of the International League of Goss Collectors and at around the same time two further models were issued by the Goss factory and these together with the Wembley Lion were put on sale at the 1924 and 1925 British Empire Exhibition.

Cairo, Port Said or Alexandria may also be considered matching on any Egyptian piece.

Durham Sanctury Flower Holder, Brown, 125mm

Durham Sanctury Knocker Cup, 118mm

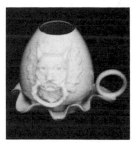

Durham Abbey Knocker Nightlight

Durham Sanctuary Knocker Mug

Dutch Sabot

Eddystone Lighthouse

Egyptian Water Jur

Egyptian Canopic Jar with Anubis Head No. 1

Egyptian Kohl Pot No. 4

Egyptian Kohl Pot No. 5

Egyptian Kohl Pot No. 6

Egyptian Alabaster Vase No. 7

Model		With any Arms £ p	With Matching Arms £ p
EGYPTIAN WATER JAR (Goss Record. 9th Edition: Page 37) *Matching Arms: EGYPT*	56mm	5.25	12.00
EGYPTIAN CANOPIC JAR WITH ANUBIS HEAD No.1 (Goss Record. 9th Edition: Page 37) This most unusual model is marked COPYRIGHT. The anubis head is detachable and the model is incomplete without this lid, which is worth £30.00 See also THIRD PERIOD (S) for a later one-piece variety. *Matching Arms: EGYPT.*	76mm	60.00	110.00
EGYPTIAN KOHL POT No 4 (Goss Record. 9th Edition: Page 37) This model is marked COPYRIGHT *Matching Arms: EGYPT*	66mm	21.75	40.00
EGYPTIAN KOHL POT No 5 (Goss Record. 9th Edition: Page 37) This model is marked COPYRIGHT *Matching Arms: EGYPT*	60mm	13.00	47.50
EGYPTIAN KOHL POT No 6 (Goss Record. 9th Edition: Page 37) This model is marked COPYRIGHT *Matching Arms: EGYPT*	Dia. 70mm	14.50	47.50
EGYPTIAN ALABASTER VASE No 7 (Goss Record. 9th Edition: Page 37) This model is marked COPYRIGHT *Matching Arms: EGYPT*	105mm	17.00	47.50
EGYPTIAN ALABASTER VASE No 8 (Goss Record. 9th Edition: Page 37) This model is marked COPYRIGHT *Matching Arms: EGYPT*	105mm	17.00	47.50
EGYPTIAN ALABASTER BOWL No 9 (Goss Record. 9th Edition: Page 37) This model is marked COPYRIGHT *Matching Arms: EGYPT*	58mm	13.50	47.50

Egyptian Alabaster Vase No. 8

Egyptian Alabaster Bowl No. 9

Egyptian Wooden Ewer No. 10

Egyptian Porcelain Ewer No. 11

Egyptian Porcelain Bottle No. 16

Egyptian Lotus Vase

Egyptian Mocha Cup (Bowl Shaped)

Egyptian Mocha Cup (Egg-cup Shaped)

Elizabethan Jug

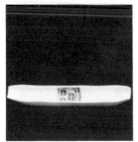

Ellesmere Ancient British Canoe

Eton Vase

Exeter Goblet

145

Model		With any Arms £ p	With Matching Arms £ p
EGYPTIAN WOODEN EWER No 10 (Goss Record. 9th Edition: Page 37) This model is marked COPYRIGHT *Matching Arms: EGYPT*	66mm	13.00	47.50
EGYPTIAN PORCELAIN EWER No 11 (Goss Record. 9th Edition: Page 37) This model is marked COPYRIGHT *Matching Arms: EGYPT*	58mm	17.00	47.50
EGYPTIAN PORCELAIN BOTTLE No 16 (Goss Record. 9th Edition: Page 37) This model is marked COPYRIGHT, and is the rarest of the Egyptian models. *Matching Arms: EGYPT*	68mm	35.00	65.00
EGYPTIAN LOTUS VASE International League model for 1923 *Correct Arms: THE INTERNATIONAL LEAGUE OF GOSS COLLECTORS*	80mm		145.00

EGYPTIAN MOCHA CUP (Bowl Shaped) Named 40mm 6.50 19.50
Matching Arms: EGYPT Un-named 40mm 4.25 12.50
This model is not listed in any edition of the Goss Record. It is described as Bowl shaped so as to distinguish it from the Egg Cup shaped variety, also named Egyptian Mocha Cup. This piece always appears to be particularly finely modelled, the porcelain being very thin and delicate. It is found both named and un-named.

EGYPTIAN MOCHA CUP (Egg Cup Shaped) Named 52mm 7.50 19.50
Matching Arms: EGYPT Un-named 52mm 5.50 12.50
This model is not listed in any edition of the Goss Record. It is described as Egg Cup shaped so as to distinguish it from the Bowl shaped version, also named Egyptian Mocha Cup. It is found both named and un-named.

for EGYPTIAN PYRAMID
see Great Pryamid

for ELIZABETHAN BUSHEL MEASURE
see Appleby Elizabethan Bushel Measure

Model		With any Arms £ p	With Matching Arms £ p

ELIZABETHAN JUG   95mm[1]   17.00   30.00
(Goss Record. 8th Edition: Page 13)
This model is listed as 'Miscellaneous' in the Goss
Record under the heading at the end of the listing of
special historical shapes, that is, it was available to any
agent but was stocked with matching arms by the
Stratford-on-Avon agent. It is difficult to find this
model in fine condition as it is first period, indeed it
was one of the first models issued and the gilding and
enamels of the coat of arms are invariably worn. Few
large size models can have been manufactured after
1895 when the newer models with specific local con-
nections became so much more popular. Frequently
found impressed, W.H. GOSS only, i.e. without the
Goshawk.
Matching Arms: QUEEN ELIZABETH

ELLESMERE ANCIENT BRITISH CANOE
(Goss Record. 8th Edition: Page 31)

(a) White glazed	length 149mm	43.50	75.00
(b) Brown†	length 149mm	220.00	

This model is listed as bearing no arms in the 9th
Edition of the Goss Record. After 1921, a white glazed
version of this model was issued and it is more commonly seen bearing a coat of arms.
Matching Arms: ELLESMERE

for ENGLISH WINE FLAGON
see London Christ's Hospital English Wine Flagon

ETON VASE   86mm   6.50   12.00
This model is identical the the Greenwich Vase
(Goss Record. 8th Edition: Page 16)
Matching Arms: FLOREAT ETONA (or WINDSOR)

EXETER GOBLET   (a) 130mm   14.00   21.00
(Goss Record. 8th Edition: Page 20)   (b) 130mm   23.00   45.00
This is inscribed: *A model of a 16th century Flemish stone-
ware goblet found in a well in the Cathedral Close, Exeter.* (a)
Matching Arms: EXETER
It can also rarely be found inscribed: *Similar ones are to
be seen in the Steen Museum, Antwerpen* (b)
*Matching Arms: ANTWERPEN or PROVINCIE
ANTWERPEN*

Exeter Vase

Felixstowe Roman Ewer

Felixstowe Roman Cinerary Urn

Fenny Stratford Popper

Fimber Ancient British Cinerary Urn

Flemish Melk Pot

Folkstone Saltwood Roman Ewer

Fountains Abbey Abbot's Cup

Four Shire Stone

Fraser Cuach

Froxfield Roman Bronze Drinking Bowl

Gibraltar Alcaraza or Spanish Carafe

148

Model		With any Arms £ p	With Matching Arms £ p
EXETER VASE (Goss Record. 8th Edition: Page 20) *Matching Arms: EXETER*	63mm 101mm	4.50 10.50	12.00 19.50
for FARM LABOURER'S BOTTLE see Luton Bottle			
for FEEDING BOTTLE see Wilderspool Roman Tetinae			
FELIXSTOWE ROMAN EWER (Goss Record. 8th Edition: Page 24) *Matching Arms: FELIXSTOWE*	73mm 114mm	5.50 10.50	12.50 21.50
FELIXSTOWE ROMAN CINERARY URN (Goss Record. 8th Edition: Page 34) *Matching Arms: FELIXSTOWE*	47mm	5.50	17.00
FENNY STRATFORD POPPER (Goss Record. 9th Edition: Page 11) This model is marked COPYRIGHT *Matching Arms: FENNY STRATFORD*	58mm	10.50	25.00
FIMBER ANCIENT BRITISH CINERARY URN International League Model for 1928. *Correct Arms: THE INTERNATIONAL LEAGUE OF GOSS COLLECTORS*	106mm		140.00
for FISH BASKET see Alderney, Guernsey, Jersey, Sark or Welsh Fish Basket			
(OLD) FLEMISH MELK POT (Goss Record. 8th Edition: Page 42)	Max. Dia. 118mm	12.00	30.00

(OLD) FLEMISH MELK POT (Goss Record. 8th Edition: Page 42)
The name of this model is spelt as above in the 8th Edition of the Goss Record (page 42) and on every model produced from the Goss factory. This being Flemish for milk, it is obviously correct. However, it is incorrectly spelt 'milk' in the 9th Edition (page 37).
Matching Arms: ANTWERPEN

for FLOATING MINE
see Contact Mine

German Smoking Pipe

Gerrans Celtic Cinerary Urn

Glastonbury (Abbot Beere's) Jack

Glastonbury Bronze Bowl

Glastonbury Vase (or Urn)

Glastonbury Roman Ewer

Glastonbury Ancient Salt Cellar

Glastonbury Terracotta Bowl

Gloucester Jug

Gnossus Ashmolean Vase

Godalming Ancient Ewer

Gravesend Oriental Water Cooler

Model		With any Arms £ p	With Matching Arms £ p
FOLKESTONE SALTWOOD ROMAN EWER (Goss Record. 8th Edition: Page 27) *Matching Arms: FOLKESTONE*	88mm[1]	8.25	15.25
FOUNTAINS ABBEY, ABBOT'S CUP (Goss Record, 8th Edition: Page 38) also see POSTCARDS Chapter *Matching Arms: FOUNTAINS ABBEY*	44mm 76mm[1]	4.75 10.50	16.00 20.00
FOUR SHIRE STONE (Goss Record. 8th Edition: Page 31) This model has a delicate finial, which is particularly prone to damage. *Matching Arms: CHIPPING NORTON*	118mm	35.00	60.00
FRASER CUACH (Goss Record. 9th Edition: Page 35) *Matching Arms: FORT AUGUSTUS*	Length 104mm	9.50	19.50
for FRID STOL see Hexham Abbey Frid Stol			
FROXFIELD ROMAN BRONZE DRINKING BOWL (Goss Record. 8th Edition: Page 36) This model was originally sold without arms, and subsequently with those of *MARLBOROUGH which are considered matching.*	Dia. 72mm	30.00	43.00
for GERMAN INCENDIARY BOMB see Maldon (Essex) German Incendiary Bomb			
GERMAN SMOKING PIPE (Goss Record. 8th Edition: Page 45) Although manufactured as an ornamental object, it merits inclusion in this section as an 'Historic Object or Shape'. It consists of a wooden stem with a black Bakelite mouthpiece, a porcelain bowl and separate porcelain pipe, which bears the coat of arms. All these parts are joined by push-fitting into cork rings. *It has no correct arms unless perhaps German*	Overall Length 252mm	56.50	
for GERMAN ZEPPELIN BOMB see Bury St. Edmunds German Bomb			

Model		With any Arms £ p	With Matching Arms £ p
GERRANS CELTIC CINERARY URN			
(Goss Record. 8th Edition: Page 18)			
With 1 coat of arms	57mm	5.50	11.25
With 1 coat of arms	127mm[1]	14.00	21.50
With 3 coats of arms	57mm	8.75	15.50
With 3 coats of arms	127mm[1]	19.50	30.00
Matching Arms: FALMOUTH			

GIBRALTAR ALCARAZA or SPANISH CARAFE   68mm   4.75   19.50
(Goss Record. 8th Edition: Page 42)
This model can also be found
labelled 'Gibraltar Carafe'.
Matching Arms: GIBRALTAR or SPAIN

Glastonbury collectors should see the marvellous two-page advertisement in the Goss Record. 8th Edition: Pages 80–81.

GLASTONBURY (ABBOT BEERE'S) JACK   56mm   4.75   13.50
(Goss Record. 8th Edition: Page 32)
Matching Arms: GLASTONBURY

GLASTONBURY ANCIENT SALT CELLAR   82mm   12.50   21.75
(Goss Record. 8th Edition: Page 32)
Matching Arms: GLASTONBURY

GLASTONBURY BRONZE BOWL   44mm   10.50   14.00
(Goss Record. 8th Edition: Page 31)   127mm[1]   23.00   45.00
Matching Arms: GLASTONBURY
The larger version can be found with or without three
ball feet, and earlier models may be found uncrested.

GLASTONBURY ROMAN EWER   71mm   5.50   12.50
(Goss Record. 8th Edition: Page 32)
Matching Arms: GLASTONBURY

GLASTONBURY TERRACOTTA BOWL   36mm   4.25   11.25
(Goss Record. 8th Edition: Page 31)
Matching Arms: GLASTONBURY

GLASTONBURY VASE (OR URN)   45mm   4.25   11.25
(Goss Record. 8th Edition: Page 31)
Matching Arms: GLASTONBURY

Goodwin Sands Carafe

Greek Amphora Vase

Great Pyramid

Greenwich Vase

Grinlow Tower

Guernsey Fish Basket

Guernsey Milk Can and Lid

Guildford Roman Vase

Guillemot Egg, open and closed

Guy's Porridge Pot

Guy's Porridge Pot (identical to Irish Bronze Pot)

Haamoga Amaui, Tonga

Model		With any Arms £ p	With Matching Arms £ p

for GLEN DORGAL CINERARY URN
see Truro Glen Dorgal Cinerary Urn

GLOUCESTER JUG	44mm	4.75	12.50
(Goss Record. 8th Edition: Page 22)	95mm[1]	11.50	21.75
Matching Arms: GLOUCESTER			

GNOSSUS ASHMOLEAN VASE 60mm 56.50
(Goss Record. 9th Edition: Pages 22, 41 and Plate C)
International League Model for 1920.
*Correct Arms: THE INTERNATIONAL LEAGUE OF
   GOSS COLLECTORS*

GODALMING ANCIENT EWER 55mm 7.00 14.00
(Goss Record. 8th Edition: Page 34)
Matching Arms: GODALMING

for GOGARTH ANCIENT VASE
see Llandudno (Gogarth) Ancient Vase

GOODWIN SANDS CARAFE 61mm 4.50 9.50
(Goss Record. 8th Edition: Page 27)
*Matching Arms: RAMSGATE, DEAL or
   WALMER*

GRAVESEND ORIENTAL WATER-COOLER 72mm 14.00 25.00
This model is marked COPYRIGHT
Matching Arms: GRAVESEND

(THE) GREAT PYRAMID 60mm 47.50 82.50
(Goss Record. 8th Edition: Page 42)
Could be considered as a Monument or Building –
often appears chipped at the corners.
Matching Arms: EGYPT

GREEK AMPHORA VASE 138mm 56.50
(Goss Record. 9th Edition: Page 40 and Plate A)
International League Model for 1921.
*Correct Arms: THE INTERNATIONAL LEAGUE OF
   GOSS COLLECTORS*

GREENWICH VASE 86mm 30.00 43.50
This model, which is uncommon, is exactly the
same as the Eton Vase (and says so on its base).
Matching Arms: GREENWICH

Model		With any Arms £ p	With Matching Arms £ p
GRINLOW TOWER	95mm	157.50	220.00
Probably the rarest white glazed Tower.			
Matching Arms: BUXTON			
GUERNSEY FISH BASKET	45mm	13.00	20.00
(Goss Record. 8th Edition: Page 17)	58mm	17.50	26.00
Matching Arms: GUERNSEY			
GUERNSEY MILK CAN and lid	70mm		15.25
(Goss Record. 9th Edition: Page 11)	108mm	15.00	21.75
This model is incomplete without	140mm	19.50	25.75
its lid, value £8.00			
Matching Arms: GUERNSEY			
GUILDFORD ROMAN VASE	63mm	7.50	15.25
(Goss Record. 8th Edition: Page 34)			
Matching Arms: GUILDFORD			
GUILLEMOT EGG (See also BIRD'S EGG,			
first period C Ornamental)	(a) Closed 93mm	52.50	
Found closed, or open as hanging posy	(b) Open 83mm	52.50	
vase either with or without arms, none of			
which may be considered matching. It is			
however preferable to have the arms of a			
coastal town where such birds are found.			
GUY'S PORRIDGE POT	50mm	7.50	14.00
(Goss Record. 8th Edition: Page 35)			
Matching Arms: WARWICK			
GUY'S PORRIDGE POT	40mm		60.00
Better known as a small Irish Bronze Pot but named in			
large Gothic script on side. Only one example has been			
seen with the arms of Stratford-On-Avon.			
HAAMOGA AMAUI, TONGA	82mm		950.00
This model is marked COPYRIGHT			
Made for the agent in Tonga, only one example is			
known to exist, although shards have been found in the			
factory spoilheap.			

Hafod Vase and Lid

Hambledon Cricket Stone

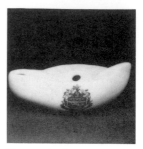

Hamworthy Lamp

Harrogate Ancient Ewer

Hastings Kettle

Hawes Ancient British Urn

Hawkins Henley Sculls in Presentation Box

Hereford Terracotta Kettle and Lid

Herne Bay Reculver Towers

Herne Bay Ancient Ewer

Hertford Ancient Ewer

Hexham Abbey Frid Stol

Model			With any Arms £ p	With Matching Arms £ p
HAFOD VASE and lid		82mm	50.00	80.00

This model is marked COPYRIGHT. The lid has a knob on top which tends to get chipped. Can be found also with a sepia transfer of DEVIL'S BRIDGE – the matching arms value of which is given here as there are no correct arms.
Both the lid and the base are worth £25.00 each.

Model			With any Arms £ p	With Matching Arms £ p
HAMBLEDON CRICKET STONE	Grey	80mm†	830.00	

(Goss Record. 9th Edition: Page 16)

HAMWORTHY LAMP	Length	100mm	8.00	17.00

(Goss Record. 8th Edition: Page 21)
Matching Arms: POOLE

HARROGATE ANCIENT EWER		62mm	4.50	16.00

(Goss Record. 8th Edition: Page 38)
Matching Arms: HARROGATE

HASTINGS KETTLE		51mm	4.25	8.25

(Goss Record. 8th Edition: Page 34)
Matching Arms: HASTINGS

HAWES ANCIENT BRITISH URN	Dia.	95mm	11.25	21.00

(Goss Record. 8th Edition: Page 38)
Matching Arms: HAWES

HAWKINS' HENLEY SCULL	Length	152mm		52.50

(Goss Record. 9th Edition: Page 25)
These sculls have never been seen other than with either of the two Henley coats of arms. The local agent had 'presentation' boxes made to sell them individually, or, more commonly, in pairs. The correct box is worth an additional £20.00
Matching Arms: HENLEY-ON-THAMES ANCIENT or HENLEY-ON-THAMES 1624

for HEN CLOUD LEEK URN
see Leek Urn

for HENLEY HAWKINS' SCULL
see Hawkins' Henley Scull

Model			With any Arms £ p	With Matching Arms £ p
HEREFORD TERRACOTTA KETTLE and lid		70mm	14.50	24.50
(Goss Record. 8th Edition: Page 24 and		121mm[1]	20.50	33.50
advertisement page 66)				
This model is incomplete without its lid, worth £4.00				
Matching Arms: HEREFORD				
HERNE BAY RECULVER TOWERS				
(Goss Record. 8th Edition: Page 27)				
	(a) White glazed	101mm	80.00	125.00
	(b) Grey†	101mm	175.00	
	(c) Brown†	101mm	195.00	
Matching Arms: HERNE BAY				
HERNE BAY ANCIENT EWER		78mm	4.50	16.00
(Goss Record. 8th Edition: Page 27)				
Matching Arms: HERNE BAY				
HERTFORD ANCIENT EWER		69mm	7.00	16.50
(Goss Record. 8th Edition: Page 24)				
Matching Arms: HERTFORD				
HEXHAM ABBEY FRID STOL	(a) White unglazed	60mm	25.75	32.50
(Goss Record. 8th Edition:	(b) White glazed	60mm	25.75	32.50
Page 30)	(c) Brown	60mm	40.00	47.50
	(d) Brown, two-piece as pin box and lid	60mm	85.00	85.00

Each of the three basic versions of this model can be found both with and without a coat of arms, and occasionally in the original box in which they were sold. The two-piece variety has only recently come to light.
Matching Arms: HEXHAM ABBEY

for HIGHLAND CUACH or WHISKEY CUP
see National Highland Cuach or Whiskey Cup

for HIGHLAND MILK CROGAN
see Stornoway Highland Milk Crogan

HITCHIN POSSET CUP		51mm	5.50	13.00
(Goss Record. 8th Edition: Page 24)				
Matching Arms: HITCHIN				

Hitchin Posset Cup

Hornsea Atwick Roman Vase

(The Old) Horse Shoe

Horsham Jug

Hunstanton Ewer

Hythe Cromwellian Mortar

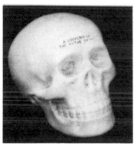

Hythe Crypt Skull

Ilkley Roman Ewer

Ipswich Ancient Ewer

Ipswich Roman Ewer

Irish Bronze Pot

(Ancient) Irish Cruisken

Model		With any Arms £ p	With Matching Arms £ p
HORNSEA ATWICK ROMAN VASE (Goss Record. 8th Edition: Page 38) *Matching Arms: HORNSEA*	51mm	5.25	13.00
(THE OLD) HORSE SHOE (Goss Record. 8th Edition: Page 43) This model is classified under the heading 'Miscellaneous' at the end of the special historical shapes list in the 9th Edition of the Goss Record. If the decoration is large, then the descriptive matter is printed on the reverse. *It has no matching arms*	115mm	15.50	
HORSHAM JUG (Goss Record. 8th Edition: Page 34) *Matching Arms: HORSHAM*	60mm	4.50	12.00
HUNSTANTON EWER (Goss Record. 8th Edition: Page 29) *Matching Arms: HUNSTANTON*	65mm	5.00	13.00
HYTHE CROMWELLIAN MORTAR (Goss Record. 8th Edition: Page 27) *Matching Arms: HYTHE*	38mm	7.00	14.00
HYTHE CRYPT SKULL (Goss Record. 9th Edition: Page 20)			
(a) Small pale yellow†	38mm	33.00	
(b) Large white†	72mm	100.00	
(c) Large pale yellow†	72mm	125.00	
ILKLEY ROMAN EWER (Goss Record. 8th Edition: Page 38) *Matching Arms: ILKLEY*	60mm 132mm	4.50 18.50	13.00 28.00
IPSWICH ANCIENT EWER (Goss Record. 8th Edition: Page 34) *Matching Arms: IPSWICH*	60mm	5.25	13.50
IPSWICH ROMAN EWER (Goss Record. 8th Edition: Page 34) *Matching Arms: IPSWICH*	98mm	14.00	24.50

Irish Mather

Irish Wooden Noggin

Italian Krater

Itford Urn

Japan Ewer

Jersey Fish Basket

Jersey Milk Can and Lid

Kendal Jug

Kettering Urn

King Richard's Well Cover

King's Newton Anglo-Saxon Cinerary Urn

Kininmonth Moss Ancient Pot

Model		With any Arms £ p	With Matching Arms £ p

Any Irish Arms may be considered matching on Irish Models

IRISH BRONZE POT   43mm   4.25   13.00
(Goss Record. 8th Edition: Page 40)   72mm   9.50   18.00
Matching Arms: ARMS OF IRELAND

(ANCIENT) IRISH CRUISKEN   95mm   157.50
International League Model for 1929
Correct Arms: THE INTERNATIONAL LEAGUE OF
  GOSS COLLECTORS

IRISH MATHER   76mm   6.50   14.50
(Goss Record. 8th Edition: Page 40 and   152mm   45.00   65.00
advertisement page 61)
See also POSTCARDS chapter
The large size is usually multi-crested and often carries a verse.
Matching Arms: ARMS OF IRELAND

IRISH WOODEN NOGGIN   63mm   6.50   14.50
(Goss Record. 8th Edition: Page 40)
Matching Arms: ARMS OF IRELAND

for ISLE OF WIGHT ROMAN EWER
see Brading Ewer

for ITALIAN EWER
see Pompeian Ewer

ITALIAN KRATER   100mm   65.00
International League Model for 1922
Correct Arms: THE INTERNATIONAL LEAGUE OF
  GOSS COLLECTORS

ITFORD LEWES URN   66mm   5.50   14.00
(Goss Record. 8th Edition: Page 35)   111mm[1] 15.00   26.00
Matching Arms: LEWES

JAPAN EWER   90mm   8.25   19.50
(Goss Record. 8th Edition: Page 42)   200mm   19.50   50.00
Both sizes are found named and un-named.
Same price
Matching Arms: JAPAN

Model		With any Arms £ p	With Matching Arms £ p
JERSEY FISH BASKET	45mm	8.25	16.50
(Goss Record. 8th Edition: Page 17)	58mm[1]	16.00	24.50
This model can be found without a coat of arms but			
this has little or no bearing on the catalogue price.			
Matching Arms: JERSEY			
JERSEY MILK CAN and lid	70mm		14.50
(Goss Record. 9th Edition: Page 11)	108mm	13.00	22.00
This model is incomplete without	136mm	17.00	26.00
its lid which is worth £8.00			
Matching Arms: JERSEY			
for JOHN BARROW'S MONUMENT			
see Sir John Barrow's Monument, Ulverston			
KENDAL JUG	86mm	5.50	15.00
(Goss Record. 8th Edition: Page 36)	145mm[1]	19.50	30.00
Matching Arms: KENDAL			
KETTERING URN	43mm	4.25	13.50
(Goss Record. 8th Edition: Page 30)			
Matching Arms: KETTERING			
KING RICHARD'S WELL COVER	100mm	130.00	215.00
(Goss Record. 9th Edition: Page 21)			
Matching Arms: MARKET BOSWORTH			
KING'S NEWTON ANGLO-SAXON			
CINERARY URN	(a) 60mm		30.00
(Goss Record. 9th Edition: Pages 22, 41 and	(b) 60mm		47.50
Plate B)			
This model was first introduced bearing the LEAGUE			
OF GOSS COLLECTORS Motif (a) and re-			
introduced later bearing the INTERNATIONAL			
LEAGUE OF GOSS COLLECTORS Motif (b).			
KININMONTH MOSS ANCIENT POT	49mm	13.00	26.00
(Goss Record. 9th Edition: Page 35 and Plate M)			
This model is marked COPYRIGHT			
Matching Arms: OLD DEER			
for KIRKPARK URN			
see Musselburgh Urn			

Lancashire Clog

Lancaster Jug

Lanlawren Celtic Sepulchral Urn

(Battle of) Largs Memorial Tower

Las Palmas Ancient Covered Jarra and Lid

Las Palmas Ancient Earthen Jar

Las Palmas Ancient Jarra

Laxey Urn

Leek Urn

Leicester Tyg

Leiston Abbey Pitcher

Letchworth Celtic Cinerary Urn

Model			With any Arms £ p	With Matching Arms £ p
LANCASHIRE CLOG		Length 93mm	34.50	47.50
(Goss Record. 9th Edition: Page 21)				
This model is marked COPYRIGHT				
Matching Arms: LANCASHIRE				
LANCASTER JUG		68mm	4.50	13.00
(Goss Record. 8th Edition: Page 27)				
Matching Arms: LANCASTER				

for LANDGATE CANNON BALL
see Rye Cannon Ball

LANLAWREN CELTIC SEPULCHRAL URN		50mm	4.25	14.00
(Goss Record. 8th Edition: Page 18)		102mm[1]	14.00	28.00

There are no correct arms for this model but any
Cornish arms would be considered as local. Lanlawren
is part of Falmouth and this must therefore be considered the 'correct' arms although the Goss Record does
not give the Falmouth agency as being stockists of this
model.
Matching Arms: FALMOUTH

(BATTLE OF) LARGS MEMORIAL TOWER				
(Goss Record: 8th Edition: Page 40)	(a) White glazed 128mm		28.00	47.50
Matching Arms: LARGS	(b) Grey glazed 128mm		300.00	

LAS PALMAS ANCIENT COVERED JARRA and lid		58mm	11.00	21.75
(Goss Record. 8th Edition: Page 42)				
This model is incomplete without its lid, value £6.00				
Matching arms: LAS PALMAS				

LAS PALMAS ANCIENT EARTHEN JAR		58mm	6.00	21.75
(Goss Record. 8th Edition: Page 42)				
Matching Arms: LAS PALMAS				

LAS PALMAS ANCIENT JARRA		53mm	6.00	21.75
(Goss Record. 8th Edition: Page 42)				
Matching Arms: LAS PALMAS				

for LAS PALMAS CANARY PORRON
see Canary Porron

*Letchworth Carinated
Roman Vase*

Lewes Vase

Lichfield Jug

*Lincoln Leather Jack, small
with City Ringers Decoration*

*Black Lincoln Leather Jack,
large*

Lincoln Vase

Littlehampton Roman Ewer

*Llandudno (Little Orme)
Roman Vase*

*Llandudno (Gogarth)
Ancient Vase*

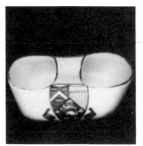

Llangollen Coracle

Lobster Trap

*London Christ's Hospital
English Wine Flagon*

Model			With any Arms £ p	With Matching Arms £ p
LAXEY GRETCH-VEG URN		Dia. 55mm	6.00	13.00

(Goss Record. 9th Edition: Page 19)
This model can be found bearing arms on the base (on
the inside) or in the usual position on the outside.
Matching Arms: LAXEY, ISLE OF MAN

for LEEK
see Welsh Leek

LEEK URN		63mm	6.00	15.50 ✓

(Goss Record. 8th Edition: Page 32)
Matching Arms: LEEK

LEICESTER TYG	(a) with 1 coat of arms	59mm	8.00	15.25 ✓
(Goss Record. 8th Edn:Page 28)	(b) with 3 coats of arms	59mm	11.25	20.00

Matching Arms: LEICESTER

LEISTON ABBEY PITCHER	61mm	4.75	14.50
(Goss Record. 8th Edition: Page 34)	107mm	12.50	21.75

Matching Arms: LEISTON ABBEY

LETCHWORTH CELTIC CINERARY URN	97mm	23.00	34.50

(Goss Record. 9th Edition: Page 19 and Plate J)
This model is marked COPYRIGHT
Matching Arms: LETCHWORTH

LETCHWORTH CARINATED ROMAN VASE	60mm	52.50	110.00

This model is marked COPYRIGHT
Matching Arms: LETCHWORTH

LEWES ROMAN VASE	35mm[1]	4.25	11.25

(Goss Record. 8th Edition: Page 35)
Matching Arms: LEWES

for LEWES URN
see Itford Urn

for LHANNAN SHEE CUP
see Ballafletcher (Cup of)

LICHFIELD JUG	57mm	4.50	13.00
(Goss Record. 8th Edition: Page 32)	121mm[1]	17.50	30.00

Matching Arms: LICHFIELD

for LIMPET SHELL
see 10K5 ORNAMENTAL or 9C ORNAMENTAL

Model		With any Arms £ p	With Matching Arms £ p

LINCOLN LEATHER JACK
(Goss Record. 8th Edition: Page 28)

(a) White glazed	56mm	4.25	13.00
(b) Correct marking-coloured bell and shield, no arms	56mm		34.50
(c) White glazed	153mm	17.50	32.50
(d) Matt black with multi-coloured bells, no arms	153mm		870.00

Matching Arms: LINCOLN

LINCOLN VASE 67mm 4.75 13.00
(Goss Record. 8th Edition: Page 28) 88mm 10.50 22.50
Matching Arms: LINCOLN

LITTLEHAMPTON ROMAN EWER 73mm 5.50 14.00
(Goss Record. 8th Edition: Page 35)
Matching Arms: LITTLEHAMPTON

LLANDUDNO (LITTLE ORME) ROMAN VASE 82mm 11.25 21.75
(Goss Record. 9th Edition: Page 34 and Plate K)
This model is marked COPYRIGHT
Matching Arms: LLANDUDNO

LLANDUDNO (GOGARTH) ANCIENT VASE 84mm 10.50 21.75
(Goss Record. 9th Edition: Page 34 and Plate K)
This model is marked COPYRIGHT
Matching Arms: LLANDUDNO

LLANGOLLEN CORACLE Length 77mm 17.50 28.00
(Goss Record. 8th Edition: Page 39 and advertisement,
page 101)
Matching Arms: LLANGOLLEN
Up until 1903, the Welsh Coracle was called thus and
listed in *Goss Record* as a national model having no
particular town or city arms. From 1904 onwards, it
was re-named The Llangollen Coracle with Llangollen
given as the matching arms, which explains the confusion of the two descriptions which can be found on the
same piece.
See also WELSH CORACLE

LOBSTER TRAP 51mm 10.50 15.50
(Goss Record. 8th Edition: Page 17) 84mm[1] 16.00 24.50
Matching Arms: ANY OF THE CHANNEL ISLANDS

London Stone

Longships Lighthouse,
Lands End

Looe Ewer

Louth Ancient Ewer

Ludlow Sack Bottle

Luton Bottle or Costrel

Lyme Regis Ammonite

Madeira Bullock Car

Maidstone Roman Ewer

Maldon (Essex) German
Incendiary Bomb

Maltese Carafe

Maltese Double-mouthed
Vase

Model		With any Arms £ p	With Matching Arms £ p
LONDON CHRIST'S HOSPITAL ENGLISH WINE FLAGON (Goss Record. 8th Edition: Page 29) *Matching Arms: CHRIST'S HOSPITAL*	90mm	8.75	19.50
LONDON STONE (a) White† (Goss Record. 9th Edition: Page 22) (b) Brown†	109mm 109mm	82.50 135.00	
LONGSHIPS LIGHTHOUSE, LAND'S END (Goss Record. 8th Edition: Page 18) *Matching Arms: LAND'S END*	122mm	26.00	37.50
LOOE EWER (Goss Record. 8th Edition: Page 18) *Matching Arms: LOOE*	65mm	4.25	13.00
for LOTUS VASE see Egyptian Lotus Vase			
LOUTH ANCIENT EWER (Goss Record. 8th Edition: Page 28) *Matching Arms: LOUTH*	43mm 113mm	4.50 17.00	13.00 25.00
LUDLOW SACK BOTTLE (Goss Record. 8th Edition: Page 31) *Matching Arms: LUDLOW*	75mm[1]	12.00	21.00
LUTON BOTTLE OR COSTREL (Goss Record. 8th Edition: Page 16) *Matching Arms: LUTON*	Length 65mm	11.00	22.50
for LUTON COSTREL see Luton Bottle or Costrel			
LYME REGIS AMMONITE (Goss Record. 9th Edition: Page 14) This model is identical to the Whitby Ammonite *Matching Arms: LYME REGIS*	73mm	23.00	34.50
MADEIRA BULLOCK CAR This model is marked COPYRIGHT *Matching Arms: FUNCHAL, MADEIRA*	55mm		600.00

Model		With any Arms £ p	With Matching Arms £ p
MAIDSTONE ROMAN EWER	82mm	6.00	14.00
(Goss Record. 8th Edition: Page 27)	130mm	11.25	26.00
Matching Arms: MAIDSTONE			

MALDON (ESSEX) GERMAN INCENDIARY BOMB   75mm   19.50   28.00
(Goss Record. 9th Edition: Page 16)
This model is marked COPYRIGHT. It has a delicate
handle which is frequently found broken, in which
condition it is of little value.
Matching Arms: MALDON

**Either MALTA or VALLETTA would be considered
matching on any Maltese Model**

MALTESE CARAFE   105mm   14.50   26.00
(Goss Record. 8th Edition: Page 42)
Matching Arms: MALTA

MALTESE DOUBLE-MOUTHED VASE   60mm   19.50   28.50
(Goss Record. 9th Edition: Page 36 and Plate P)
Matching Arms: MALTA

MALTESE FIRE GRATE   53mm   12.00   23.00
(Goss Record. 8th Edition: Page 42)
Matching Arms: MALTA

MALTESE FUNEREAL URN   61mm   5.50   13.00
(Goss Record. 8th Edition: Page 42)
Matching Arms: MALTA

MALTESE TWIN VASE   50mm   32.50   40.00
(Goss Record. 9th Edition: Page 36 and Plate P)
Matching Arms: MALTA

MALTESE TWO-WICK LAMP   Length 81mm   12.00   21.00
(Goss Record. 8th Edition: Page 42)
Matching Arms: MALTA

MALTESE VASE à CANARD   45mm   8.00   16.50
(Goss Record. 9th Edition: Page 36)
Matching Arms: MALTA

MANX LOBSTER POT   Dia. 67mm   40.00
This model is identical to the Lobster Trap.
Matching Arms: ISLE OF MAN

Maltese Fire Grate

Maltese Funereal Urn

Maltese Twin Vase

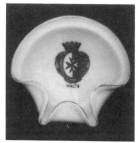

Maltese Two-wick Lamp

Maltese Vase à Canard

Manx Lobster Trap

Manx Peel Pot

Manx Spirit Measure

The Maple Leaf of Canada

*Mary Queen of Scots
Nightlight*

Melrose Cup

Minster Ancient Ewer

Model		With any Arms £ p	With Matching Arms £ p
MANX PEEL POT (Goss Record. 8th Edition: Page 26) *Matching Arms: PEEL, ISLE OF MAN*	49mm	5.50	14.00
(ANCIENT) MANX SPIRIT MEASURE (Goss Record. 8th Edition: Page 26) *Matching Arms: PEEL, ISLE OF MAN*	68mm	8.25	20.00
(THE) MAPLE LEAF OF CANADA This model is marked COPYRIGHT and numbered 813. *Matching Arms: CANADA or any Canadian coat of arms.*	118mm	70.00	130.00
MARY, QUEEN OF SCOTS Face in high relief on (a) two-piece night-light (b) two or three-handled mug For illustration see page 172. *Correct Arms: MARY QUEEN OF SCOTS*	78mm 118mm	130.00 75.00	145.00 105.00
MELROSE CUP (Goss Record. 8th Edition: Page 40) Not really a model in the true sense of the word, it was designed by the Melrose Agent and first marketed exclusively by him. The bowl of the cup incorporates the same leaf design that can be found at the top of the pillars in Melrose Abbey. *Matching Arms: MELROSE ABBEY*	128mm	40.00	55.00
for MILK CROGAN see Stornoway Highland Milk Crogan			
MINSTER ANCIENT EWER This model is marked COPYRIGHT *Matching Arms: MINSTER*	88mm	12.50	24.00
MINSTER ANCIENT URN This model is marked COPYRIGHT *Matching Arms: MINSTER*	65mm	8.75	24.75
for MONMOUTH MASK See FIRST PERIOD C ORNAMENTAL Chapter			
for MONNOW GATE see Old Gateway on Monnow Bridge			

Minster Ancient Urn

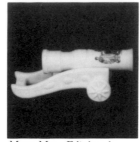

Mons Meg, Edinburgh Castle

Munich Beer Seidel

Musselburgh Kirkpark Ancient Urn

National Highland Cauch or Whiskey Cup

Newbury Leather Bottle, small

Newbury Leather Bottle, (large) with Stopper

Newcastle (Staffordshire) Cup

Newcastle Castle

Newcastle Roman Jug

North Foreland Lighthouse

Northwich Sepulchral Urn

Model			With any Arms £ p	With Matching Arms £ p
MONS MEG, EDINBURGH CASTLE (Goss Record. 8th Edition: Page 40) *Matching Arms: EDINBURGH*	Length 122mm		33.50	42.50
MUNICH BEER SEIDEL *Matching Arms: MUNICH (MUNCHEN)*	52mm		25.75	52.50
MUSSELBURGH KIRKPARK ANCIENT URN (Goss Record. 8th Edition: Page 40) *Matching Arms: MUSSELBURGH*	51mm		4.25	14.00

for MYCENAEAN VASE
see Cyprus Mycenaean Vase

NATIONAL HIGHLAND CUACH or WHISKEY CUP
(Goss Record. 8th Edition: Page 40)   Width 94mm   6.50   13.00
Any 'Highland' Arms are considered matching.

for NAUTILUS SHELL
see Second Period 10K5 Ornamental and First Period 9C Ornamental chapters.

Model			With any Arms £ p	With Matching Arms £ p
NEWBURY LEATHER BOTTLE (Goss Record. 8th Edition: Page 16) (a) *Matching Arms: NEWBURY* (b)	58mm 114mm[1]		4.25 13.00	11.00 21.00
(c) With Stopper	125mm[1]		35.00	43.50
NEWCASTLE (STAFFORDSHIRE) CUP (Goss Record. 8th Edition: Page 32) *Matching Arms: NEWCASTLE-UNDER-LYME*	70mm[1]		12.00	24.00
NEWCASTLE CASTLE (a) White glazed *Matching Arms: NEWCASTLE* (b) Brown†	88mm 88mm		130.00 300.00	165.00
NEWCASTLE ROMAN JUG (Goss Record. 8th Edition: Page 30) *Matching Arms: NEWCASTLE*	63mm		4.25	13.50

for NORMAN TOWER, CHRISTCHURCH
see Christchurch Priory Church Norman Tower

NORTH FORELAND LIGHTHOUSE   108mm   41.50   56.50
(Goss Record. 8th Edition: Page 27)
Matching Arms: BROADSTAIRS or RAMSGATE

Norwegian Bucket

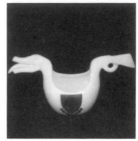

Norwegian Dragon-shaped Beer Bowl

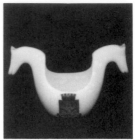

Norwegian Horse-shaped Beer Bowl

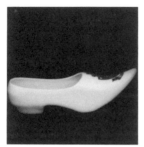

Norwegian Wooden Shoe

Norwich Urn

Nottingham Ewer

Nottingham Urn

Old Gateway on Monnow Bridge

Orkney Craisie

Ostend Flemish Bottle

Ostend Flemish Tobacco Jar

Ostend Vase

Model			With any Arms £ p	With Matching Arms £ p
NORTHWICH SEPULCHRAL URN		85mm		215.00

NORTHWICH SEPULCHRAL URN 85mm 215.00
International League Model for 1930.
Correct Arms: THE INTERNATIONAL LEAGUE OF
  GOSS COLLECTORS

NORWEGIAN BUCKET 58mm 11.50 47.50 ⚡
(Goss Record. 8th Edition: Page 42)
Matching Arms: NORWAY (NORGE)

NORWEGIAN DRAGON-SHAPED BEER BOWL
(Goss Record. 8th Edition: Page 42) Length 155mm 17.00 47.50
Matching Arms: NORWAY (NORGE)

NORWEGIAN HORSE-SHAPED BEER BOWL
(Goss Record. 8th Edition: Page 42) (a) Length 115mm 16.00 47.50 /
Matching Arms: NORWAY (NORGE) (b) Length 115mm 56.50
Can rarely be found (b) with the following inscription
in Norwegian: *Model af Norsk ølbolle (kjengé) med*
Dragehoved. Rd.No. 526382, which actually applies to
the Dragon-shaped beer bowl.

NORWEGIAN WOODEN SHOE Length 103mm 19.00 47.50
(Goss Record. 8th Edition: Page 42)
Matching Arms: NORWAY (NORGE)

**The Arms of any Norwegian Town would also be considered matching.
BERGEN is the most common.**

NORWICH URN 51mm 4.25 12.00
(Goss Record. 8th Edition: Page 29) 62mm 6.00 14.00 ∨
Matching Arms: NORWICH 88mm[1] 10.50 17.50

for NOSE OF BRASENOSE
see (The Nose of) Brasenose

NOTTINGHAM EWER (a) 1 crest 63mm 4.50 12.00 ✓
(Goss Record. 8th Edition: Page 30) (b) 2 crests 63mm 6.00 13.00
Matching Arms: NOTTINGHAM

NOTTINGHAM URN 40mm 4.25 11.00 ✓✓
(Goss Record. 8th Edition: Page 30 and advertisement
page 79)
Matching Arms: NOTTINGHAM

Oxford Ewer

Oxford Jug

Painswick Pot

Panama Vase

Penmaenmawr Urn

Perth Coronation Chair

Peterborough Tripod

Plymouth Jug

Pompeian Ewer

Portland Lighthouse

Portland Vase

Preston Old Bushel Measure

Model		With any Arms £ p	With Matching Arms £ p

for OLD BRAZIER (SCILLY ISLES)
see Tresco Old Brazier

OLD GATEWAY ON MONNOW BRIDGE
(Goss Record. 9th Edition: Page 23
and Plate J)

(a) White glazed	95mm	75.00	110.00
(b) Brown†	95mm	215.00	

This model is the MONNOW GATE and not MON-
MOW GATE as mis-spelt in the 9th Edition of the
Goss Record and on the model itself. The side gates are
found both open and closed.
Matching Arms: MONMOUTH

for OLD HORSESHOE
see Horseshoe (The Old)

for OLD PILLION STONE, FLOWERGATE, WHITBY
see Whitby Pillion Stone

for OLD SARUM KETTLE
see Salisbury Kettle

ORKNEY CRAISIE   80mm   17.00   30.00
(Goss Record. 9th Edition: Page 35)
This model has a high thin handle which can frequently
be found either cracked or completely broken off, in
which condition it is of little value.
Matching Arms: ORKNEY

OSTEND FLEMISH BOTTLE   65mm   5.50   19.50 ✓
(Goss Record. 8th Edition: Page 42)
Matching Arms: OSTENDE

OSTEND FLEMISH TOBACCO JAR   54mm   4.25   16.00 ✓
(Goss Record. 8th Edition: Page 42)
Matching Arms: OSTENDE

OSTEND VASE   57mm   4.25   16.00 ✓
(Goss Record. 8th Edition: Page 42)
Matching Arms: OSTENDE

OSTEND VASE   57mm   4.25   13.00
(Goss Record. 8th Edition: Page 42)
Matching Arms: OSTENDE

Model			With any Arms £ p	With Matching Arms £ p	
OXFORD EWER		76mm	5.25	13.00	
(Goss Record. 8th Edition: Page 31)		126mm[1]	12.00	19.50	✔
Matching Arms: OXFORD					
OXFORD JUG		173mm[1]	17.00	28.00	
(Goss Record. 8th Edition: Page 31)					
Matching Arms: OXFORD					
PAINSWICK POT		50mm	4.25	13.00	✔✔
(Goss Record. 8th Edition: Page 22)					
Matching Arms: PAINSWICK					
PANAMA VASE		128mm	26.00	50.00	
Matching Arms: PANAMA					
PENMAENMAWR URN		45mm	4.25	13.00	✔
(Goss Record. 8th Edition: Page 39)					
Matching Arms: PENMAENMAWR					
PERTH CORONATION CHAIR	(a) White glazed	87mm	75.00	110.00	
(Goss Record. 9th Edition: Page 36)	(a) Stone in brown	87mm	117.50	157.50	
This model is the same as the	(c) Brown†	87mm	150.00		
Westminster Abbey Coronation Chair					
except that it carries the following					
inscription:					
The chair contains the ancient stone					
on which the Kings and Queens of					
Scotland were formerly crowned at					
Scone, Perthshire.					
Matching Arms: PERTH					
PETERBOROUGH TRIPOD		47mm	8.25	14.50	
(Goss Record. 8th Edition: Page 30)					
Matching Arms: PETERBOROUGH					

for PILGRIM'S BOTTLE
see Ancient Costril

for PINE CONE
see Bournemouth Pine Cone

for PIPE
see German Smoking Pipe or Twickenham Antique Pipe

Model			With any Arms £ p	With Matching Arms £ p
PLYMOUTH (SPANISH) JUG		55mm	4.25	12.00
(Goss Record. 8th Edition: Page 20)				
Matching Arms: PLYMOUTH				
POMPEIAN EWER		91mm	8.75	
(Goss Record. 8th Edition: Page 42)		208mm	21.75	
Both sizes are also found un-named – same price.				
Italian Arms have yet to be recorded on this model but				
they would certainly be matching were they to exist.				

for POPE'S PIPE, TWICKENHAM
see Twickenham Antique Pipe

				With any Arms £ p	With Matching Arms £ p
PORTLAND LIGHTHOUSE	(a) Black band		120mm	67.50	80.00
(Goss Record. 8th Edition: Page 21)	(b) Brown band		120mm	40.00	65.00
Matching Arms: ROYAL MANOR	(c) Orange band		120mm	100.00	140.00
or U.D.C. OF PORTLAND					
PORTLAND VASE		(a)	51mm	4.50	10.50
		(b)	51mm	26.00	31.50
		(c)	51mm	35.00	

This is one of the most interesting models. All are inscribed on the base *Model of The Portland Vase in The British Museum* and some have commemorative wording on the base marking the anniversary of the death of Josiah Wedgwood as follows *MEMORIAL OF JOSIAH WEDGWOOD* (b) and are much sought after. This variety is thought to have been part of a limited edition (possibly 1,000) and collectors picking up every Portland Vase could easily have a pleasant surprise. Mr. J.J. Jarvis, when starting the League of Goss Collectors, chose this as the first 'League' model (c).

Collectors may read about the discovery and history of the original in the Goss Record. 8th Edition: Page 28. There are no correct town arms for this model as the Goss original is currently in the British Museum. As the original was purchased by the Duchess of Portland, the arms of the Duke of Portland could be considered matching, or perhaps also those of the Royal Manor or U.D.C. of Portland

Matching Arms for (a) DUKE OF PORTLAND
          (b) JOSIAH WEDGWOOD
          (c) THE LEAGUE OF GOSS COLLECTORS

Queen Elizabeth's Riding Shoe

Queen Philippa's Record Chest

Queen Victoria's First Shoe

Ramsey Cronk Aust Cinerary Urn

Ramsgate Romano-British Ewer

Ramsgate Romano-British Jug

Ramsgate Urn

Rayleigh Ancient Cooking Pot

Reading Jug

Reading (Silchester) Urn

Reading (Silchester) Vase

Rochester Bellarmine Jug

Model		With any Arms £ p	With Matching Arms £ p

PRESTON OLD BUSHEL MEASURE   Dia. 58mm   56.50   110.00
(Goss Record. 9th Edition: Page 21 and Plate M)
This model is marked COPYRIGHT. It is the rarest of
the 'small' bushels.
Matching Arms: PRESTON

for PRINCESS VICTORIA'S FIRST SLIPPER
see Queen Victoria's First Shoe

for PYRAMID
see Great Pyramid (The)

for QUEEN CHARLOTTE'S KETTLE
see Windsor Kettle

QUEEN ELIZABETH'S RIDING SHOE   Length 105mm   82.50   110.00
(Goss Record, 9th Edition: Page 16 and Plate L)
On page 16 of the Goss Record it is referred to as a
slipper and under Plate L as a shoe.
This model is by far the rarest shoe.
It is marked COPYRIGHT
Matching Arms: THAXTED

QUEEN PHILIPPA'S RECORD CHEST
(Goss Record. 8th Edition. Page 99)   Length (a) 80mm   26.00   32.50
Matching Arms: KNARESBOROUGH (ABBEY)   (b) 94mm   26.00   32.50

QUEEN VICTORIA'S FIRST SHOE (a) Without Arms 102mm   27.00†
(Goss Record. 8th Edition: Page 20)   (b) Pre-1901   102mm   26.00   34.50
                         (c) Post-1901   102mm   26.00   34.50
Can sometimes be found with a hole in the back of the
shoe for hanging.
A descriptive leaflet was issued with this model and is
valued at £10.00
Matching Arms: QUEEN VICTORIA or SIDMOUTH

RAMSEY CRONK AUST CINERARY URN   59mm   6.00   14.00
(Goss Record. 8th Edition: Page 26)
Matching Arms: RAMSEY, ISLE OF MAN

RAMSGATE ROMANO-BRITISH EWER   47mm   13.50   22.00
This model is marked COPYRIGHT and 794.
Matching Arms: RAMSGATE

Model			With any Arms £ p	With Matching Arms £ p
RAMSGATE ROMANO-BRITISH JUG This model is marked COPYRIGHT and 795. *Matching Arms: RAMSGATE*		70mm	12.50	22.00
RAMSGATE URN This model is marked COPYRIGHT and 787. *Matching Arms: RAMSGATE*		75mm	8.00	22.00
RAYLEIGH ANCIENT COOKING POT (Goss Record. 8th Edition: Page 22) *Matching Arms: RAYLEIGH*		33mm	4.50	14.00
READING JUG (Goss Record. 8th Edition: Page 16) *Matching Arms: READING*		82mm 140mm	4.25 12.00	10.50 20.00
READING (SILCHESTER) URN (Goss Record. 8th Edition: Page 16) *Matching Arms: READING*		50mm	4.25	10.50
READING (SILCHESTER) VASE (Goss Record. 8th Edition: Page 16) *Matching Arms: READING*		50mm	4.25	10.50
for RECULVER TOWERS see Herne Bay Reculver Towers				
ROCHESTER BELLARMINE JUG (Goss Record. 8th Edition: Page 27) *Matching Arms: ROCHESTER*		65mm	4.75	13.00
for ROMAN EWER see Cirencester Roman Ewer				
ROMAN MORTARIUM (Goss Record. 8th Edition: Page 43) *This model has no matching arms.*	(a) Named (b) Un-named	Dia. 95mm	33.00 11.00	
For ROMAN TETINAE see Wilderspool Roman Tetinae				
ROMAN VASE This model is marked COPYRIGHT and 783. *It has no matching arms.*	(a) White glazed (b) Lustre †	160mm 160mm	47.50 56.50	

Roman Mortarium

Roman Vase No. 783

Romsey Bushel

Rothesay Stone

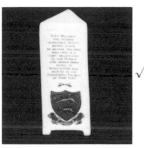

Rufus Stone

Russian Shrapnel Shell

Rye Cannon Ball with Plinth

Rye Cannon Ball without Plinth

Suffron Walden Covered Urn and lid

St. Albans Ancient Cooking Pot

St. Mary's Lighthouse, Whitley Bay

St. Neots Ancient Urn

Model		With any Arms £ p	With Matching Arms £ p
ROMSEY BUSHEL	Dia. 68mm	9.50	18.50
(Goss Record. 8th Edition: Page 23)			
Matching Arms: ROMSEY			
ROTHESAY STONE	Brown† Length 95mm	875.00	
(Goss Record. 9th Edition: Page 35 and Plate G)			
Only two examples of this rare model are known to exist			
RUFUS STONE	94mm	10.00	19.50
(Goss Record. 8th Edition: Page 23 and advertisement page 64)			
The nearest Agency to the Rufus Stone is Lyndhurst and this may also be considered matching.			
Matching Arms: KING WILLIAM RUFUS			
RUSSIAN SHRAPNEL SHELL	110mm	16.00	40.00
(Goss Record. War Edition. Page 5 [illustrated] and 7)			
Matching Arms: RUSSIA or ANY ARTILLERY REGI-MENT could add £10–£40			
RYE CANNON BALL, Multi-coloured			
(Goss Record. 8th Edition: Page 35)			
(a) On plinth	106mm	75.00	120.00
(b) Without plinth	68mm	30.00	56.50
Matching Arms: RYE			
SAFFRON WALDEN COVERED URN and lid	70mm	13.50	22.50
(Goss Record. 8th Edition: Page 22)	121mm	19.50	32.50
This model has a lid that looks very like an Egyptian Mummy's Head without which it is incomplete, value £8.00			
Matching Arms: SAFFRON WALDEN			
With Egyptian Arms add £10.00			
ST. ALBANS ANCIENT COOKING POT	58mm	8.25	15.50
(Goss Record. 8th Edition: Page 24)			
Matching Arms: ST. ALBANS			
ST. MARY'S LIGHTHOUSE, WHITLEY BAY	135mm	400.00	495.00
This model is not listed in any edition of the Goss Record and is the second rarest lighthouse.			
Matching Arms: WHITLEY BAY			

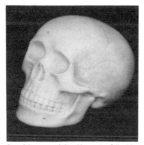

St. Simon of Sudbury's Skull

Salisbury (Old Sarum) Kettle

Salisbury Leather Jack

Salisbury Leather Gill

Model			With any Arms £ p	With Matching Arms £ p
ST. NEOTS ANCIENT URN (Goss Record. 8th Edition: Page 24) *Matching Arms: ST. NEOTS*		63mm	4.75	15.25
ST. SIMON OF SUDBURY'S SKULL	(a) White† (b) Brown†	72mm 72mm	175.00 285.00	
SALISBURY KETTLE (Goss Record. 8th Edition: Page 36 and advertisement page 114) Also known as the Old Sarum Kettle *Matching Arms: SALISBURY*		88mm 133mm	11.50 17.50	17.50 22.50
SALISBURY LEATHER JACK (Goss Record. 8th Edition: Page 36) The large size is always and the small size is sometimes found with CR 1646 on the side under a crown. In addition, it appears both crested and uncrested. Same price. *Matching Arms: SALISBURY*		☞ 44mm 140mm[1]	4.25 16.00	13.00 26.50
SALISBURY LEATHER GILL (Goss Record. 8th Edition: Page 36) This model is always found with RSM 1658 in red and blue letters on the side. It can be found both crested and uncrested. Same price. *Matching Arms: SALISBURY*		75mm	10.00	24.50

The Salisbury Jack and Gill are thought to be the inspiration for the popular nursery rhyme, with the broken crown being that of Charles I. The initials C R (Carolus Rex) 1646 on the Salisbury Jack is held to be a commemoration of the visit by Charles I to the neighbourhood, and the loyal owner of the Jack marked it thus. 1658 on the gill is the year of Oliver Cromwell's death. R S M stands for 'Resurgam' meaning 'I shall rise again', referring to the rising hopes of the Loyalists on hearing of the death of Cromwell. The originals should still be in Salisbury Museum.

for SALTWOOD EWER
see Folkestone Roman Ewer

Model		With any Arms	With Matching Arms
SARK FISH BASKET (Goss Record. 8th Edition: Page 17) *Matching Arms: SARK (SERCQ)*	45mm 58mm		26.00 31.50

Sark Fish Basket

Sark Milk Can and Lid

Scarborough Jug

Scarborough Kettle

Seaford Urn

Shakespeare's Jug

*Shrewsbury 'Uriconium'
Ewer*

*Shrewsbury
Romano-Salopian Ewer*

*Sir John Barrow's
Monument, Ulverston*

Skegness Clock Tower

Southampton Ancient Pipkin

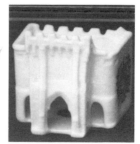

Southampton Bargate

Model		With any Arms £ p	With Matching Arms £ p
SARK MILK CAN and lid	70mm	20.00	30.00
(Goss Record. 9th Edition: Page 11)	108mm		34.50
This would be incomplete without its lid, value £8.00	140mm		40.00
Matching Arms: SARK (SERCQ)			
SCARBOROUGH JUG	51mm	4.75	13.00
(Goss Record. 8th Edition: Page 38)	70mm	10.50	19.50
Matching Arms: SCARBOROUGH			
SCARBOROUGH KETTLE	66mm	8.00	15.25
(Goss Record. 8th Edition: Page 38)	88mm	14.00	24.50

This model can be found labelled as a *Scarborough Jug*, same price.
Matching Arms: SCARBOROUGH
Up until 1911–1916, the two Scarborough models were both known as 'Scarborough Jugs'. The name of one was changed, probably to avoid confusion. Originally one jug was named as follows:
Model of jug found in old moat at the back of Huntress Row 600 years old
and the other
Model of jug found near Ancient Pottery.
It was the latter which was re-named a kettle between 1911 and 1916. Goss Records prior to 1911 list both as Scarborough Jugs. Both shapes were in production before 1900.

Model		With any Arms £ p	With Matching Arms £ p
SEAFORD URN	48mm[1]	6.00	14.50
(Goss Record. 8th Edition: Page 35)			
Matching Arms: SEAFORD			
SHAKESPEARE'S JUG	51mm	8.00	15.50
(Goss Record. 8th Edition: Page 35)	76mm	12.00	20.00
Matching Arms: WILLIAM SHAKESPEARE or	88mm	17.50	30.00
STRATFORD-ON-AVON			

for SHEPHERD'S CROWN SEA URCHIN
see Steyning Shepherd's Crown

Model		With any Arms £ p	With Matching Arms £ p
SHREWSBURY EWER	97mm	17.00	26.00
First Period Variety – The Uriconium Ewer [1]			
(Goss Record. 8th Edition: Page 31)			

One of the first models to be introduced.
Matching Arms: SHREWSBURY

Model		With any Arms £ p	With Matching Arms £ p
SHREWSBURY ROMANO-SALOPIAN EWER (Goss Record. 8th Edition: Page 31) *Matching Arms: SHREWSBURY*	68mm	5.25	13.00 ✓
for SILCHESTER URN ✓ see Reading (Silchester) Urn			
for SILCHESTER VASE see Reading (Silchester) Vase			
for SIMON OF SUDBURY'S SKULL see St. Simon of Sudbury's Skull			
SIR JOHN BARROW'S MONUMENT, ULVERSTON *Matching Arms: ULVERSTON*	120mm	70.00	110.00
SKEGNESS CLOCK TOWER *Matching Arms: SKEGNESS*	132mm	80.00	130.00
for SKULL see Hythe Crypt Skull, Yorick's Skull or St. Simon of Sudbury's Skull			
for SOLDIER'S WATER BOTTLE see Waterlooville Soldier's Water Bottle			
SOUTHAMPTON ANCIENT PIPKIN (Goss Record. 8th Edition: Page 23) *Matching Arms: SOUTHAMPTON*	56mm 76mm 101mm[1]	4.25 12.00 21.50	9.00 19.50 ✓ 28.00
SOUTHAMPTON BARGATE (Goss Record. 8th Edition: Page 23)			
(a) Small, white glazed	55mm	47.50	82.50
(b) Small, grey†	55mm	87.50	
(c) Large, white glazed or unglazed†	87mm	65.00	110.00
(d) Large, grey†	87mm	110.00	
(e) Large, brown†	87mm	185.00	
Matching Arms: SOUTHAMPTON			
SOUTHDOWN SHEEP BELL This model is identical to the Small Swiss Cow Bell and is marked COPYRIGHT *It has no correct arms – any Sussex downland arms are to be considered as matching*	54mm	52.50	85.00

Southport Vase

Southwold Ancient Gun

Southwold Jar

Staffordshire Drinking Cup

Staffordshire One-handled Tyg

Staffordshire Two-handled Tyg

Southdown Sheep Bell

Staffordshire Tyg League Model

Steyning Shepherd's Crown Sea Urchin

Stirling Pint Measure

Stockport Plague Stone

Stockton Ancient Salt Pot

192

Model		With any Arms £ p	With Matching Arms £ p
SOUTHPORT VASE (Goss Record. 8th Edition: Page 27) *Matching Arms: SOUTHPORT*	50mm	4.25	12.00
SOUTHWOLD ANCIENT GUN (Goss Record. 9th Edition: Page 28) *Matching Arms: SOUTHWOLD*	Length 94mm	160.00	275.00
SOUTHWOLD JAR (Goss Record. 8th Edition: Page 34) *Matching Arms: SOUTHWOLD*	88mm 140mm[1]	4.50 15.00	14.00 26.00
for SPANISH CARAFE see Gibraltar Alcaraza			
for SPANISH (EDDYSTONE) JUG see Plymouth Jug			
STAFFORDSHIRE DRINKING CUP International League Model for 1926. *Correct Arms: THE INTERNATIONAL LEAGUE OF GOSS COLLECTORS*	111mm		80.00
(STAFFORDSHIRE) ONE-HANDLED TYG (Goss Record. 8th Edition: Page 32) *Matching Arms: STAFFORDSHIRE*	65mm	4.25	12.00
(STAFFORDSHIRE) TWO-HANDLED TYG (Goss Record. 8th Edition: Page 32) *Matching Arms: STAFFORDSHIRE*	65mm	4.25	12.00
STAFFORDSHIRE TYG (Goss Record. 9th Edition: Pages 22 and 28 and Plate B) This model was first introduced bearing the LEAGUE OF GOSS COLLECTORS Motif (a) and re-introduced later bearing the INTERNATIONAL LEAGUE OF GOSS COLLECTORS Motif (b).	(a) 70mm (b) 70mm		40.00 47.50
STEYNING SHEPHERD'S CROWN SEA URCHIN (Goss Record. 9th Edition: Page 29) This model is marked COPYRIGHT *Matching Arms: STEYNING*	50mm	21.75	34.50

Stornoway Highland Milk
Crogan

Stratford-on-Avon Sanctuary
Knocker

Stratford-on-Avon Toby
Basin

Stratford-on-Avon Toby Jug

Sunderland Bottle

Swindon Vase

Swiss Cow Bell

Swiss Milk Bucket

Swiss Milk Pot and lid

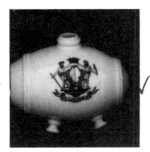

Swiss Vinegar Bottle

Teignmouth Lighthouse

Tenby Gateway

Model		With any Arms £ p	With Matching Arms £ p
STIRLING PINT MEASURE (Goss Record. 8th Edition: Page 40) *Matching Arms: STIRLING*	61mm	7.50	16.50 ✓
STOCKPORT PLAGUE STONE (Goss Record. 8th Edition: Page 17) *Matching Arms: STOCKPORT*	Length 75mm	15.50	26.00
STOCKTON ANCIENT SALT POT (Goss Record. 8th Edition: Page 21) *Matching Arms: STOCKTON-ON-TEES*	73mm	6.50	16.50
STORNOWAY HIGHLAND MILK CROGAN (Goss Record. 8th Edition: Page 40) *Matching Arms: STORNOWAY*	56mm	7.50	23.50

During the Goss family ownership of the pottery, Stratford models could only be obtained from the Stratford agency. This is why the Shakespeare's Font is rarely found without matching arms.

STRATFORD-ON-AVON SANCTUARY KNOCKER **in high relief on two-handled mug** (Goss Record. 9th Edition: page 30) This Model is marked COPYRIGHT *Matching Arms: STRATFORD-ON-AVON*	Height of detail 62mm	145.00	225.00
STRATFORD-ON-AVON TOBY BASIN **Multi-coloured** (Goss Record. 8th Edition. Page 35)	53mm	80.00†	
STRATFORD-ON-AVON TOBY JUG **Multi-coloured** (Goss Record. 8th Edition: Page 35)	78mm	65.00†	
SUNDERLAND BOTTLE (Goss Record. 8th Edition: Page 21 and advertisement page 65) *Matching Arms: SUNDERLAND*	58mm	4.25	12.50 ✓
SWINDON VASE (Goss Record. 8th Edition: Page 36) *Matching Arms: SWINDON*	55mm 110mm[1]	4.25 11.25	13.00 19.50

Model			With any Arms £ p	With Matching Arms £ p
SWISS COW BELL		51mm	9.50	22.50
(Goss Record. 8th Edition: Page 43)		73mm	11.50	28.00
Only the 73mm size listed in the Goss Record. *Matching Arms: SWITZERLAND or any arms in that country*				
SWISS MILK BUCKET		56mm	7.50	31.50
(Goss Record. 8th Edition: Page 43)		82mm	10.00	41.50
Matching Arms: SWITZERLAND or any arms in that country				
SWISS MILK POT and lid		82mm	11.50	43.00
(Goss Record. 8th Edition: Page 43) Often found cracked in the base. This model is incomplete without its lid which is valued at £6.00 *Matching Arms: SWITZERLAND or any Arms in that country*				
SWISS VINEGAR BOTTLE	Length	75mm	7.50	42.50
(Goss Record. 8th Edition: Page 43) *Matching Arms: SWITZERLAND or any Arms in that country*				
TEIGNMOUTH LIGHTHOUSE		115mm	37.50	49.50
(Goss Record. 8th Edition: Page 20) *Matching Arms: TEIGNMOUTH*				
TENBY GATEWAY	(a) White glazed	65mm	87.50	175.00
Matching Arms: TENBY	(b) Brown	65mm	175.00	275.00
	(c) Brown	65mm	275.00†	
TEWKESBURY SAXON URN		45mm	4.25	13.00
(Goss Record. 8th Edition: Page 22) *Matching Arms: TEWKESBURY*				
TINTERN ANCIENT WATER BOTTLE		76mm	6.00	21.00
(Goss Record. 8th Edition: Page 29) *Matching Arms: TINTERN ABBEY*				

for TOBY BASIN
see Stratford-on-Avon Toby Basin

for TOBY JUG
see Stratford-on-Avon Toby Jug

Tewksbury Saxon Urn

Tintern Ancient Water Bottle

Tonbridge Eastcheap Ancient Ewer

Tresco Old Brazier

Tresvannack Ancient Urn

Tuscan Vase, 785

Truro Glen Dorgal Cinerary Urn

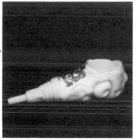

Twickenham Antique Pope's Pipe

Walmer Roman Vase

Wareham Bottle

Waterlooville Soldier's Water Bottle

Welsh Crochon

Model			With any Arms £ p	With Matching Arms £ p
TONBRIDGE EASTCHEAP ROMAN EWER (Goss Record. 8th Edition: Page 27) *Matching Arms: TONBRIDGE*		63mm	4.75	14.00
TRESCO OLD BRAZIER (Goss Record. 8th Edition: Page 18) *Matching Arms: SCILLY ISLES (DORRIEN-SMITH)*		69mm	13.00	30.00
TRESVANNACK ANCIENT URN (Goss Record. 8th Edition: Page 18) *Matching Arms: PENZANCE (PENSANS A.D.)*		55mm	6.50	15.00
TRURO GLEN DORGAL CINERARY URN (Goss Record. 8th Edition: Page 18) *Matching Arms: TRURO*		54mm	4.50	14.50 ✓
TUSCAN VASE This model is marked 'COPYRIGHT 785' *It has no matching arms*	(a) White glazed (b) Lustre	150mm 150mm	125.00 125.00	
TWICKENHAM ANTIQUE POPE'S PIPE (Goss Record. 8th Edition: Page 29) *Matching Arms: TWICKENHAM*	Length	118mm	40.00	55.00

for TYG (ONE HANDLE)
see Staffordshire One-Handled Tyg

for TYG (TWO HANDLES)
see Staffordshire Two-Handled Tyg

for URICONIUM EWER (First Period models so marked)
see Sir John Barrow's Monument, Ulverston

for ULVERSTON, SIR JOHN BARROW'S MONUMENT
see Sir John Barrow's Monument, Ulverston

for URICONIUM EWER (First Period models so marked)
see Shrewsbury Ewer

for WALDEN ABBEY COVERED URN
see Saffron Walden Covered Urn

Model		With any Arms £ p	With Matching Arms £ p
WALMER ROMAN VASE (Goss Record. 8th Edition: Page 27) *Matching Arms: WALMER or DEAL*	65mm	4.25	11.50 ✓

Model		With any Arms £ p	With Matching Arms £ p
WAREHAM BOTTLE	67mm	4.75	13.00

(Goss Record. 8th Edition: Page 21)
Matching Arms: WAREHAM

for WARWICK – GUY'S PORRIDGE POT
see Guy's Porridge Pot

WATERLOOVILLE SOLDIER'S WATER BOTTLE	83mm	11.00	24.75

(Goss Record. 8th Edition: Page 24)
Matching Arms: WATERLOOVILLE

Any Welsh arms may be considered matching on Welsh models

WELSH CORACLE	Length 77mm	17.50	28.00

(Goss Record. 8th Edition: Page 39)
Matching Arms: LLANGOLLEN
Up until 1903, the Welsh Coracle was called thus and listed in *Goss Record* as a national model having no particular town or city arms. From 1904 onwards, it was re-named The Llangollen Coracle with Llangollen given as the matching arms, which explains the confusion of the two descriptions which can be found on the same piece.

WELSH CROCHON	50mm	5.50	14.00
(Goss Record. 8th Edition: Page 39)	61mm	7.50	19.50
also see POSTCARDS Chapter	76mm[1]	17.00	25.00
Matching Arms: CONWAY	107mm[1]	28.50	33.50

WELSH FISH BASKET	58mm		55.00

Matching Arms: ARMS OF WALES

WELSH HAT	(a) Plain brim	Dia. 74mm	11.50	17.50
	(b) Llanfair P.G. on brim		28.50	46.50

Matching Arms: ARMS OF WALES

WELSH JACK and lid	120mm	17.00	28.50

(Goss Record. 8th Edition: Page 39)
This model is not complete without its lid, value £9.00
Matching Arms: ARMS OF WALES

Welsh Fish Basket

Welsh Hat

Welsh Jack and Lid

Welsh Leek

Welsh Milk Can and Lid

Welsh Picyn

Wensleydale Leyburn Leather Jack

Westminster Abbey Coronation Chair, Brown

Weymouth Roman Vase

Whitby Ammonite

Whitby Pillion Stone

Whitstable Roman Patera

Model		With any Arms £ p	With Matching Arms £ p
WELSH LEEK (Goss Record. 8th Edition: Page 39) *Matching Arms: ARMS OF WALES*	90mm	11.50	17.00
WELSH MILK CAN and lid (Goss Record. 8th Edition: Page 39) This model is incomplete without its lid which is worth £8.00 *Matching Arms: ARMS OF WALES*	70mm 108mm 140mm	12.00 14.00 17.00	17.00 19.50 26.00
WELSH PICYN (Goss Record. 8th Edition: Page 39) *Matching Arms: ARMS OF WALES*	62mm	9.00	17.00
for WELSH PORRIDGE BOWL see Welsh Picyn			
WENSLEYDALE LEYBURN LEATHER JACK (Goss record. 8th Edition: Page 38) *Matching Arms: LEYBURN*	67mm	6.00	19.50

WESTMINSTER ABBEY CORONATION CHAIR
(Goss Record. 8th Edition: Page 29)
see also Perth Coronation Chair

(a) White	87mm	31.50	43.00
(b) Stone in brown	87mm	82.50	117.50
(c) Brown	87mm	250.00	285.00
(d) Blue	87mm		unpriced

A blue version is thought to exist but has not yet been seen.
Matching Arms: WESTMINSTER ABBEY

Model			
WEYMOUTH ROMAN VASE (Goss Record. 8th Edition: Page 21 and advertisement page 61) *Matching Arms: WEYMOUTH*	56mm 94mm[1]	6.50 12.00	15.00 23.50
for WHISKEY CUP see National Highland Cuach or Whiskey Cup			
WHITBY AMMONITE (Goss Record. 7th Edition: Page 52–Illustrated) Identical to the rarer Lyme Regis Ammonite *Matching Arms: WHITBY*	73mm	19.50	30.00

Model		With any Arms £ p	With Matching Arms £ p

WHITBY PILLION STONE   Length 72mm   19.50   30.00
(Goss Record. 9th Edition: Page 33)
Matching Arms: WHITBY

for WHITLEY BAY, ST. MARY'S LIGHTHOUSE
see St. Mary's Lighthouse, Whitley Bay

WHITSTABLE ROMAN PATERA   Dia. 88mm   12.50   25.00
(Goss Record. 8th Edition: Page 27)
Matching Arms: THE SEAL OF THE CORPORATION
OF THE DREDGERS OF WHITSTABLE, 1793

WILDERSPOOL ROMAN TETINAE   105mm   82.50
International League Model for 1924
Correct Arms: THE INTERNATIONAL LEAGUE OF
  GOSS COLLECTORS.

Up until 1903, Winchester shapes could only be purchased at the Winchester Agency. This accounts for their scarcity and the preponderance of matching arms. Any Winchester or associated arms may be considered matching.

WINCHESTER BUSHEL	38mm	65.00	117.00
(Goss Record. 8th Edition: Page 24)	51mm	87.00	175.00
Matching Arms: WINCHESTER	58mm[1]	225.00	500.00

WINCHESTER FLAGON   100mm[1]   13.00   28.00
This model is not listed in any edition of the Goss   130mm[1]   17.00   32.00
Record. It is an un-named historical shape and traditional to the Winchester Agent who stocked this model manufactured by the Copeland works until Goss set up on his own and was able to meet his requirements.
See also FIRST PERIOD 9C ORNAMENTAL WARE
Matching Arms: WINCHESTER

for WINCHESTER BLACK JACK
see Winchester Jack

WINCHESTER JACK	32mm	17.50	26.00
(Goss Record. 8th Edition: Page 23)	44mm	5.25	11.00
Matching Arms: WINCHESTER	83mm[1]	9.50	19.50
	121mm[1]	21.50	40.00

Wilderspool Roman Tetinae

Winchester Bushel

Winchester Flagon

Winchester Jack

Winchester Pot

Winchester Quart

*Winchester Castle
Warden's Horn on plinth*

*Winchester Castle
Warden's Horn*

Windsor Round Tower

Windsor Urn

Windsor Kettle and Lid

Windleshaw Chantry

Model			With any Arms £ p	With Matching Arms £ p

WINCHESTER POT — 74mm — 13.00 — 25.00
(Goss Record. 8th Edition: Page 24)
Matching Arms: WINCHESTER

WINCHESTER QUART — 92mm†[1] — 400.00
(Goss Record. 8th Edition: Page 24)
This model is not known bearing a coat of arms. It is a
most impressive piece – rare and desirable.

WINCHESTER CASTLE WARDEN'S HORN   Length
(Goss Record. 8th Edition: Page 24) (a) on plinth† 152mm 300.00
Found named as Warder's or (b) without plinth† 152mm 175.00
Warden's Horn
A beautiful piece in either form which
carries no arms.

WINDLESHAW CHANTRY — 128mm — 75.00 — 145.00
On the base it is stated that this was a souvenir of the
1920 Church Bazaar. (Near St. Helens, Lancs.)
Matching Arms: EN DIEU ET MON ESPERANCE
(Sir Thomas Gerard of Kingsley & Bryn)

WINDSOR KETTLE and lid — 170mm — 110.00 — 157.50
(Goss Record. 8th Edition: Page 17)
Also known as Queen Charlotte's favourite
Windsor Kettle.
This model should have a circular lid with a flat top
surmounted by a round knob. Value £35.00
Matching Arms: WINDSOR

**for WINDSOR – QUEEN CHARLOTTE'S
FAVOURITE KETTLE**
see Windsor Kettle

WINDSOR ROUND TOWER (a) Large white† 145mm 425.00
Two-piece, unglazed night-light (b) Large brown† 145mm 650.00
  (c) Large grey† 145mm 525.00
(This model is illustrated in the
Goss Record, 9th Edition: Page 40, Plate I)

WINDSOR URN — 38mm — 4.25 — 11.50
(Goss Record. 8th Edition: Page 16) — 82mm — 10.50 — 22.00
Matching Arms: WINDSOR or ETON (FLOREAT
ETONA)

Wisbech Jug

Winsford Salt Lump

Witch's Cauldron

Worcester Jug

Wymondham Ancient Jar

Yarmouth Ewer

Yarmouth Jug

York Roman Ewer

York Roman Urn

York Roman Vessel

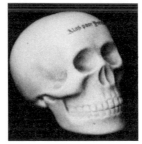

Yorick's Skull (Small)

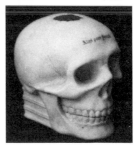

Yorick's Skull (Large)
Two-piece Nightlight

Model			With any Arms £ p	With Matching Arms £ p
WINSFORD SALT LUMP This is identical to the Cheshire Salt Block, and appears with the Arms of Winsford either glazed or unglazed (a). A rare variety (b) has been seen with holes for pouring in the top and SALT in script on the front. *Matching Arms: WINSFORD*	(a) (b)	80mm 80mm		43.50 56.50
WISBECH JUG (Goss Record. 8th Edition: Page 17) *Matching Arms: WISBECH*		82mm[1]	20.50	32.50
WITCH'S CAULDRON (Goss Record. 9th Edition: Page 30) This model is identical to the Peterborough Tripod and carries a quotation from Macbeth. *Matching with either Scottish or Shakespeare's arms.*		47mm	11.25	14.50
WORCESTER JUG (Goss Record. 8th Edition: Page 38) *Matching Arms: WORCESTER*		64mm 101mm[1]	5.50 11.25	16.00 26.00
WYMONDHAM ANCIENT JAR (Goss Record. 8th Edition: Page 29) *Matching Arms: WYMONDHAM*		61mm	9.50	19.50
YARMOUTH EWER (Goss Record. 8th Edition: Page 29 and advertisement page 77) *Matching Arms: GREAT YARMOUTH*		62mm	4.50	13.50
YARMOUTH JUG (Goss Record. 8th Edition: Page 29 and advertisement page 77) *Matching Arms: GREAT YARMOUTH*		132mm	35.00	65.00
YORICK'S SKULL (Goss Record. 8th Edition: Page 35)	(a) Pale yellow† (b) White unglazed† (c) Pale yellow† (d) White unglazed† (e) Pale yellow† (f) White glazed†	38mm 70mm 70mm 102mm 102mm 102mm	35.00 82.50 100.00 125.00 175.00 130.00	

The 102mm version is in two pieces
and can be used as a night-light.

Model		With any Arms £ p	With Matching Arms £ p
YORK ROMAN EWER	63mm	4.75	13.00
(Goss Record. 8th Edition: Page 38)	127mm[1]	14.00	26.00
see also POSTCARDS Chapter			
Matching Arms: YORK			
YORK ROMAN URN	51mm	4.25	13.00
(Goss Record. 8th Edition: Page 38)	101mm[1]	12.50	26.00
Matching Arms: YORK			
YORK ROMAN VESSEL	73mm[1]	11.50	24.50
(Goss Record. 8th Edition: Page 38)			
Matching Arms: YORK			

F   Cottages and Coloured Buildings

In 1893 Adolphus Goss introduced a new range that was to prove highly successful. These were reproductions in miniature of historic buildings, famous cottages and churches of an exact likeness and colouring. The first seven models were nightlights and those surviving today can often be found with candlewax still inside or with heat cracks, as they were sold to be used at bedtime. The smoke came out of the hollow chimneys and the light shone out through the extra thin porcelain windows and half-open doors when a candle was placed inside. Initially the three most popular were the famous Shakespeare's Birthplace and Ann Hathaway's Cottage, both at Stratford on Avon, and Burns' Cottage, Ayrshire.

Heavy demand for these coloured houses led to the range being gradually extended to 42 buildings with a variety of sizes, some half-size versions and nightlight burners. In the latter half of the firm's life, some cottages were glazed and this intensifies the colouring. £10.00 should be added to values for glazed varieties.

Other changes in the moulds occurred when the original buildings that the models were reproduced from were altered in any significant way. For example, the extensions to 'The First and Last House at Land's End' and 'Lloyd George's Home'. Both these appear in the original and extended forms.

Charles Dickens's House at Gads Hill in Rochester was originally moulded with no porch windows due to ivy completely covering the walls. When the Goss artists discovered that there was a small window either side of the front door after the ivy had been cut away, future models incorporated these windows. Keen collectors of cottages would probably like to have an example of each variation. The coloured houses were not normally crested but the 'First and Last House in England' can be found with a glass or enamel badge containing the Arms of Cornwall affixed to one end wall. Plain white cottages are rare, and were possibly taken home by employees.

There were slight differences in the colours used over the years, hardly surprising with some models like the two Stratford cottages which were in production for over 40 years, a succession of different paintresses, new batches of enamels being mixed every week and differences in firing temperatures. But generally the sizes, colours and moulds were consistent. Most of the cottages were made up from sketches by Adolphus Goss, then later his son Clarence Richard (Dick), Noel and John Goss (Dick's cousins), and a few of the pottery's best workmen.

The Cat and Fiddle Inn at Buxton was measured up by Noel Goss and workman Alfred Mollart in 1925, modelled by John Goss and out on the production line all in the same year. John also modelled Isaac Walton's cottage, Shallowford, between 1925 and 1928 using photographs, the original building having burned down completely long before. During the 1920's Noel and Alfred measured up several buildings including the pretty John Knox's House in Edinburgh in 1929.

Several new models were in preparation at the end such as the An Clachan in 1938, and the later smaller sizes of Shakespeare's and Hathaway's cottages which are all third period Goss and can be found listed in that section. Designs have been found for Plas Newydd, Llangollen, and Atlantic View Hotel, Land's End, but these have never been seen and it is not now thought that even one example of each exists.

Some of the white glazed buildings, for example, Massachusetts Hall, with the Blackpool crest are seconds and although no other variation of this piece has been found to date, it has been established that it did go into production in coloured form as small fragments of the building have been unearthed at the site of the factory. Perhaps this, Land's End, Atlantic View or may be even Plas Newydd, Llangollen will appear in colour in the future.

Cottages and Buildings in this section have been listed alphabetically by person, town or title. All sizes are given by *length* unless otherwise stated. Buildings that are not recorded in this section will appear either under **THIRD PERIOD 11O** or **SECOND PERIOD 10E** Chapters

Bunyan's Cottage, Elstow

Burns' Cottage, small

Burns' Cottage, nightlight

Buxton, Cat and Fiddle Inn

*Old Court House,
Christchurch*

*Dickens' House, Rochester,
without Porch Windows*

*First and Last House with
Annexe*

*First and Last House, Land's
End*

*Dickens' House, Rochester,
with Porch Windows*

*First and Last Post Office,
Sennen*

*Glastonbury, Church of Joseph
of Arimathoea*

Goss Oven, Stoke-on-Trent

£   p

Exceptionally, all dimensions given in this chapter are the length

for ABBOT'S KITCHEN, GLASTONBURY ABBEY
see Glastonbury Abbey, Abbot's Kitchen

for AN CLACHAN COTTAGE
see THIRD PERIOD 11.0 BUILDINGS AND MONUMENTS

for ANN HATHAWAY'S COTTAGE, SHOTTERY
see Hathaway's Cottage, Shottery

for ATLANTIC VIEW HOTEL, LAND'S END
see Land's End, Atlantic View Hotel

for BEDDGELERT, PRINCE LLEWELLYN'S HOUSE
see Prince Llewellyn's House, Beddgelert

for BOURNEMOUTH, PORTMAN LODGE
see Portman Lodge, Bournemouth

(JOHN) BUNYAN'S COTTAGE, ELSTOW   Length 60mm   750.00
Unglazed

(ROBERT) BURNS' COTTAGE, AYRSHIRE
(Goss Record. 8th Edition: Page 40) glazed or unglazed
   (a) Small   62mm   82.50
   (b) Night-light, blue windows with brown glazing bars   145mm   145.00
   (c) as (b) but with no windows, unglazed only   145mm   265.00

BUXTON, CAT AND FIDDLE INN   Length 68mm   205.00
Unglazed

for CHARLES DICKENS' HOUSE, GADS HILL PLACE
see (Charles) Dickens' House, Gads Hill

CHRISTCHURCH, OLD COURT HOUSE   Length 76mm   300.00
(Not listed in any edition of the Goss Record, but advertised by
Ritchie & Co. on the back cover of the Eighth Edition.)
Unglazed.

for COCKERMOUTH, WORDSWORTH'S HOUSE
see Wordsworth's Birthplace, Cockermouth

for COURTHOUSE, CHRISTCHURCH
see Christchurch Old Court House

£ p

(CHARLES) DICKENS' HOUSE, GADS HILL, ROCHESTER

65mm   115.00

(Goss Record. 8th Edition: Page 27)
There are two varieties of this model – with and without small windows on either side of the front door. The value is unaffected. Unglazed.

for DOVE COTTAGE, GRASMERE

see (William) Wordsworth's Home, 'Dove Cottage', Grasmere

for ELLEN TERRY'S FARM, TENTERDEN, KENT

see (Miss Ellen) Terry's Farm, Tenterden, Kent

for FEATHERS HOTEL

see Ledbury, The Feathers Hotel

FIRST AND LAST HOUSE IN ENGLAND

(Goss Record. 8th Edition: Page 18)
Can be found with the badge of Cornwall on one end for which £20 should be added. The small model can be found with either a green or black door.
This model can be found glazed or unglazed and sometimes bears the Penzance agent's name, Stevens and Sons, Western Esplanade, on the base. A box of these cottages was sold from this shop for 7/6d in the 1960's!

(a) Small, cream or brown roof, green door	64mm	80.00
(b) Small, grey roof, black or green door	64mm	95.00
(c) Night-light, cream roof, green door	117mm	220.00
(d) Night-light, grey roof, black door	117mm	220.00
(e) Night-light, white, green door, brown chimney	117mm	240.00

FIRST AND LAST HOUSE IN ENGLAND – WITH ANNEXE

Unglazed   Length 140mm   650.00
Can be found with the matching arms of Land's End on roof for which £50.00 should be added.

FIRST AND LAST POST OFFICE IN ENGLAND, SENNEN

(Goss Record. 8th Edition: Page 18)   Length 73mm   135.00
Unglazed
Sometimes has the badge of Cornwall on one end for which £20.00 should be added.

GLASTONBURY ABBEY – THE ABBOT'S KITCHEN

(Goss Record. 9th Edition: Pages 26 & 27)   Length 70mm   600.00
Can be found with either black or brown door.   Height 88mm
Unglazed

GLASTONBURY – CHURCH OF JOSEPH OF ARIMATHOEA

Unglazed   70mm   600.00

Glastonbury Abbey, Abbot's Kitchen

Gullane Smithy

Thomas Hardy's Birthplace

Ann Hathaway's Cottage, small

Ann Hathaway's Cottage, large

Holden Chapel, Boston, U.S.A.

Hop Kiln, Headcorn

Dr. Johnson's House, Lichfield

The Feathers Hotel, Ledbury

Old Market House, Ledbury

Lloyd George's Early Home without Annexe

Lloyd George's Early Home with Annexe

213

£ p

GOSS OVEN

(Goss Record. 9th Edition: Pages 27 & 28.   Length
Plate G) There are two varieties: (a) Orange chimney unglazed 75mm   185.00
                            (b) Brown chimney part-glazed 75mm   200.00
The ovens were situated in Sturgess Street, Stoke-on-Trent and
are still standing today.

GRETNA GREEN, OLD TOLL BAR
                                      Length 125mm   1750.00
Unglazed, sometimes found not marked W.H.Goss

GULLANE, THE OLD SMITHY
                                      Length 75mm   475.00
(Goss Record, 9th Edition: Page 35 and advertisement
in the 8th Edition, Page 98)
Unglazed

(THOMAS) HARDY'S BIRTHPLACE, DORCHESTER
(Goss Record. 9th Edition: Page 14)   Length 100mm   325.00
Unglazed

(ANN) HATHAWAY'S COTTAGE, SHOTTERY
(Goss Record. 8th Edition: Page 35)
Glazed or unglazed
                        (a) Small   64mm   65.00
                        (b) Night-light   148mm   150.00
                        (c) Night-light white unglazed only 148mm   225.00
This model was in constant production from the mid-1890s and
minor variations will be found as moulds were replaced. These
variations do not affect values.
For later examples see THIRD PERIOD 11.0 BUILDINGS
AND MONUMENTS.

for HEADCORN HOP KILN
see Hop Kiln, Headcorn, Kent

HOLDEN CHAPEL, HARVARD UNIVERSITY, BOSTON, USA
(Goss Record. 8th Edition: Page 43)   Length 137mm   1800.00
Sold by the Boston Mass. agent, Jones, McDuffee and Stratton
Co. Ltd.
Unglazed

HOP KILN, HEADCORN, KENT
                                    Height 89mm   1200.00
(Goss Record. 9th Edition: Page 20)
Unglazed

for HUER'S HOUSE
see Newquay Huer's House

£ p

for ISAAC WALTON'S COTTAGE or BIRTHPLACE, SHALLOWFORD
see Walton's Cottage, (Birthplace), Shallowford

for JOHN BUNYAN'S COTTAGE, ELSTOW
see Bunyan's Cottage, Elstow

(DR. SAMUEL) JOHNSON'S HOUSE, LICHFIELD   Height 75mm   140.00
(Goss Record. 8th Edition: Page 32)   Length 47mm
Glazed or unglazed

for JOHN KNOX'S HOUSE, EDINBURGH
see THIRD PERIOD 11.0. BUILDINGS AND MONUMENTS

LAND'S END, ATLANTIC VIEW HOTEL   Unpriced
(Goss Record. 8th Edition: Page 18)
Although this model was listed as being 'in the course of
preparation' in the Eighth Edition, it was apparently never
produced, and was omitted from the Ninth Edition.

LEDBURY, THE FEATHERS HOTEL   Length 114mm   700.00
Unglazed
Rumour has it that the Hotel owner purchased the entire
remaining output of this model when the Ledbury agency closed
and presented them to couples honeymooning at the Hotel.

LEDBURY, OLD MARKET HOUSE   Length 68mm   275.00
(Goss Record. 9th Edition: Page 18. Plate H)
Unglazed

for LLANGOLLEN, PLAS NEWYDD
see Plas Newydd, Llangollen

for LLEWELLYN'S HOUSE, BEDDGELERT
see Prince Llewellyn's House, Beddgelert

(RT.HON.) LLOYD GEORGE'S EARLY HOME   Length 62mm   125.00
Llanstymdwy, Criccieth
(Goss Record. 8th Edition: Page 39)
Glazed or unglazed

(RT.HON.) LLOYD GEORGE'S EARLY HOME   Length 102mm   105.00
– WITH ANNEXE, Llanstymdwy, Criccieth
Unglazed

for LOOK-OUT HOUSE
see Newquay Look-Out House

Manx Cottage

Huer's House, Newquay

Look-out House, Newquay

Old Maids' Cottage, Lee, Devon

Old Thatched Cottage, Poole

Old Toll Bar, Gretna Green

Portman Lodge, Bournemouth

Priest's House, Prestbury

Prince Llewellyn's House, Beddgelert

St. Catherine's Chapel, Abbotsbury

St. Nicholas Chapel, Lantern Hill, Ilfracombe

St. Nicholas Chapel, St. Ives

				£ p
MANX COTTAGE	(a) Small	Length	62mm	85.00
(Goss Record. 8th Edition: Page 26)	(b) Night-light	Length	122mm	150.00
Glazed or unglazed				

MASSACHUSETTS HALL, HARVARD UNIVERSITY,
BOSTON, USA   Length 175mm   2000.00
(Goss Record. 8th Edition: Page 43)
The only variety known to exist is white glazed and bears the
Blackpool arms. Shards of a coloured variety have been found on
the factory spoil heap, but to date a perfect coloured example has
not come to light.

NEWQUAY, HUER'S HOUSE				
(Goss Record. 8th Edition: Page 18)	(a) Grey	Length	70mm	100.00
Glazed and unglazed	(b) White		70mm	65.00

NEWQUAY, LOOK-OUT HOUSE	(a) 4 windows	Height	65mm	85.00
(Goss Record. 8th Edition: Page 18)	(b) 5 windows	Height	65mm	85.00
Glazed only				

for OLD COURTHOUSE, CHRISTCHURCH
see Christchurch, Old Courthouse

OLD MAIDS' COTTAGE, LEE, DEVON   Length 73mm   115.00
(Goss Record. 8th Edition: Page 20)
Glazed and unglazed

for OLD MARKET HOUSE, LEDBURY
see Ledbury – Old Market House

for OLD SMITHY, GULLANE
see Gullane, The Old Smithy

OLD THATCHED COTTAGE, POOLE   Length 68mm   350.00
(Goss Record. 9th Edition: Page 14)
Unglazed

for OLD TOLL BAR, GRETNA GREEN
see Gretna Green, Old Toll Bar

PLAS NEWYDD, LLANGOLLEN   Unpriced
(Goss Record. 8th Edition: Page 39)
It is said that seven of these models were produced, and sold by
the local agent. Apparently no more were made, and none has
as yet been discovered.

for POOLE, OLD THATCHED COTTAGE
see Old Thatched Cottage, Poole

Shakespeare's House, small

Shakespeare's House,
Half-length

Shakespeare's House,
Two-piece Nightlight

Southampton Tudor House

Sulgrave Manor

Ellen Terry's Farm,
Tenterden, Kent

Isaac Walton's Birthplace,
Shallowford

A Window in Thrums small

A Window in Thrums
Nightlight

Wordsworth's Birthplace,
Cockermouth

Wordsworth's Home, Dove
Cottage, Grasmere

Massachusett's Hall,
Harvard University

		£ p
PORTMAN LODGE, BOURNEMOUTH	84mm × 72mm	325.00

Appears with either open or closed door.
Unglazed

for PRESTBURY, PRIEST'S HOUSE
see Priest's House, Prestbury

PRIEST'S HOUSE, PRESTBURY   Height 71mm   900.00
This model is marked COPYRIGHT and   Length 90mm
numbered 786
Unglazed

PRINCE LLEWELLYN'S HOUSE, BEDDGELERT   63mm   120.00
(Goss Record. 8th Edition: Page 38)
Glazed and unglazed

ST. CATHERINE'S CHAPEL, ABBOTSBURY   Length 87mm   400.00
(Goss Record. 9th Edition: Page 14) Unglazed

for ST. IVES, ANCIENT CHAPEL OF ST. NICHOLAS
see St. Nicholas Chapel, St. Ives

ST. NICHOLAS CHAPEL, LANTERN HILL, ILFRACOMBE
(Goss Record. 8th Edition: Page 20)   74mm   145.00
Glazed and unglazed

ST. NICHOLAS CHAPEL, ST. IVES
(Goss Record. 8th Edition: Page 18)
      (a) White, glazed   55mm   100.00
      (b) Coloured, glazed or unglazed   55mm   185.00

SHAKESPEARE'S HOUSE, STRATFORD-ON-AVON
(Goss Record. 8th Edition: Page 35)
Many variations in size may be found, both glazed and un-
glazed. These are the only models made from Goss moulds; for
all other sizes see THIRD PERIOD 11.0 BUILDINGS AND
MONUMENTS
      (a) Small. Full-length   Length 65mm   65.00
      (b) Small. Full-length   78mm   65.00
      (c) Medium. Full-length   110mm   85.00
      (d) Medium. Full-length   140mm   95.00
      (e) Night-light. Full-length   185mm   150.00
      (f) Small. Half-length open door   70mm   80.00
      (g) Large. Half-length closed door   83mm   135.00
      (h) Night-light. Half-length. Separate base   105mm   110.00

SOUTHAMPTON TUDOR HOUSE   Length 83mm   265.00
(Goss Record. 8th Edition: Page 23)
Unglazed

£ p

SULGRAVE MANOR, NORTHAMPTONSHIRE
(Goss Record. 8th Edition: Page 30)   Overall length 125mm   875.00
There are many restored and few perfect examples of this model.
Remember that sub-standard models are worth less than half of
the perfect price.
Unglazed

(MISS ELLEN) TERRY'S FARM, TENTERDEN, KENT
(Goss Record. 8th Edition: Page 27)   Length   70mm   290.00
This cottage is unglazed with a glazed, brown roof.

for THOMAS HARDY'S HOUSE
see Hardy's Birthplace

(ISAAC) WALTON'S COTTAGE (BIRTHPLACE), SHALLOWFORD
There are two sizes of this model, but the vari-   Length (a) 86mm   325.00
ations in size are minimal   Length (b) 95mm   675.00
Unglazed

A WINDOW IN THRUMS   (a) Small   60mm   115.00
(Goss Record. 8th Edition: Page 40)   (b) Night-light   130mm   220.00
Both varieties found glazed and unglazed.
This cottage in Kirriemuir was the subject of a novel by author
J.M. Barrie

(WILLIAM) WORDSWORTH'S BIRTHPLACE, COCKERMOUTH
(Goss Record. 8th Edition: Page 18)   81mm   200.00
Unglazed

(WILLIAM) WORDSWORTH'S HOME, DOVE COTTAGE,
   GRASMERE   Overall length 102mm   375.00
(Goss Record. 9th Edition: Page 31)
Unglazed

G Crosses

The unglazed brown crosses are nearly all pre-1900. Possibly the first cross was the Sandbach model, which was made in three parts, the two crosses being held to the base with large corks. William Henry Goss himself was very fond of the Sandbach Crosses and often paid them a visit. The chosen originals were usually in the country and well off the beaten track. This inaccessability to the potential customer may account for their rarity, although they could be obtained at the Stoke Agency of Ritchie and Co as well as agencies local to the site of the original. They were somewhat expensive at up to 4/-, when small crested models sold for between 1/- and 1/6 each. No brown crosses bore arms, and their colouring was as natural as the artists could make them, with green tinges of moss and brown shading.

The Richmond Market Cross was introduced much later, in 1916, with the St Buryan, St Columb Major and Buxton, being introduced after the Great War. The white glazed and unglazed varieties are also post 1900. Another of Mr Goss's favourite crosses was the St Martin's Cross, Iona, a large stone replica of which was used as his memorial in Hartshill Cemetery, Stoke-upon-Trent.

All crosses are uncrested with the exception of the Richmond Market Place Cross

Bakewell Cross

Buxton Market Cross

Campbeltown Cross

Carew Cross

Eyam Cross

Llandaff Cross

St. Martins Cross, Iona

Kirk Braddan Cross

Inverary Cross of the Nobles

Richmond Market Place Cross

St. Buryan Cross

St. Columb Major Cross

Model		With any Arms £ p	With Matching Arms £ p

BANBURY CROSS
See THIRD PERIOD O – BUILDINGS AND MONUMENTS

BAKEWELL ANCIENT CROSS
(Goss Record. 8th Edition: Page 18)

(a) White		145mm	180.00
(b) Brown		145 mm	225.00

BUXTON, OLD MARKET CROSS

Grey 88mm 1300.00

CAMPBELTOWN ANCIENT CROSS
(Goss Record. 8th Edition: Page 40)

Brown 152mm 550.00

CAREW ANCIENT CROSS
(Goss Record. 9th Edition: Page 34)

(a) White unglazed	150mm	90.00
(b) Brown	150mm	100.00
(c) White glazed	216mm	130.00
(d) Brown	216mm	240.00

EYAM ANCIENT CROSS
(Goss Record. 8th Edition: Page 18)

(a) White glazed	168mm	150.00
(b) White unglazed	168mm	175.00
(c) Brown	168mm	285.00

INVERARY ANCIENT CROSS OF THE NOBLES
(Goss Record. 8th Edition: Page 40)

Brown 141mm 600.00

for IONA CROSS
see St. Martin's Cross, Iona

KIRK BRADDAN CROSS
(Goss Record. 8th Edition: Page 26)

(a) Brown	84mm	80.00
(b) White unglazed	84mm	175.00

LLANDAFF ANCIENT CROSS
(Goss Record. 8th Edition: Page 39)

(a) White unglazed	147mm	265.00
(b) Brown	147mm	525.00

RICHMOND MARKET PLACE CROSS
(Goss Record. 8th Edition: Page 38)

(a) White glazed	130mm	35.00	56.50
(b) Brown	130mm	300.00	

Matching Arms: RICHMOND (YORKS)

Model		With any Arms £ p	With Matching Arms £ p
ST. BURYAN ANCIENT CROSS			
(a) White glazed	43mm	56.50	
(b) White unglazed	43mm	70.00	
(c) Brown	43mm	100.00	
ST. COLUMB MAJOR ANCIENT CROSS			
(Goss Record. 8th Edition: Page 18)			
(a) White glazed	90mm	47.50	
(b) White unglazed	90mm	60.00	
(c) Brown	90mm	120.00	

Variety (a) and (b) can be found with the Blackpool
arms which would halve their values.

ST. IVES ANCIENT CROSS (a) White	140mm	185.00	
(Goss Record. 8th Edition: Page 18) (b) Brown	140mm	285.00	
(c) White	204mm	210.00	
(d) Brown	204mm	300.00	

ST. MARTIN'S CROSS, IONA
(Goss Record. 8th Edition: Page 40)

(a) White glazed, flat back	142mm	95.00	
(b) Brown, detailed back	142mm	160.00	
(c) White glazed, flat back	216mm	145.00	
(d) White unglazed	216mm	150.00	
(e) Brown, detailed back	216mm	195.00	

SANDBACH CROSSES
(Goss Record. 8th Edition: Page 17)   260mm 1100.00
This model is made in three sections, the two brown
crosses being held in place by cork plugs.

H Fonts

Twelve fonts were produced, none in great numbers, and are highly prized by collectors. Like crosses, the bulk of the fonts were made before 1900 in brown unglazed form. After 1900 other varieties were introduced including white unglazed and glazed crested. Between 1904 and 1916 the Avebury, St Iltyd's and St Ives were produced, with the Buckland Monachorum following later in the 1920s.

Shakespeare's Font could only be obtained from the Stratford agency up until 1929 which explains why that particular model is almost always found with matching arms.

Those fonts which were also produced during the First Period are denoted thus: [1]

Model			With any Arms £ p	With Matching Arms £ p

AVEBURY ANCIENT SAXON FONT (CALNE)
(Goss Record. 8th Edition: Page 36 and Page 91
photo and advertisement) | (a) White glazed | 86mm | 100.00 | 155.00
Matching Arms: CALNE (b) Brown† 86mm 300.00

| | (a) White glazed | 86mm | 100.00 | 155.00 |
| | (b) Brown† | 86mm | 300.00 | |

BUCKLAND MONACHORUM FONT 75mm 375.00
Matching Arms: BUCKLAND ABBEY, Nr YELVERTON

for CALNE FONT
see Avebury Ancient Saxon Font

for CANTERBURY FONT
see St. Martin's Church Font, Canterbury

HADDON HALL NORMAN FONT [1]
(Goss Record. 8th Edition: Page 18)

| | (a) White glazed | 92mm | 47.50 | 65.00 |
| | (b) Brown† | 92mm | 285.00 | |

Matching Arms: BAKEWELL or DUKE OF RUTLAND

HEREFORD CATHEDRAL FONT
(Goss Record. 8th Edition:

| | (a) White glazed | 96mm | 120.00 | 145.00 |
| Page 24 and Page 66 photo | (b) Brown | 96mm | 285.00 | 285.00 |

and advertisement)
*Matching Arms: HEREFORD CATHEDRAL
or SEE OF HEREFORD A.D. 1275*

**for LLANTWIT MAJOR NORMAN FONT IN ST.
ILTYD'S CHURCH**
see St. Iltyd's Church Font (Llantwit Major)

for MONMOUTH FONT
see Warwick Font, Troy House, Monmouth

ST. ILTYD'S CHURCH FONT (LLANTWIT MAJOR)
(Goss Record. 8th Edition: Page 39)

(a) Brown†	88mm	435.00	
(b) White unglazed†	88mm	875.00	
(c) White glazed, Blackpool Arms or Llantwit Major	88mm	300.00	875.00

Avebury Ancient Saxon Font (Calne)

Buckland Monachorum Font

Haddon Hall Norman Font

Hereford Cathedral Font

St. Iltyd's Church Font, Llantwit Major

St. Ives Church Font

St. Martins Font, Canterbury, Closed

St. Martins Font, Canterbury, Dished

St. Martins Font, Canterbury, Open

St. Tudno's Church Font

Southwell Cathedral Font

Stratford-on-Avon Church Font

			With any Arms £ p	With Matching Arms £ p
Model				

ST. IVES CHURCH ANCIENT FONT
(Goss Record. 8th Edition: Page 18)

(a) White glazed	88mm	26.00	47.00
(b) White unglazed†	88mm	95.00	
(c) Brown†	88mm	150.00	

Matching Arms: ST. IVES (CORNWALL)

ST. MARTIN'S CHURCH FONT, CANTERBURY [1]
(Goss Record. 8th Edition: Page 26)

(a) lidded, white glazed†	75mm	40.00	
(b) lidded, white unglazed†	75mm	65.00	
(c) lidded, brown†	75mm	90.00	
(d) dished, white glazed	69mm	35.00	50.00
(e) open, white glazed†	74mm	42.50	
(f) open, brown†	74mm	90.00	

There are three varieties of this font:
Lidded, dished, and open.
Matching Arms: CITY or SEE OF CANTERBURY

ST. TUDNO'S CHURCH FONT, LLANDUDNO
(Goss Record. 8th Edition: Page 91 photo and advertisement)

(a) White glazed	95mm	26.00	37.50
(b) White unglazed†	95mm	47.50	
(c) Brown†	95mm	185.00	

Matching Arms: LLANDUDNO

for SHAKESPEARE'S FONT
see Stratford-on-Avon Church Font

SOUTHWELL CATHEDRAL FONT
(Goss Record. 8th Edition: Page 30)

(a) White glazed†	95mm	75.00	
(b) White unglazed†	95mm	105.00	
(c) Brown†	95mm	240.00	

Model			With any Arms £ p	With Matching Arms £ p

STRATFORD-ON-AVON CHURCH FONT
(Goss Record. 8th Edition: Page 35)

	(a) White unglazed	54mm	21.50	28.00
	(b) Brown†	54mm	325.00	

The following inscription appears inside bowl in Gothic lettering surrounding arms:
Model of font in which Shakespeare was baptized
Matching Arms: STRATFORD-ON-AVON,
SHAKESPEARE'S ARMS or SHAKESPEARE's CHURCH
During the Goss family ownership of the pottery, the Stratford models could only be obtained from the Stratford agency. This is why the Shakespeare's Font is rarely found without matching arms.

for TROY HOUSE FONT
see Warwick Font, Troy House, Monmouth

WARWICK FONT, TROY HOUSE, MONMOUTH [1]
(Goss Record. 8th Edition: page 36)

	(a) White glazed†	55mm	56.50
	(b) White unglazed†	55mm	65.00
	(c) White glazed but with coloured shields†	55mm	75.00
	(d) Brown†	55mm	195.00

WINCHESTER CATHEDRAL FONT [1]

	(a) White glazed†	415.00
	(b) White unglazed†	525.00
	(c) Black†	650.00

This model was made in two sizes: Heights 115mm and 125mm. Same value.

I Animals and Birds

The majority of animals were produced during the latter half of the second period, mainly in the 1920's. John Goss, youngest son of Huntley, designed most of these including the lion, rhino, hippo and an alsatian lying on a plinth. They were exhibited and sold at the British Empire Exhibition held at Wembley, Middlesex in 1924 and 1925. Of particular interest would have been the Wembley Lion, produced especially for the exhibition and sold bearing the 1925 B.E.E. Motif.

First period animals include the Elephant, Bear and Ragged Staff, Sheep, Bullock and Sheep group and Swan. These will be found listed in the First Period 9C ORNAMENTAL Ware chapter.

After the sale of the Goss pottery in 1929, animals continued to be manufactured during the third period until 1934 but in no great numbers.

Matching Arms are given where known failing which B.E.E. Wembley are the most desirable.

Model			With any Arms £ p	With Matching Arms £ p
AYLESBURY DUCK		Length 100mm	175.00	220.00
Matching Arms: AYLESBURY				
BEAR, POLAR	(a) Glazed	Length	300.00	
	(b) Unglazed	125mm	195.00	
for BEAR AND RAGGED STAFF				
see FIRST PERIOD 9C ORNAMENTAL CHAPTER				
BULL		Length 135mm	300.00	400.00
Any Spanish arms could be considered matching				
CALF		Length 117mm	265.00	300.00
Possible matching arms: COWES				
CHESHIRE CAT		Length 83mm		
(Goss Record. 9th Edition: Page 11, Plate M)	(a) Glazed		85.00	130.00
	(b) Unglazed		110.00	

Inscribed *He grins like a Cheshire Cat chewing gravel.*
This cat often has a firing flaw in one or both ears,
which reduces the price by around one-third.
Matching Arms: CHESHIRE

COW		Length 135mm	325.00	350.00
Possible Matching Arms: COWES				
DOG		Length 133mm	325.00	
See also Prince Llewellyn's Dog				
ELEPHANT with Howdah				
see FIRST PERIOD 9C ORNAMENTAL CHAPTER				
HIPPOPOTAMUS		Length 127mm	350.00	
KANGAROO		Height 94mm	550.00	
LION, STANDING		Length 135mm	265.00	

Sandbach Crosses

St. Ives Cross

Warwick Font, Troy House, Monmouth

Winchester Cathedral Font large, white

Winchester Font, Black, Small

Aylesbury Duck

Polar Bear

Bull

Calf

Cheshire Cat

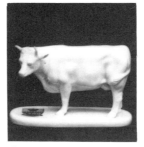

Cow

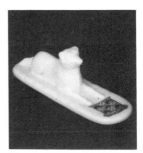

Dog

Model		With any Arms £ p	With Matching Arms £ p

LION, LUCERNE

(Goss Record. 9th Edition: Page 38)   Length

		Length		
(a) White glazed & crested (at front or rear, usually Blackpool)	110mm	35.00	80.00
(b) White glazed with Latin wording	110mm	70.00†	
(c) White unglazed with Latin wording	110mm	87.00	140.00
(d) Brown unglazed with Latin wording	110mm	265.00†	

This model should have a spear protruding 7mm out of the centre of the back. Often the spear is broken off level with the lion's back in manufacture and is glazed over. Beasts without the 7mm spear are worth some 50% less than the varieties priced here.
Matching Arms: LUCERNE

for LION SCOTTISH
see Third Period 11R

for LION (WEMBLEY)
see Wembley Lion

for LUCERNE LION
see Lion, Lucerne

PENGUIN

		Length		
(a) Black colouring	83mm	205.00	350.00
(b) White glazed	83mm	165.00	200.00

The strong Goss family connection with the Falkland Islands probably prompted the appearance of this model.
Matching Arms: FALKLAND ISLANDS

PRINCE LLEWELLYN'S DOG – GELERT
This is an identical model to the DOG   Length 133mm   700.00†
listed above, but coloured, and named
on the plinth.

RACEHORSE   Length 120mm   315.00   400.00
Possible Matching Arms: NEWMARKET

RHINOCEROS   Length 129mm   350.00

SHEEP On Plinth   Length 147mm   175.00   215.00
Possible correct arms would be those of any sheep farming areas, e.g. Tavistock. A First Period variation of the sheep not on a plinth will be found in C ORNAMENTAL Chapter

Hippopotamus

Kangaroo

Standing Lion

Lucerne Lion

Penguin

Prince Llewellyn's Dog, 'Gelert'

Racehorse

Rhinoceros

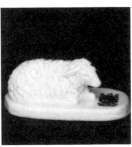

Sheep

Shetland Pony

Tiger

Wembley Lion

234

Model		With any Arms £ p	With Matching Arms £ p
SHETLAND PONY	Length 103mm	130.00	175.00

(Goss Record. 9th Edition: Page 36)
The model also appears with arms of places on Dartmoor and
Exmoor and was obviously sold in these areas as a model of a
local pony.
Matching Arms: LERWICK

SWAN
see First Period 9C. ORNAMENTAL Chapter

TIGER on rocky base (a) White	Length 170mm	575.00	
(b) Coloured†	Length 170mm	850.00	

**WEMBLEY LION (made for the
  British Empire Exhibition 1925)**
*Matching Arms: BRITISH EMPIRE
EXHIBITION 1924 or 1925* — Length 100mm   120.00   170.00

J Miniatures

The range of Goss miniatures was the result of experiments in the 1860's with egg-shell porcelain which was chiefly made by Thomas Boden, a highly skilled craftsman. This range of tiny shapes included a variety of delicate jugs and matching bowls and Tea sets with tiny blue and gold butterfly handles on the cups, less than half an inch high! Yet they are so very strong that even now it is unusual to find a broken miniature.

Llewellyn Jewitt waxed lyrical over his friend's best egg-shell in his *Ceramic Art of Great Britain*, hailing it as 'yet another achievement in the plastic art in which W H Goss stood pre-eminent. The pieces produced in this almost ethereal and very difficult ware are so light as to be devoid of gravity, and yet the body is of such extreme hardness and firmness as to be as strong as thicker and more massive wares, of a finer and purer body than the Sevres, thinner and far more translucent than Belleek, more delicate in tone than Worcester and more dainty to the touch than any other, the 'egg-shell' produced by Mr Goss is an achievement in ceramics of which he may be justly proud. Lighter and more delicate than even the shell itself, and of perfect form down to the minutest detail, nature has in this instance been outdone by imitative art. The specimens of Mr Goss's egg-shell porcelain are worthy of a place in the choicest cabinets!'

Most of the miniatures are first and second period and embrace a choice variety of decorations, the best known perhaps being forget-me-nots. Others include a jug decorated with blue and gold dots which matches a plain bowl, thistles and The Trusty Servant. A later decoration was the Good Luck Shamrock with a horseshoe. Crested miniatures were third period and rather thicker and cruder in quality. The second period tea sets are particularly sought after. The lid of the tea pot is so small it is never found factory marked, it being too small to carry the Goshawk.

KEY TO DECORATIONS
A   Forget-Me-Nots
B   Blackpool or other Coats of Arms
C   No decoration (except blue and gold dots on Jugs only)
D   Shamrock, Horseshoe and GOOD LUCK
E   Trusty Servant
F   Thistles
G   Shamrocks

Miniature Tea Service on oval tray
Comprising Oval Crinkle Tray, 165mm long, two or four cups and saucers, teapot with lid, sugar basin and milk jug. Four 38mm Dia. plates can also be found but are as rare as is the 60mm cake plate.

Miniature Tea Service on square tray
Comprising 70mm square tray, cup and saucer 35mm Dia.,
tea pot with lid, sugar basin and milk jug.

Prices for each piece:

Decoration	Teapot and Lid Height 35mm	Cup and Saucer Height 16mm	Milk Jug Height 20mm	Sugar Basin Dia. 28mm	Tea Plate Dia. 38mm	Cake Plate Dia. 60mm	Square Tray Width 70mm	Oval Tray Length 165mm	Addition for Complete Set
A	35.00	30.00	22.00	22.00	35.00	45.00	22.00	25.00	25.00
B					25.00				
C	35.00	22.00	15.00	17.50	30.00				
D									
E	45.00	30.00	27.50	27.50	45.00		25.00	35.00	25.00
F	45.00	30.00	27.50	27.50			25.00	35.00	30.00
G	45.00	30.00	27.50	27.50			20.00	35.00	25.00

Jug and Bowl Set
All sizes are the same price with the exception of the jug bearing decoration A
Height of Jug 20mm Diameter of Bowl 35mm
    25mm   40mm
    30mm   45mm

Each item priced separately. No premium is to be added for a matched set. The 20mm
Jug doubles as the milk jug in tea services.

Decoration	Jug or Bowl £ p	Jug only £ p
A	17.50	22.00
B	7.00 [3]	
C	15.00	
D	15.00	
E	22.00	
F	25.00	
G	15.00	

Miniature Tea Service on Oval Tray, forget-me-nots

Oval Tray, forget-me-nots

Miniature Beaker, Trusty Servant

Miniature Tea Service on Square Tray, Trusty Servant

Miniature Teaplate, forget-me-nots

Miniature Vase Two Handles, Shamrock, Horseshoe and Good Luck

Miniature Jug, Thistles

Miniature Bowl, plain

Cup and Saucer forget-me-nots

Milk Jug and Sugar Basin forget-me-nots

Jug and Bowl Blue and Gold dots

Teapot and lid, Trusty Servant

Vase, Two-handled All same price regardless of size

	20mm
	25mm
	30mm

	£ p
A	25.00
B	20.00 [3]
C	20.00
D	25.00
E	30.00
F	35.00
G	25.00

Miniature Beaker   19mm

E	£40.00

Bottle and Four-beaker set on 70mm square tray

E	£250.00

A miniature is not known to have a particular decoration where no letter or price is given

K Ornamental Articles

Many of the pieces in this section were made during both first and second periods. They most naturally fall in the second chapter and to avoid double listing are all shown here. Pieces also produced during the first period are suffixed thus [1].

1 FAIRY SHAPES UP TO 60 mm HIGH
2 VASES 50 mm TO 75 mm HIGH
3 VASES 76 mm HIGH UP TO 100 mm HIGH
4 VASES OVER 100 mm HIGH
5 MISCELLANEOUS ITEMS
6 WALL POCKETS
7 HOLY WATER STOUPS

Adolphus's photograph with his own notes. Look at the unusual nightlight

First period heraldic and transfer ware

Bag Vase

Frilled Bowl

Cylinder Vase, Three Tiny Feet

Early Squat Vase 43mm

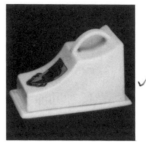

Rectangular Cheese Dish and Cover, Miniature

Bagware Vase 70mm

Ball Vase Two Handles

Ball Vase Three Handles

Club Vase 56mm

Cone Vase 56mm

Taper Vase, Curved Base

Taper Vase, Curved Base

£ p

1 FAIRY SHAPES UP TO 60mm HIGH:

Bag Vase		45mm	5.50
Ball Vase		46mm	4.50
		50mm	4.50
Beaker		40mm	4.00
Bowl, narrow base identical to Holy Water Bowl page 252 Dia.		52mm	5.00
Bowl. Shallow frilled		28mm	4.50
Tumbler with three small feet		40mm	4.00
Squat Vase [1]		40mm	5.00
Wide Taper Vase [1]		45mm	5.50
Taper Vase Curved Base		45mm	5.50
		50mm	5.50
Miniature Cheese Dish and Cover	Length 80mm Height	50mm	20.00
Miniature Taper Cup and Saucer		38mm	8.50
Miniature Bagware Teapot and lid	Cord not blue	60mm	19.50

2 VASES 50mm TO 75mm HIGH:

Amphora Vase with 2 butterfly handles	70mm	24.50
Bag Vase with white, green or blue cord	70mm	14.00
Ball Vase	55mm	6.50
	71mm	8.25
Ball Vase. With 2 handles	57mm	8.00
Ball Vase. With 3 handles	56mm	8.50
	67mm	11.25
Club Vase	56mm	4.00
Cone Vase	56mm	4.00
Crinkle Vase. Conical. Flat base	71mm	5.50

Conical Crinkle Vase, Flat Base

Conical Crinkle Vase, Rounded Base

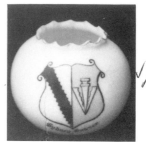
Ball Vase, Crinkle Top

High Lipped Ewer

Jar with Decoration in Relief 57mm

Narrow Taper Vase with Everted Rim

Thistle Vase, Two Handles

Trumpet Top Vase, Two Handles

Urn with Handle 69mm

Wide Taper Vase with Everted Rim

Bag Vase Narrow

Urn 70mm

244

		£ p
Crinkle Vase. Conical. Rounded base	70mm	5.50
High-Lipped Ewer	72mm	4.25 ✓
Jar, with decoration in relief. Sometimes called Ali-Baba Vase	57mm	4.25
Narrow Taper Vase with everted rim	75mm	5.25
Thistle Vase. Two Handles	64mm	5.25
Trumpet-top Vase. Two handles	75mm	5.25
Squat Taper Vase	64mm	5.25
Urn with or without handle	69mm	5.25
Wide Taper Vase, everted rim, narrow neck [1]	65mm	5.25

3   VASES 76mm TO 100mm HIGH:

Amphora Jar	80mm	12.00
Amphora Vase with three butterfly handles	85mm	26.00
Amphora Vase mounted on three Blue Balls and Plinth	93mm	19.50
Amphora Vase on blue or orange coral feet	85mm	19.50 ✓
Amphora Vase on 3 coral feet, with 3 butterfly handles	85mm	28.50
Bag Vase. Narrow	93mm	18.50
Bag Vase. Circular	97mm	18.50
Bag Vase. Circular Dia. 100mm	98mm	18.50
Ball Vase. With two handles	76mm	10.50
Ball Vase. With three handles	76mm	12.00
Bulbous vase, curved base, medium width crinkle top. Known as a 'Violet Vase' by the factory.	76mm	11.00
Diamond-mouthed Vase [1]	81mm	6.00 ✓
Diamond Vase. Old pattern, with 'foot' [1]	79mm	13.00
Jar, Flat base, wide top	86mm	6.50

Amphora with Three Butterfly Handles

Amphora Vase mounted on three Blue Balls and plinth

Amphora on Three Coral Feet

Diamond Mouthed Vase 80mm

Bulbous, Medium-mouthed Crinkle Top 'Violet' Vase

Oviform Vase 80mm

Scallop Edge Fern Pot

Early Lozenge Vase, Oval Top

Taper Vase Rounded Base

Thistle (Vase) 80mm

Vase with Two Butterfly Handles

Jar 86mm

		£ p
Oviform Vase	80mm	6.00
Oviform Vase with crinkle top	80mm	6.00
Oviform Vase. With crinkle top and two blue butterfly handles	88mm	40.00
Lozenge-shaped Vase. With moulded bows at neck. Oval top [1]	86mm	35.00
Taper Vase, rounded base	83mm	7.00
Thistle Vase with 'pineapple' moulding in relief	79mm	6.50
Urn	96mm	6.50
Urn with two butterfly handles [1]	85mm	26.00

4   VASES OVER 100mm HIGH:

Amphora Vase. With	(a) No butterfly handles	100mm	30.00
	(b) Two butterfly handles	120mm	40.00
	(c) Three butterfly handles	120mm	40.00
Ball Vase		114mm	16.00
Ball Vase. With four handles		125mm	25.00
Club Specimen Vase		114mm	4.50
Cone Specimen Vase		117mm	4.50
Four Ball Group		114mm	75.00
		146mm	82.00
Globe Vase, narrow neck		196mm	28.00
Globe Vase. With two small knurled handles, narrow neck		196mm	32.50
Globe Vase. With three small knurled handles, narrow neck		196mm	34.50
Goblet with central stem		162mm	30.00
Jar, curved base, narrow top		109mm	12.50
Lozenge-shaped Vase. Upright with diamond top [1]		139mm	40.00

Ball Vase, Crinkle Top

Ball Vase Four Handles

Club Specimen Vase 114mm

Cone Specimen Vase 117mm

Four Ball Group

Globe Vase with Three Small Knurled Handles, Narrow Neck

Goblet 162mm

Jar, Curved Base, Narrow Top 109mm

Early Lozenge-shaped Vase, Upright with Diamond Top

Pear Shaped Vase

Pompeian Centre Piece 125mm

Pompeian Centre Piece 340mm

		£ p
Pear Shaped Vase. Flat with rectangular top[1]	106mm	20.00
	122mm	22.50
	130mm	26.00
As above but with red or green grapevine decoration and sepia transfer of Windsor or Balmoral Castle	130mm	175.00
Pompeian Centrepiece On Plinth	125mm	28.00
(Illustrated. Goss Record. 8th Edition: Pages 4 and 75)	340mm	165.00
Pompeian Centrepiece. No plinth.	111mm	26.00
Quadruple Amphora Group. On plinth	150mm	67.50
Sack. Bagware	110mm	33.50
Taper Vase	110mm	12.50
Taper Vase. Crinkle top	170mm	12.00
Taper Vase. Crinkle top. With two blue angular handles and blue cord around neck	115mm	28.00
Taper Vase. With two high angular handles and fluted, everted rim	172mm	26.50
Triple Amphora. Three joined vases	110mm	40.00
Triple Bag Centrepiece	200mm	130.00
With four oval bag vases, central one elongated		
(Goss Record. 8th Edition: Page 4)		
Triple Bag and Shell Centrepiece. Having three glazed 66mm bag vases fixed together with a cone-shaped shell held centrally	159mm	130.00
Vase. Bell-shaped on socle base. Rare. May also be found with two handles	203mm	55.00
Vase. Bulbous. With cup top and strap handle	176mm	22.00
	218mm	26.00
Vase. With cup top and two strap handles	218mm	26.50
Vase, globular with two high handles and circular mouth	200mm	30.00
Vase, Oviform. numbered 849 Dia. 100mm	225mm	40.00

Quadruple Amphora Group on Plinth

Bagware Sack Vase

Taper Vase, Crinkle Top, 2 Blue Handles 107mm

Triple Amphora

Triple Bag and Shell Centrepiece

Vase, Bell-shaped on Socle Base 203mm

Bulbous Vase with Cup Top and Strap Handle

Large Vase with Two Curved Handles

Bass Basket small 64 mm

Bass Basket Medium 80mm

Early 94mm Bass Basket

Taper Vase, 2 High Handles 172mm

Circular Unglazed Button

Circular Button. One side Blue Glazed

Oval Cameo

Circular Disc

Limpet Shell, Orange Coral Legs

Nautilus Shell, large

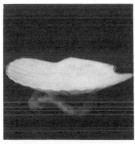

Scallop Shell on Coral Ring

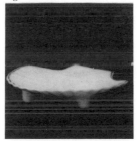

Scallop Shell 76mm on Three Short Legs

Pot-pourri Bowl small 41mm

Pot-pourri Bowl, large 80mm

Churchill Toby Jug

Scarborough Flags Plate

5 MISCELLANEOUS ITEMS:

			£ p
Bass Basket.		64mm	10.00
The smallest 64mm size has 'pinched in' sides at the centre of		80mm	12.00
the top edges. The largest size is early and carries no arms.		94mm[1]	20.00

Buttons Circular with central hole

All found unmarked	(a) Unglazed	Dia. 15mm	15.00
	(b) blue glazed one side	Dia. 15mm	25.00

Cameo Oval with bust of a lady in bas-relief

All found unmarked	White glazed	20mm	30.00

Churchill Toby Jug with blue or green coat, marked COPYRIGHT
1927 and inscribed on top hat *Any Odds – Bar one That's
me who Kissed the Blarney Stone*   164mm   115.00

Cigarette Holder not marked but several have recently
been discovered in the factory spoil heap   Length 75mm   20.00

Disc, circular, probably originally mounted in a silver ring.   Dia. 50mm   4.00
see also M METALWARE

Limpet Shell, coral legs   Dia. 74mm   Height 36mm   11.00
see also 9C ORNAMENTAL for the eggshell variety.

Nautilus Shell
Glazed and crested with orange or yellow coral legs on white
glazed rocky base   150mm   75.00
See also FIRST PERIOD C. ORNAMENTAL for the smaller
eggshell variety

Scallop Shell.	(a) 3 short legs	Length	76mm	8.00
	(b) on coral legs	Length	76mm	22.00
	(c) on coral ring	Length	76mm	25.00
	(d) 3 short legs	Length	101mm	10.00
	(e) No legs	Length	140mm	12.00
	(f) 3 short legs	Length	140mm	12.00

Pot-pourri Bowl. Small   Dia. 98mm   Height 40mm   15.00

Pot-pourri Bowl or Rose Bowl. Large.

(a) With rim around centre and no decoration	80mm	17.50
(b) Without rim and having a colourful star decoration on top	80mm	22.00

Holy Water Bowl, used in a travelling communion
set, with IHS in red Gothic lettering on the side.

Also found without lettering (b)	(a) Dia.	52mm	12.00
	(b)		4.00

Toilet Salt Mortar

Wall Pocket

Flower Holder or Hair Tidy

Largest Wall Pocket 173mm

Slipper Wall Pocket

Toilet Salt Mortar, underside

£ p

Salt Vase & Pestle. In Gothic script on 55mm club vase.

Toilet Salt Mortar in Gothic Script on a circular dish,
an un-named Roman Mortarium with inscription on base in
handwriting of W.H. Goss extolling the virtues of cleaning the
teeth with ground salt. Dia. 95mm Priced as a pair 75.00

Scarborough Flags Plate. Specially shaped plate made for the
Southport Agent, J.G. Nairn Width 105mm 265.00

Plate, Specially Decorated, one of only four produced in
bagware, with coloured cartoon of two doctors, Major Embleton
and Major Goss. This was specially designed by Margaret Goss
around 1920 Dia. 150mm 200.00

6 WALL POCKETS

Shield shaped

Usually named FLOWERHOLDER or (a) 60mm 5.00
HAIR TIDY (b) 75mm 6.00
With arms other those those below (c) 80mm 6.50
  (d) 92mm 8.50
  (e) 101mm 10.00
  (f) 122mm 11.00
  (g) 173mm 26.00

Shield shaped Wallpockets or Posy Holders. With arms of
Cambridge University, Eton College or Harvard University,
Boston, Mass. USA. Motto *Veritas*, fully covering piece
(Goss Record. 8th Edition: Page 4) 173mm 45.00

Slipper. To hang on wall as posy vase Length 96mm 5.50

Flower Holder with profile of Shakespeare in bas-relief.
  Glazed 122mm 100.00
see also 10E NAMED MODELS AND SPECIAL SHAPES
for Durham Sanctuary Knocker Flowerholder

7 HOLY WATER STOUPS

These are found in five sizes, normally carrying the letters I.H.S. in red at the centre of the cross. This is the familiar monogram of the first three letters of the Greek word for Jesus, Iesus Hominum Salvador. Some examples carry normal coats of arms. The design comprises a shell-type water container surmounted by a cross pierced for wall-mounting.

	Height	With any arms £ p	With I.H.S. £ p
(a)	124mm	20.00	30.00
(b)	142mm	26.00	35.00
(c)	190mm	30.00	40.00
(d)	219mm	35.00	45.00
(e)	256mm	40.00	50.00

Holy Water Stoups

L Domestic and Utility Wares

This section has been arranged into the various headings listed below. Ornamental ware will be found in Chapter K. As these pieces all date from the second period, please check the first or third periods where an item cannot be found. Pieces known to have also been produced during different periods are denoted here thus: [1] or [3].

Wherever possible given names for shapes have been taken from the Goss Records. Its compiler, J J Jarvis, obtained information from the Goss factory between 1900 and 1921, so that in the absence of any official catalogues, these publications provide us with the only source of correct terminology. However, recent discoveries among the photographs and papers belonging to Adolphus Goss have provided further information. Mugs and loving cups were known at the time of manufacture as ½ pint, pint, quart mugs etc. Domestic shapes too small for daily use have been catalogued in the Ornamental Section as fairy shapes, which is how the factory originally termed them.

1 Bagware Tea Service
2 Taper Tea Service
3 Melon Tea Service
4 Octagonal Coffee Service
5 Other Cups and Saucers
6 Cream and Milk Jugs
7 Sugar Basins
8 Teapots and lids
9 Teapot Stands
10 Preserve Jars and Lids
11 Other Items of Tableware
12 Trinket and Pin Trays
13 Boxes and Bowls with Lids
14 Candleholders and Nightlights
15 Candlesnuffers and stands
16 Inkwells
17 Match Holders and Tobacco Jars
18 Ashtrays and Pipe Trays
19 Miscellaneous
20 Loving Cups and Mugs
21 Margaret Goss Decorations
22 Decorations in Relief

An early factory sales photograph showing part of the range of cream and milk jugs

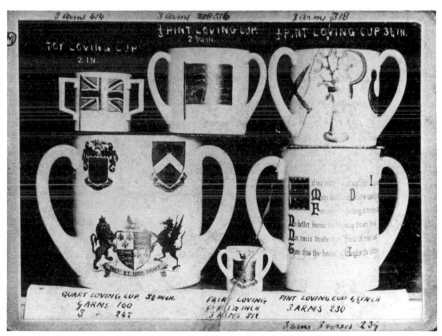

Early 1880's Adolphus Goss photograph

Table Ware

1 BAGWARE TEA SERVICE

£ p

This ware is in the form of a tied bag, gathered in by a blue cord with gilded tassels and having a matching blue cord handle. Some items have words, in illuminated Gothic script, emblazoned on the side or lid.

Cup and Saucer		50mm	14.00
		60mm	15.00
Cream Jug		60mm	12.50
		75mm	14.00
Milk Jug		105mm	17.50
		114mm	17.50
Slop Bowl	Dia. 110mm	Height 55mm	12.50
	Dia. 140mm	Height 65mm	16.00
Sugar Basin	Dia. 88mm	Height 40mm	10.00
	Dia. 103mm	Height 47mm	11.50
Jam Dish and Lid		86mm	17.00
Marmalade Dish and Lid		86mm	17.00
Preserve Jar and Lid		105mm	13.50
Tea Pot and lid		115mm	34.50
		140mm	34.50
		155mm	37.50

for **Miniature Teapot** see FAIRY SHAPES

Tea Plate		Dia. 100mm	6.50
		Dia. 115mm	6.50
		Dia. 125mm	6.50
		Dia. 135mm	6.50
		Dia. 150mm	7.50

The 150mm size also appears with a 5mm blue band around the edge with the gilding inset.   15.00

Cake Plate	Dia. 250mm	18.00

Add around £5.00 for each additional crest

For Bagware Vases see 10K ORNAMENTAL Chapter

High Melon Cup and Saucer
115mm

Bagware Cup and Saucer
60mm

Low Melon Cup and Saucer
55mm

Taper Cup and Saucer

Early Straight Sided Cup and
Saucer

Coffee Can and Saucer

Individual Morning Set
Cup on Platter

Octagonal Coffee Cup and
Saucer

Octagonal Sugar Bowl,
Probably Late

Octagonal Coffee Pot and Lid

Octagonal Milk Jug

Butter Dish, Ears of Corn in
Relief

£ p

2 TAPER TEA SERVICE

		£ p
Cup and Saucer	69mm	5.50
	82mm	5.50

For Miniature Cup and Saucer see 10K1 ORNAMENTAL Chapter

Cream Jug	81mm	5.25
	85mm	5.25
	95mm	6.50
Milk Jug	108mm	6.50
	145mm	7.50
	159mm	9.50
	176mm	15.50
Hot Water Jug with lip and lid	176mm	20.00
Sugar basin	Dia. 80mm Height 42mm	4.25
	Dia. 85mm Height 48mm	4.25
Slop Bowl	Dia. 95mm Height 55mm	5.00
	Dia. 105mm Height 75mm	8.00
Tea Pot and lid	112mm	24.50
	140mm	28.00
Coffee Pot often named Taper Coffee Pot and lid	118mm	20.00
	160mm	20.00

3 MELON TEA SERVICE

Low Melon Cup and Saucer	44mm	6.50
	53mm	6.50
Medium Melon Cup and Saucer	55mm	6.50
	75mm	6.50
High Melon Cup and Saucer	70mm	6.50
	115mm	6.50
Cream Jug	53mm	4.75
	60mm	5.50
	72mm	6.00
Milk Jug	85mm	6.50
	100mm	6.50
	118mm	7.00
Hot Water Jug	155mm	16.00

Tankard Cream Jug Early, Angular Handle

Ribbed Milk Jug

Welsh Lady Cream Jug

Fluted Cream Jug

Manx Legs Cream Jug

Big-lipped Cream Jug

Urn-Shaped Cream Jug, Early, Butterfly Handle

Ball Cream Jug

Shaped Low Melon Cream Jug

Shaped High Melon Milk Jug

Bagware Cream Jug

Bagware Milk Jug

		£ p
Hot Water Jug with thumb lip and lid	165mm	20.00
Slop Bowl	48mm	5.25
Sugar Basin	42mm	4.50
	54mm	5.25
Tea Pot	93mm	19.50
	114mm	22.00
	140mm	26.00
Tea Plate	Dia. 100mm	4.50
	Dia. 130mm	4.50
	Dia. 150mm	4.50
	Dia. 160mm	5.50
Cake Plate	Dia. 250mm	14.00

Add around £5.00 for each additional crest

4 OCTAGONAL COFFEE SERVICE
With heavily gilded rims and handles

Cup and Saucer	62mm	25.50
Milk Jug	77mm	25.50
Sugar Basin	46mm	25.00
Coffee Pot and lid	192mm	55.00

5 OTHER CUPS AND SAUCERS
See also 11 THIRD PERIOD S for late examples.

Coffee Can and Saucer	52mm	6.50
Straight-sided Cup and Saucer, square handle [1]	70mm	12.50
Curved Cup and Saucer	70mm	6.50
Two-handled Straight-sided Cup and Saucer with two blue square handles [1]	68mm	20.00
Moustache Cup and Saucer	98mm	30.00

Taper Milk Jug

Giant 176mm Taper Jug

Ribbed Sugar Basin

Taper Sugar Basin

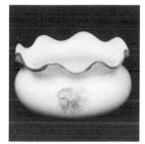

Fluted Sugar Basin

Melon Sugar Basin

Ball Shaped Sugar Basin

Bagware Sugar Basin

Frilled Sugar Basin

Bagware Marmalade Dish and Lid

Taper Sugar Basin

Circular Tea Pot Stand

£ p

6 CREAM AND MILK JUGS
See also 11 THIRD PERIOD S for late examples.

		£ p
Ball	47mm	4.25
	55mm	5.00
	60mm	5.25
	65mm	8.00
Big-lipped	60mm	5.25
	67mm	6.00
Cylindrical	100mm	12.50
Fluted	55mm	6.00
Frilled	57mm	5.00
Kneeling – Manx legs and handle in yellow	67mm	17.50
Ribbed	86mm	7.50

Sometimes found with a blue, pink or yellow handle. Add £10.00

Tankard with everted rim [1]	67mm	6.50
Urn-shaped with butterfly handle [1]	65mm	14.00
Welsh Lady (Coloured)	94mm	30.00

7 SUGAR BASINS

Ball			48mm	4.00	
			55mm	5.00	
Crinkle			25mm	4.25	
Fluted			40mm	6.00	
Frilled	Dia.	50mm	Height 25mm	5.00	
	Dia.	85mm	Height 35mm	6.00	
Kneeling – Manx legs in yellow			67mm	17.50	
Ribbed			50mm	7.00	
			58mm	8.00	

8 TEA POTS and lids

Kneeling Manx Legs in yellow	110mm	65.00

Add £20 for Manx arms

Globular, having straight spout, curved handle, and 3 small feet [1]	116mm	45.00

Early Teapot with Three Small Feet

Bagware Teapot

Taper Coffee Pot

Manx Legs Teapot

Melon Teapot and Lid

Taper Tea Pot and Lid

Preserve Jar and Lid, Strawberries

Circular Jar and Lid, Bees and Clover

Preserve Pot and Lid as Timbered Cottage

Cheese Dish and Cover with Dolphin Handle

Butter Dish and Cover with Dolphin Handle

Butter Dish 'Waste Not'

£ p

9 TEA POT STANDS

Circular		Dia. 82mm	5.00
		Dia. 102mm	6.50
		Dia. 118mm	7.50
		Dia. 144mm	8.50
		Dia. 160mm	9.50
Square	With one crest	144mm sq	11.00
	With up to four crests and verse	144mm sq	20.00

10 PRESERVE JARS AND LIDS

These are decorated with colour transfers of the following fruits
and have either plain white or coloured fruit knobs on the lids.
Spoon cut outs are to be found on either the lid or the base.

Cylindrical	Dia. 57mm	Height 100mm	18.00
	Dia. 72mm	Height 110mm	15.00

Add the following premium to base price for these decorations:

Apples (on a branch)	40.00
Blackberries	40.00
Cherries (on a branch)	40.00
Grapefruit	45.00
Grapes (red and white bunches)	40.00
Honey (bees and clover, clover as knob)	40.00
Lemons	45.00
Plums	45.00
Strawberries	40.00

Appropriately decorated base plates may be found for the above. Dia. 110mm   20.00

for Orange Preserve Pot and Lid
See 11 THIRD PERIOD S.

**Preserve Pot and Lid in the shape of a timbered
cottage with thatched roof**   115mm   60.00

**Honey Section Dish – Square, with
bee as knob on lid** [3]   140mm square   26.00

11 OTHER ITEMS OF TABLE WARE

Bowl, octagonal	Width 128mm	13.00
Bowl, soup or dessert	Dia. 185mm	6.00
Butter Dish with ears of corn in relief	Dia. 143mm	14.00

Late Tea Plate

Bagware Teaplate
115mm Dia.

Melon Tea Plate
100mm Dia.

Late Tea Plate Side View

Bagware Tea Plate Side View

Melon Tea Plate Side View

Egg Cup, Cylindrical

Egg Cup, Goblet

Egg Cup on Plate 62mm

Fruit Basket With
Coral Handle

Invalid Feeding Cup

Jam Dish or Nut Tray

			£ p
Butter Dish 'Waste not' and ears of corn in relief		Dia. 143mm	14.00
Butter Dish, with carved wooden surround 'BUTTER'		Dia. 150mm	15.00
Butter Dish circular lid and dolphin handle	Height 90mm	Dia. 152mm	18.50
Cheese dish circular lid and dolphin handle	Height 90mm	Dia. 152mm	18.50
Cheese Dish. With carved wooden surround 'CHEESE'		Dia. 150mm	15.00
Child's Feeding Bowl		Dia. 130mm	10.00

Dinner Service:
Two 61-piece dinner services were made for the Goss agent in Malta. Upon his death they passed to his two daughters living in England. Made from earthenware, each piece carries the arms of Malta and comprises:

One soup tureen and cover with base plate
Two vegetable dishes and covers with base plates
One gravy boat and stand
One cheese dish and cover
Twelve dinner plates
Twelve side plates
Twelve soup dishes
Twelve dessert bowls

Approximate value £300.00

Dish Oval, fluted. When decorated	200mm	20.00
with strawberries add £30.00	250mm	20.00
Egg Cup, Cylindrical	60mm	6.00
Egg Cup, Goblet	50mm	6.00
Several patterns, one scalloped	60mm	6.00
Egg Cup, Mounted on plate	62mm	8.00
Fruit Basket. With coral handle [1]	212mm	100.00
(Illustrated. Goss Record. 8th Edition: Page 4. Upper Shelf.)		
See also FIRST PERIOD C ORNAMENTAL		
Individual Morning Set – Cup on elongated platter[1]	203mm	20.00
Invalid Feeding Cup	76mm	14.50
Jam Dish	Dia. 145mm	8.00

Napkin Ring

Egg-shaped Cruet in Stand

Beaker

Taper Beaker with Handle

Salt Castor

Child's Feeding Bowl

Porcelain Spoon

Tea Infuser and Lid

Toastrack, Four section

Trinket Tray small 230mm

Trinket Tray large 310mm

Bagware Preserve Jar and Lid

269

		£ p
Mustard pot and lid, one handle	85mm	8.50
Napkin Ring	40mm	9.00
Nut Tray	Dia. 125mm	6.50
Octagonal Bowl	Width 128mm	13.00
Oviform Mustard Pot and lid	60mm	8.00
Oviform Pepper Castor	60mm	8.00
Oviform Salt Castor	60mm	8.00

The above three items are found also in a stand
with tall handle   Price Complete: 100mm   30.00

Plate, scallop edge	112mm	15.00

Beakers (or Tumblers) (For 44mm Fairy	(a)	80mm	5.50
size see 10K.1 ORNAMENTAL	(b)	95mm	6.50
	(c)	115mm	7.50
	(d)	145mm	11.00
Barrel-shaped	(e)	72mm	8.00
Lincoln Imp in High relief	(f)	80mm	50.00
Cylindrical, with everted rim	(g)	135mm	7.00

Note: Some of (a) (b) and (c) varieties are occasionally found
with handles – same price.

Pepper Castor Shaped – PEPPER in blue	87mm	10.00
Salt Castor Shaped – SALT in blue	87mm	10.00

Can be found with either one or several holes in top.   110mm   12.00

Sugar Castor Shaped – SUGAR in blue	115mm	12.00
Spoon Coat of arms in bowl	Length 150mm	85.00

for Tankard Mugs
see L.20 LOVING CUPS AND MUGS

Tea Infuser and Lid	Dia. 82mm Height 35mm	12.50
Toast Rack	Length 170mm	30.00

Four section on fluted edge oval base with central circular
handle

Tray, elongated and heavily fluted	Length 345mm	35.00

Oval Crinkle Tray Length 158mm

Round Dish Plain Rim

Square Teapot Stand

Crinkle Edge Pin Tray

Pin Tray on Three Coral Legs

Round Dish, with Turned Under Rim

Square Pintray, Plain

Square Pintray with Tassels

Lip Salve Pot and Lid, Cylinder

Lip Salve Pot and Lid, Ball

Rectangular Stamp Box and Lid

Cylindrical Pot and Lid, Dia, 90mm

£ p

12   TRINKET AND PIN TRAYS

				£ p
Trinket Tray	(a) One crest	Length	230mm	17.50
	(b) Multi-crested			30.00
	(a) One crest	Length	310mm	20.00
	(b) Multi-crested			40.00
Oval 'Crinkle' Tray	(a) With large flutes	Length	165mm	8.00
	(b) With small flutes	Length	165mm	8.00

Round, Crinkle Dish	Dia.70mm	4.25
Sometimes found with coral legs	75mm	4.25
when £12.50 should be added	85mm	4.50
	95mm	5.50
	100mm	6.00

Round Dish. Plain rim [1]   Dia. 78mm   5.00

Round Dish. Heavy, with turned-under rim [1]   Dia. 82mm   7.00

Square Tray. Plain   70mm sq   6.00
  See also MINIATURES J CHAPTER

Square Tray. Heavy, with gilded tassel corners   70mm sq   8.00

13   BOXES AND BOWLS WITH LIDS

Cylindrical pot [1]   Dia. 90mm   15.00

Lip-Salve Box, Ball   Dia. 43mm   Height 33mm   6.00

Lip-Salve Pot, Cylinder   Dia. 43mm   Height 35mm   6.00

Stamp Box, Rectangular Length 52mm Width 40mm Height 18mm   6.00

Puff Box   Dia. 82mm   Height 40mm   7.00

Pomade Box with small knob on lid   Dia. 62mm   Height 50mm   5.50

Rectangular Box with forget-me-nots in relief on lid
                         Length 98mm   Width 52mm   Height 35mm

(a) Glazed	10.00
(b) Unglazed	14.00
(c) Word HAIRPINS	25.00
(d) Illustrated HAIRPINS	25.00
(e) Word MATCHES	25.00

Powder Bowl. Large with shaped knob on lid.
  Often found in lustre   Dia. 130mm   Height 100mm   20.00

Candle Holder, Round,
Frilled with Handle

Large Candleholder and
Snuffer

Candle Holder with Lincoln
Imp

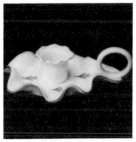

Nightlight, Fluted base
and globe

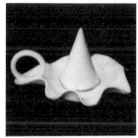

Extinguisher Holder & Snuffer
Round, Frilled with Handle

Cone Candle Snuffer

Mitre Candle Snuffer

Monk Candle Snuffer

Nun Candle Snuffer

Mr. Punch Candle Snuffer

Conical Shell Candle Snuffer

Welsh Lady Candle Snuffer

273

£ p

14 CANDLE-HOLDERS AND NIGHTLIGHTS

Candlestick. Column	89mm	10.00
	127mm	16.00
	153mm	16.00
Candlestick column with tapered base and splayed sconce over central oval decoration	180mm	65.00
Candle-Holder, Flat, round, frilled, with handle Length 106mm		11.00

Candle-Holder. Flat, oval, frilled, with handle   Length 120mm
as above with standing Lincoln Imp on sconce   Height   45mm   50.00

Candle-Holder. Flat, oval, frilled, with handle and Extinguisher (which should be plain)   Length 170mm   25.00

Candle Bracket. (To hang on wall)   Height 107mm   40.00

Night-light. Base with handle and
   Globe (in two parts)   Length 105mm   Height 80mm   80.00

Nightlight. Fluted base and Globe   Height 100mm   50.00

For Durham Abbey Knocker, Mary Queen of Scots,
   Windsor Round Tower and Yorick's Skull Nightlights
see NAMED MODELS 10E CHAPTER

for Cottage Nightlights
see 10F COTTAGES CHAPTER

15 CANDLESNUFFERS AND STANDS

Cone	53mm	6.00
Mitre	60mm	55.00
Monk	82mm	130.00
Nun	94mm	175.00
Mr. Punch	92mm	43.50
Conical Shell	81mm	60.00
Welsh Lady	(a) White glazed 95mm	45.00
	(b) Multi-coloured 95mm	60.00

Safety Inkwell

Crinkle Top Inkwell

Matchbox Holder

Match Holder

Circular Ash Tray

Pipe Tray

Hat Pin Holder

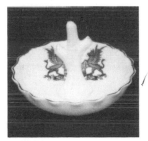

Ring Tree

Pincushion

Scent Bottle with Stopper

Vase, Identical to Scent Bottle

Shaving Mug

275

		£ p
Extinguisher Stand, On round crinkle dish	Dia. 70mm	13.50
Extinguisher Stand, Flat, round, frilled with handle	Length 106mm	11.50

16   INKWELLS

Inkwell, safety, tapered sides	57mm	12.50
Inkwell, crinkled top, glazed	76mm	14.50

17   MATCH HOLDERS AND TOBACCO JARS

Match Holder, ball-shaped, unglazed	67mm	7.50
	76mm	10.00
Match Holder, ball shaped with hallmarked silver rim, unglazed	68mm	40.00
Match-box Holder	Height 46mm Length 66mm	50.00
Tobacco Jars	(a) 3ozs. with lid 108mm	20.00
	(b) 8ozs. with lid 172mm	22.50

18   ASHTRAYS AND PIPE TRAYS

Ashtray with coloured map of the Isle of Wight standing on rear edge of the ribbed dish [3] Only found with Isle of Wight crests.	70mm	45.00
Ashtray. Circular, ribbed edge	Dia. 115mm	12.50
Ashtray. Oval with rests at each end and four thistle sprays in relief	Length 100mm	22.50
Pipe-tray	Length 112mm	8.50

19   MISCELLANEOUS

Fern Pots

Double Flower pot in circular base to hold water	90mm	15.00
Scallop Edge	92mm	15.00
Taper On flat circular base	Height 90mm Dia. 76mm	12.50

Hair Tidy – with HAIR TIDY in blue and either forget-me-nots, pink roses, thistles or leeks and shamrocks on lid	Dia. 70mm Height 93mm	15.00
	Dia. 80mm Height 93mm[1]	20.00

		£ p
Hat-Pin Holder	92mm	15.00
Menu Holder [1]	69mm	20.00

Pin Cushion. Small, squat, wide vase with circular hole in centre
to receive sawdust filling and velvet cover   Dia. 78mm   15.00
see also FIRST PERIOD 9C ORNAMENTAL CHAPTER

Ring Tree	62mm	16.50
Scent Bottle	130mm	10.00

Add £5.00 for stopper

Shaving Mug	99mm	36.50

20 LOVING CUPS AND MUGS

See also POSTCARDS chapter

Loving Cups – Three Handled

	(a)	38mm	13.00
	(b)	43mm	13.00
	(c)	51mm	13.00
	(d)	57mm	13.00
	(e)	70mm	16.00
	(f)	83mm	22.00
	(g)	95mm	22.00
	(h)	121mm	35.00
	(i)	133mm	70.00
Covered with separate lid	(j)	133mm	85.00

NOTE: As a variation, some of the above may have square
handles

Mugs – Two Handled

	(a)	38mm	5.50
	(b)	51mm	8.50
	(c)	57mm	9.50
	(d)	76mm	12.50
	(e)	82mm	16.00
	(f)	121mm	30.00

NOTE: As a variation, some of the above may have square
handles

Mugs – One handled

	(a)	38mm	4.25
	(b)	51mm	6.00
	(c)	57mm	7.00
	(d)	76mm	9.00
	(e)	82mm	12.00
	(f)	121mm	22.00

NOTE: As a variation, some of the above may have square
handles

Oviform Vase, Crinkle

Taper Fern Pot on Base

Double Fern Pot, Two-piece

One Handle Mug 62mm

Mug Two Square Handles 76mm

Loving Cup Three Handles

Loving Cup Three Square Handles

Mug Two Handles

Beaker, Barrel-shaped, Early 74mm

Barrel Shaped Mug

Mug One Handle

Tankard Mug with Everted Rim Early

		£ p
Barrel-shaped mug one square handle.	74mm	12.00
Tankard Mug with Everted rim and angular handle	70mm	7.00
Tankard Mug no rim and angular handle	75mm	7.00

N.B. See note on Minor Variations in Size. The items in this section vary considerably in size and the nearest height should be taken.

21 MARGARET GOSS DECORATIONS Normally identifiable by the monogrammed letters 'M.G.' and the date 1922. Margaret Goss was a grand-daughter of William Henry Goss and daughter of William Huntley Goss. Margaret (known as Peggy) designed a number of coloured scenes, usually depicting humourous animal and nursery rhyme themes for childrens' mugs and plates. See *Goss China Arms, Decorations and Their Values*, 2NI for a full list and additional value.

22 DECORATIONS IN RELIEF

The following may be found on two or three-handled loving cups:

			£ p
in high relief – **W.H. Goss**		110mm	75.00

Usually also bearing the arms of W.H. Goss and Stoke-on-Trent.

In bas-relief Profiles of:

			£ p
King Edward VII	two handled	90mm	75.00
King Edward VII	three handled	90mm	85.00
King Edward VII	three handled	120mm	110.00
King George V	two handled	90mm	85.00
King George V	three handled	120mm	110.00

These are usually found with corresponding commemorative devices.

The following decorations in relief may also be found, and details are given in the relevant chapters:–

Durham Abbey Knocker	10E
Mary Queen of Scots	10E
Stratford Sanctuary Knocker	10E
Shakespeare	10K6
Lincoln Imp Beaker	10L.11

Puff Box and Lid

Pomade Box and Lid

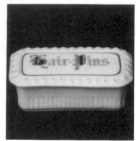
Hairpin Box

Candlestick, Column 153mm

Candlestick, Column 69mm

Candle Bracket

Tankard Mug with Everted Rim

Tankard Mug, Early

Tankard Mug, Angular Handle

Shaped Pepper Castor

Menu Holder

Hair Tidy and Lid

*W.H. Goss Face in Relief on
Loving Cup*

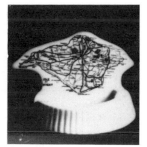

*Ashtray with Map of Isle of
Wight*

*Brass Holder Containing
Posy Vase*

*Copper and Porcelain Dish
Dia. 110mm*

Goss Plated Spoon

Brass Pipe Rack

M Metalware

A metal teaspoon was produced with the permission of W.H. Goss, bearing the name 'Goss' in the bowl, and having a handle in the shape of the Portland Vase. On this Portland Vase was an enamelled coat of arms, usually that of London, but several others are known.

One example has the word 'SILVER' clearly impressed into the shaft but the base metal is obviously nickel-silver, which takes on a dull yellowish hue unless kept regularly polished. Presumably these spoons were originally silver-plated, but time and wear have resulted in many losing their plating to some extent.

Production of these spoons is estimated to have taken place from about 1905 until the mid-1920s, and they were made in Birmingham by the firm of Arbuckle (no longer in existence). Arbuckles were large producers of such seaside souvenirs, and the 'Goss' spoons would only have represented a very small portion of the firm's total output. They were retailed by many Goss agents at 1/- each with various coats of arms enamelled in correct colours. Retailers obtained their supplies from the sole wholesale agent, Henry Jones & Co. Ltd., St. Paul's Churchyard, London.

Length of Spoon 120mm £35.00

See also 10L.11 DOMESTIC AND UTILITY WARES for porcelain spoon.

A Pipe-rack, a Posy Vase holder and a Mantel Clock, all carrying Goss porcelain inserts (usually bearing arms commemorating Queen Victoria's Diamond Jubilee, not of a design found elsewhere on Goss china), but made of Brass, can be found. The combination of porcelain and brass was the idea of William Henry Goss himself. The brass manufacturer was Harcourt, and a registered number of 128998 is quoted, which indicates a date of 1889. Possibly Harcourts were anticipating the Golden Jubilee, but there are probably other examples with normal coats of arms. (Note: it is necessary to dismantle these items to find the 'Goshawk/W.H. Goss' mark. Sometimes the corners of the plaque have been trimmed to fit the brass holder by the manufacturer).

Price range £75.00–£100.00

There are two other Goss items which have metal surrounds. In each case they have flat circular porcelain bases and raised (a) copper and (b) silver rims fitted to them, converting them to a variety of ash or pin trays.

The copper-mounted piece bears the Flags of the Allies decoration, while the silver rimmed dish carries a coat of arms.

(a) Diameter of porcelain portion of copper dish 70mm

Overall diameter 104mm £20.00

(b) Silver rim dish £30.00

N Dolls

During the First World War, Huntley Goss manufactured dolls in an attempt to save his ailing factory. He thought that the Goss Factory could become the chief source of supply for porcelain dolls' heads, arms and legs because the German firms could no longer export their ware to Great Britain as trade with the enemy had been cut off since 1914.

It took much time and expense to buy the correct equipment and make the moulds, as well as organise the sales. Goss dolls, with their mohair and beautiful hand painted faces, had only just begun to capture the English toy market, despite their high price, when the war ended in November 1918. In no time at all the German factories resumed their highly competitive exports and the trade tailed off. Noel Goss, eldest son of Huntley, said that the firm did not manage to break even with this line and the extra losses only added to the firm's financial troubles. Manufacture had commenced in 1916 and no more were made after 1918.

Goss dolls can be identified by the word 'GOSS' impressed into the base of the neck at the back, quite unlike any other Goss mark. Under this was a mould number, sometimes prefixed with the letter G.

From head to toe, lengths varied from 230 mm to 700 mm, depending on whether they were baby, child or lady dolls. All left the Goss factory dressed in Edwardian style clothing with frilly petticoats and lacy outer garments.

Value is dependent on condition, a wig being preferable to moulded hair, and glass eyes more interesting than painted ones. If a doll has its original clothing it is of higher value than one without.

The following dolls have been recorded to date. The publishers will be pleased to learn of any further varieties for inclusion in future editions of this guide.

Model Number	Type	Length	Hair	Eyes	Arms	Legs
8	Child	700mm	mohair	painted	china	china
15	Child	400mm	mohair	glass	china	china
19	Child	650mm	real	glass	china	china
25	Child	440mm	mohair	glass	china	china
30	Child	400mm	mohair	glass	china	stuffed
31	Child	340mm	red	glass	china	stuffed
G4	Baby	350mm	painted	painted	china	stuffed
G5	Baby	330mm	painted	painted	china	stuffed
G9	Child	400mm	mohair	painted	china	stuffed
G13	Baby	230mm	painted	painted	china	stuffed

The values tend to be subjective but range between £350.00 and £425.00

Doll Model D15

Doll Model D30

Doll Model G9

Doll Model 8

Doll Model G4

Doll Model 13

Doll Model 31

Doll Model 19

11 · The Third Period: 1930–1939

O   BUILDINGS AND MONUMENTS
P   FLOWER GIRLS
Q   TOBY JUGS
R   FIGURES AND ANIMALS
S   WARE CARRYING THE 'W H GOSS AND GOSHAWK' AND 'W H GOSS ENGLAND' TRADEMARKS
T   WARE MARKED 'W H GOSS COTTAGE POTTERY' OR 'ROYAL BUFF'
U   HAND PAINTED WARE

Child kneeling on a cushion, at prayer. 165mm. The third period, coloured, variety is shown here.

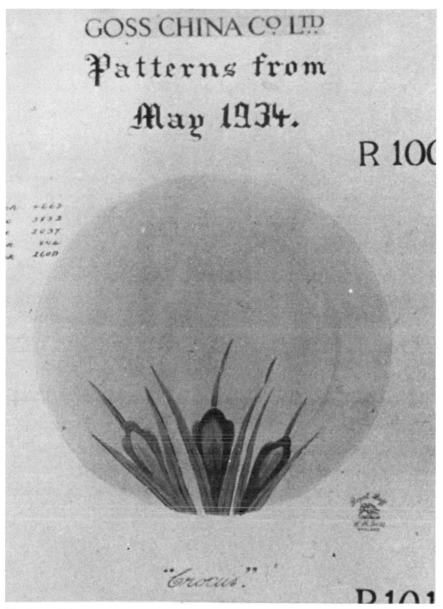

Third period Goss Crocus pattern (taken from design book) for Royal Buff *ware*

Introduction

Armorial ware continued in production until 1934, and has been listed as Second Period as the majority of pieces were produced between 1881 and 1929, during the family ownership of the pottery. After 1930, the new owner, Harold Taylor Robinson re-named the firm 'The Goss China Co Ltd' and had control over many other crested china firms including Arcadian, Coronet Ware, Swan, Robinson and Leadbeater etc. (See *Crested China* by Sandy Andrews for the full story). Moulds from these other potteries were used at the Goss Works, as well as original Goss moulds. Pieces made during this period include porcelain (glazed parian) and pottery. The latter tended to be glazed on the base, making the Goshawk blacker and darker. This situation continued until 1934, although Robinson was made bankrupt in 1932. After May 1934 when he took over Willow Art, the Goshawk appeared on china from Willow Art moulds. The word 'ENGLAND' appeared on most but not all of the factory marks, mainly after 1935. The pattern books of the 'Goss China Co Ltd' were registered in the name of Messrs Allied English Potteries Ltd and included the Royal Buff designs used on the beige earthenware tea services.

The sales of heraldic ware alone were not enough to keep the firm viable and production began to change to the brightly coloured toby jugs, comical figures and animals, Cottage Pottery Teasets, Royal Buff Ware and earthenware Commemorative mugs and ashtrays in an attempt to keep up with changing trends and fashions in the roaring twenties. During the thirties trade was grinding to a halt and one ex-works manager said that at that time, the predominant products were the famous Goss flower girls, bowls of china flowers and the like, mostly for the American market. In 1939 the factory was closed.

The Goshawk was used during Robinson's ownership in preference to other factory names because Goss had always been the market leader and stood for quality and perfection. The cataloguing of the other factories' wares for the *Price Guide to Crested China* has shown which of the Third Period Goss, or Goss England as it is popularly known, originates from Arcadian, Willow Art etc., the most common ranges being white glazed buildings and black cats.

A large amount of difficult to describe and list domestic ware of the late period is constantly coming to light. All of this is of relatively little value and the reader is advised to refer to the DOMESTIC AND ORNAMENTAL WARE Chapters and to take the value of a similar item for the piece in question.

It should be remembered that all prices in this book are for the *items* of Goss only and *not* for any decorations which may appear on them.

O   Buildings and Monuments

Except where noted, all these models were white-glazed, and
usually carried the appropriate coat of arms. Many of them
can also be found bearing the manufacturer's mark of an
associated company, usually Willow Art or Arcadian.

An Clachan Cottage – in full colour, produced solely as a
souvenir of the 1938 Empire Exhibition, at which had been
built a full size replica of this Cottage ... 100mm ... 650.00

£ p

A second version of the **An Clachan Cottage** can also be found –
but it is in fact the small version of **Robert Burns' Cottage**,
merely re-named and, on the example seen displays the motif
of the 1938 Exhibition and a GOSS ENGLAND mark

	Length 62mm	650.00

Ann Hathaway's Cottage fully coloured

Length	78mm	47.50
	110mm	65.00
	133mm	75.00

Banbury Cross

(a)	White	127mm	65.00
(b)	Brown or Blue/Brown	127mm	175.00

Burns Statue.
Seated with dog at feet ... 170mm ... 45.00

Big Ben

	100mm	35.00
With some colouring	100mm	40.00
	134mm	40.00
	152mm	40.00
	170mm	50.00

Canterbury Cathedral ... 64mm ... 55.00

Cenotaph

90mm	20.00
145mm	35.00

Chesterfield Church ... 76mm ... 60.00

Clachan Empire Exhibition Tower and Stadium
Glazed, grey, and bearing a late colour transfer of the *Clachan
Empire Exhibition*, 1938 motif. This model may have been in-
tended for use as an ash-tray, as the pictorial portion is 'dished' ... 125mm ... 100.00

Clifton Suspension Bridge ... 64mm ... 65.00

Edith Cavell Monument ... 180mm ... 65.00

Norwich Cathedral

Banbury Cross

Big Ben

Chesterfield Church

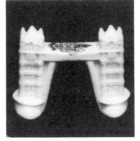

Tower Bridge

St. Paul's Cathedral

The Cenotaph

Westminster Abbey, West Front

Temple Bar

Norwich Edith Cavell Memorial

The Old Curiosity Shop

Windsor Castle, Round Tower

		£ p
Hindhead Sailor's Stone	95mm	45.00
Houses of Parliament	64mm	50.00
King Alfred's Statue	170mm	70.00
John Knox's House in full colour	102mm	350.00
Marble Arch, London	40mm	35.00
	57mm	40.00
Nelson's Column	100mm	70.00
Norwich Cathedral	Length 105mm	60.00
Old Curiosity Shop	46mm	60.00
Rock of Ages with verses of hymn on one side.	79mm	30.00
Rock of Gibraltar, menu holder See illustration on jacket rear	Length 160mm	225.00
Rufus Stone	100mm	30.00
Shakespeare's Birthplace in full colour	Length 40mm	40.00
	78mm	47.50
	102mm	65.00
	115mm	75.00
St. Paul's Cathedral	75mm	45.00
	90mm	50.00
	120mm	55.00
Temple Bar	65mm	50.00
Tower Bridge	58mm	65.00
Westminster Abbey	52mm	45.00
	133mm	55.00
Windsor Castle	53mm	55.00
Windsor Round Tower	76mm	40.00
York Minster	56mm	60.00

An Clachan Cottage

Rock of Ages

Shakespeare's Birthplace

John Knox's House

Shakespeare Bust

The Rock of Gibraltar

King Alfred's Statue

Penguin on Ash Tray

Two Babies on Tray

Father and Child Beside Open Bag 'Married Bliss'

Gin and It

Two Coloured Children on Log

P Flower Girls

The brightly coloured porcelain flower girls were the last successful series made by the Goss factory and spanned the 1930's. Several of these were made in two sizes and ranged between the tiny 68mm, often a cruet, and the more elegant 170mm.

All but one of the larger sizes of these ladies are named, the exception being the Bell lady. Small sizes were often unnamed, probably because of lack of room on the base to do so. They were all hand painted by paintresses who signed their initials in enamel on the base. No two flower girls are decorated the same and the range of colours includes purple, blue, pink, yellow, green and crimson, with great variation in colours used. The word 'ENGLAND' appears on most but not all of the factory stamp marks.

			£ p
Annette		100mm	110.00
		135mm	195.00
Balloon Seller		90mm	130.00
		130mm	175.00
Barbara seated on settee		110mm	240.00
Bell Lady		92mm	75.00
Bridesmaid		90mm	95.00
		140mm	145.00
Bunty			220.00
Cruet two ladies in full colour, one salt, one pepper,			
	(a) Bridesmaid and Granny	Each 68mm	60.00
	(b) Lorna and Peggy	Each 85mm	70.00
Daisy		120mm	160.00
Pair of 'Daisy' Flower Girls mounted on Wooden Bookends		Pair	325.00
Doris. Reputed to exist but unverified			
Dutch Girl		140mm	175.00
Edyth		140mm	170.00
Granny		90mm	115.00
Gwenda		130mm	155.00

Annette

The Balloon Seller

Barbara

Bell Lady

Bridesmaid, 140mm

Dutch Girl

Cruet Salt

Cruet Pepper

Pair of 'Daisy Bookends'
Left-Hand . . .

. . . and Right-Hand

Granny

Edyth

294

		£ p
Joan	130mm	170.00
See illustration on jacket rear		
Lady Beth		190.00
Lady Betty	160mm	190.00
Lady Freda		220.00
Lady Marie	145mm	215.00
Lady Rose	170mm	170.00
Lorna	90mm	130.00
Miss Julia	170mm	190.00
Miss Prudence	135mm	215.00
Mistress Ford	100mm	215.00
Mistress Page	105mm	215.00
Peggy	90mm	145.00
	120mm	190.00
Phyllis	95mm	215.00
Un-named Lady Pink dress, black bonnet	170mm	100.00

A series of 6 figures entitled 'The Wedding Group', modelled from the original designs of the American artist C.H. Twelvetrees, were produced as follows:

The Bride 'God Bless Her'	95mm	175.00
The Bridegroom 'God Help Him'	100mm	175.00
The Best Man 'No Wedding Bells for Him'	95mm	220.00
The Mother-in-Law 'But a Very Nice One'	105mm	220.00
The Parson 'Solemn and Businesslike'	100mm	220.00
The Bridesmaid	90mm	95.00

Gwenda

Lady Betty

Joan

Lady Marie

Lady Rose

Lorna

Miss Julia

Miss Prudence

Mistress Page

Peggy

Phyllis

Un-named Lady, Pink Dress,
Black Bonnet

The Bride

The Bridegroom

The Best Man

The Mother-in-Law

The Parson

The Bridesmaid 90mm

Toby Jug 100mm Coloured

Toby Jug 60mm Coloured

Toby Jug 85mm

Toby Jug 90mm Coloured

Toby Jug 100mm Coloured

Toby Jug, Female, 70mm

Q Toby Jugs

Apart from the Stratford Toby Jug and basin and the 'Churchill' Toby Jug, all Goss Toby Jugs are Third Period products and a wide selection of other crested china manufacturers' moulds were used. Sizes range from miniatures, little more than 30mm high, to larger sizes in the region of 200mm high. Female Toby Jugs were also made. The same jug is often found in a variety of colours.

		£ p
Toby Jug British Sailor, blue colouring	60mm	55.00
Toby Jug White glazed and crested	67mm	45.00
	80mm	50.00
Toby Jug miniature (Male and Female Figures)	40mm	60.00
Toby Jug Multi-coloured See illustration on jacket front	70mm	60.00
Toby Jug, Multi-coloured, female	70mm	60.00
Toby Jug Multi-coloured, also found with one arm forming a handle	85mm	70.00
	160mm	120.00
Toby Jug Multi-coloured	50mm	60.00
	100mm	100.00
	127mm	100.00
	160mm	120.00

For **Stratford Toby Jug** and **Stratford Toby Basin**
  See 10E NAMED MODELS AND SPECIAL SHAPES

For **Churchill Toby Jug**
  See 10K5 MISCELLANEOUS ITEMS

R Figures and Animals

Many figures were incorporated into ash-trays, cruets, posy-holders, and other domestic wares – while some appear to be purely ornamental. Ware in this section almost without exception originates from the Arcadian and Willow Art factories. Should you be unable to find a particular piece listed here, please consult *The Price Guide to Crested China* where the model should be found. The price will be similar.

		£ p
Babies (two) seated on Ash Tray *That's the one Daddy told Nurse!*	70mm	55.00
Black Baby as Ash Tray		65.00
Black Boy – *Cigarettes*	100mm	65.00
Black Boy and Girl seated on log	80mm	65.00
Black Boys, two seated on log	80mm	65.00
Black Cat in Boot	58mm	60.00
Black Cat on Dish	115mm × 70mm	50.00
Black Cat (seated) on Horse-shoe Shaped Pin Box	70mm	55.00
Black Cat Playing Golf on Golf Ball	60mm	65.00
Black Cat on Pouffe, blue handles *Good Luck*	93mm	50.00
Black Cat Seated at Head of Horseshoe as Ash Tray	Approx. 42mm	45.00
Black Cheshire Cat (identical to white variety)	90mm	85.00
Budgerigar		35.00
Burns, Bust of	136mm	17.50
Caddy, with Bag on Golf Ball		60.00
Cat, Seated		35.00
Cat, Seated, with White or Coloured Bow at Neck	60mm	35.00
Cheshire Cat (No base), white or coloured (add £10)	98mm	35.00

Black Cat in Boot

Black Cat on Horseshoe Tray

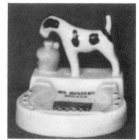

Dog and Whiskey Bottle on Ash Tray

Falstaff

English Folksong Bride

Pixie on a Toadstool

White Boy Holding Open Matchbox

Scottish Lion on Ashtray

Punch and Judy Pepper and Salt

Ashtray, Edward VIII

Box Ashtray, Burns and S.E.E. 1938

Circular Ashtray with Three Rests

			£ p
Chicken White or coloured (add £10)		50mm	35.00
Crest Faced Man with coat of arms on flat face		80mm	40.00
Cruet. Punch (Salt), Judy (Pepper) and Toby (Mustard) in full colour – all on tray			85.00
NOTE: Items from the above set may be found white glazed or in varying shades of lustre			
		Price each	20.00
Dog and Whisky Bottle on Ash Tray 'His Master's Breath'			40.00
Dog, Scottie with blue Tam O'Shanter		60mm	40.00
Dog, Scottie, Black and White with glass eyes		Length 260mm	125.00
Dog, squat, one ear up, some colouring		90mm	40.00
Dog, with one ear up. White or Coloured (add £10)		70mm	35.00
English Folksong Bride standing beside ancient chest		93mm	55.00
Falstaff	(a) Coloured	150mm	100.00
	(b) White	150mm	70.00
Fish, Plaice Two sizes		Length 78mm	30.00
		125mm	30.00
Frog		60mm	35.00
'Gin and It' Two seated ladies at side of dish, coloured.		100mm × 65mm	60.00
Golfer, standing on golf-ball, holding clubs – in centre of hexagonal dish		90mm × 75mm	50.00
Gnome, standing carrying a shell filled with produce under each arm. Fully coloured		128mm	300.00
Jester on Ashtray, coloured		64mm	60.00
(Ann) Hathaway Bust		80mm	22.00
		135mm	30.00
Hippopotamus		Length 88mm	60.00
Lady in Bathing Costume and Cap on Ash Tray			45.00

Cat, Seated with Bow

Cat, Seated

Budgerigar

Dog, with One Ear Up

Dog, Squat, One Ear Up

Scottie Dog, Length 260mm

Chicken

Rabbit

Rhinoceros

Plaice

Shetland Pony

Duck Posy Holder

302

		£ p
Lady Godiva on Horseback. Small, glazed	80mm	50.00
Lady Reclining on Top of Box coloured	100mm × 85mm	250.00
Lifeboat Man	140mm	35.00
'Married Bliss' Posy Vase (Coloured)		
(a) Girl, holding baby, with open bag in front		55.00
(b) Man ,holding baby, with open bag in front		55.00
New Forest Pony	65mm	45.00
Norwich Canary	94mm	100.00
Nude Female Seated on rock. Coloured with holes in base.		
(For flower arrangement)	190mm	70.00
Penguin	90mm	40.00
Penguin on Ash Tray	92mm	75.00
Pig, with verse	80mm	40.00
Pixie. Seated on toadstool (Coloured)	54mm	50.00
Policeman, with raised hand: 'Stop'	94mm	50.00
Rabbits, blue, yellow, green, brown or Royal Buff	40mm	22.00
	50mm	25.00
	60mm	26.00
	80mm	26.00
	100mm	26.00
Rabbit, White	60mm	30.00
Racehorse and Jockey. Oval base, some colouring	108mm	220.00
Rhinoceros Length	90mm	60.00
Royston Crow, black	66mm	125.00
Always unmarked		
Scots Boy on thistle shaped dish		
and holding bunch of heather. Some colouring	90mm	55.00
Scottish Lion. Stylized, standing on square ashtray base.		
Scottish Empire Exhibition 1938. Coloured, green trim	103mm	75.00

			£ p
Shakespeare Bust	(a) White, unglazed	80mm	22.00
	(b) White, unglazed	110mm	26.00
	(c) White, unglazed	135mm	30.00
	(d) Bronzed	135mm	50.00
	(e) White, unglazed	165mm	30.00
	(f) Bronzed	175mm	65.00

Shell — 70mm — 20.00

Shetland Pony No base — 76mm — 45.00

Swan — 50mm — 25.00

Trusty Servant. Coloured. Not to be confused with the earlier variety — 132mm — 125.00

Toucan. Coloured, on an Ash Tray shaped like a bird's foot — 61mm — 50.00

Welsh Lady. Bust. With some colouring — 62mm — 35.00

White Boy holding open matchbox as holder 'Matches' — 100mm — 35.00

S. Ware carrying the 'W.H. Goss and Goshawk' and 'W.H. Goss England' Trademarks

		£ p
Ash Tray. Circular with three rests	Dia. 70mm	10.00
	Dia. 118mm	10.00
Ash Tray. Oval, with rests at each end	Length 100mm	12.00
Ash Tray. Rectangular with rests in each corner.	Length 135mm width 103mm	15.00
Ash Tray. Square, card symbols in each corner	60mm sq.	20.00
Ash Tray. Box-shaped. Thistle, spray of heather, Bust of Burns transfer, Burns' cottage transfer and Scottish Empire Exhibition motif appear on this and similar very late pieces	Length 120mm	26.00
Ash Tray. Shamrock shaped	Length 95mm	20.00
Ash Tray Various colours – *Edward VIII, Crowned May 12 1937* in bas-relief	Dia. 132mm	30.00
Basket. Biscuit colour, with tiny flowers at base of handle	90mm × 75mm	40.00
Basket containing six milk bottles	50mm	35.00
Bass Bottle and Glass on Dish	60mm × 35mm	40.00
Bass Bottle and Silver Beer Mug on Dish	115mm × 70mm	40.00
Bon-Bon Dish Basket weave design, plain with brown handles	157mm	20.00
Boot	70mm × 40mm	30.00
Bottle with Cork	60mm × 70mm	30.00
Bottle 'One Special Irish' or 'One Special Scotch' with cork	95mm	30.00
Bowl. Matt black inside and out.	Dia. 85mm	10.00
Bucket	55mm	20.00
Butter Dish in Wooden Surround 'Butter'	Overall Dia. 155mm	15.00
Cake plate, with side tabs	Width 220mm	12.00

Bass Bottle and Glass on Tray

Ash Tray, Rectangular, 135mm long

Bowl, 85mm Dia., Matt Black

Butter Dish in Wooden Surround

Cake Plate Burns and S.E.E. 1938

Mug 80mm

Cream Jug, Double Lip, No Handle

Cup and Saucer, Taper, Shaped Handle

Cup and Saucer, Curved

Cup and Saucer, Taper

Cup and Saucer, Fluted and Patterned

Cup and Saucer, Straight

£   p

Cake Plate. Burns, thistles, heather and S.E.E. 1938
decoration — Width 250mm — 30.00

Chamber Pot — 55mm × 40mm — 20.00

Cheese Dish, green — Length 165mm — 20.00

Chess Pawn — 50mm — 30.00

Chess Rook — 50mm — 25.00

Coronation Mug 1937 – King George VI and Queen Elizabeth. — 80mm — 35.00
   This and any other item bearing this design would be worth
   approximately the same.

Cruet   Salt Castor in form of an apple, coloured — 30mm — 30.00
         Pepper Castor in form of an orange, coloured — 30mm — 30.00
         Basket, coloured beige to hold the above — Length 80mm — 20.00

Cream Jug, double lip, no handle — 40mm — 5.00

Cream Jug, one lip and handle — 60mm — 6.50

Cup and Saucer Various — Approx. 70mm — 5.00

Dish quadrifoil — Length 140mm — 8.00

Dish. Oval, with tapered sides, green trim, and rose
   decoration inside — 30.00

Dish, Circular — Dia. 105mm — 4.00

Dish, shaped, oval — Length 142mm — 8.50

Egg, with Flapper's Head — 38mm — 30.00

Egyptian Canopic Jar with Anubis Head
   one-piece, fixed head — 75mm — 40.00

Fireplace with Kettle and Black Cat – *There's No*
   Place Like Home or *Home Sweet Home* — 90mm × 90mm — 35.00

Fruit Bowl, orange lustre — Height 110mm   Dia. 245mm — 20.00

Honey section dish and cover with bee knob [2] Square 145mm × 145mm — 25.00

Lantern. Coloured, hexagonal, with handle — 200mm — 75.00

Lavatory Pan, brown seat, inscribed *Ashes* — 60mm — 18.50

Whiskey, Soda and Glass on Thistle Ashtray

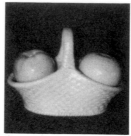

Cruet: Apple and Orange in Basket

Egyptian Canopic Jar with fixed Anubis Head

Bulbous Milk Jug

Mug with Little Red Riding Hood Scene

Green Posy Ring

Quadrifoil Dish

Octagonal Sugar Bowl, Late

Welsh Lady Teapot

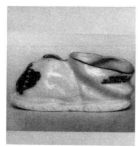

Shoe, John Waterson's Clog

Shaped Vase

Coloured Lantern

		£ p
Match Holder, octagonal *Matches*	45mm	6.00
Milk Jug, bulbous	90mm	7.00
Mug with floral decoration, two handled	118mm	20.00
	133mm	20.00
Mug, one-handled	100mm	12.00
Mug, Little Red Riding Hood Scene	100mm	70.00
Open Umbrella	50mm × 35mm	25.00
Posy Dish. Blue or green. Circular	Dia. 155mm	13.00
Preserve Jar and Lid. Shaped	60mm	30.00
Preserve Pot and Lid orange peel pattern in bas-relief. Orange colour	90mm	30.00
Prime Cheddar Cheese		30.00
Puzzle Jug	70mm	25.00
Rose Bowl. Pink, with green foliage, sometimes with rose knop on lid [1]	80mm × 50mm	30.00
Salt and Pepper Pots Bulbous, usually found with late transfer decoration (add £10)	Each 54mm	10.00
Salt and Pepper Pots octagonal	Each 88mm	8.00
Shaving Mug	100mm	45.00
Shoe (John Waterson's Clog in Arcadian)	Length 80mm	35.00
Slipper	38mm	30.00
Sugar Basin, octagonal	Dia. 70mm	10.00
	85mm	12.00
	100mm	15.00
Sugar Basin, shaped	Height 45mm Dia. 80mm	5.00
Sugar Basin, circular	Height 60mm Dia. 95mm	5.00
Sweetmeat Dish, green	Length 165mm	15.00
Tankard, shaped with curved handle. Huntsman with hounds and fox in bas-relief. Coloured	95mm	55.00

		£ p
Tea-pot and lid in form of Welsh Lady, coloured Her arms forming handle and spout	152mm	65.00
Teaplates Various	Dia. 150mm	3.00
Thimble	38mm	35.00
Thistle Vase	44mm	10.00
Toast-Rack, green	Length 100mm	15.00
Vases. Various shapes and sizes under 70mm	Each around	4.00
Weston-Super-Mare Floral Clock Surround coloured Can be found with original clock for which add £25.00	Length 230mm	70.00
Whisky Bottle, Soda Syphon and Glass on		
(a) Horse-shoe Ash Tray	87mm	40.00
(b) Thistle Ash Tray	87mm	40.00
Whisky Bottle. Hip-flask type – two-piece	120mm	60.00

COLOURED AND LUSTRE ITEMS

Items such as coffee and tea cups and saucers, sugar basins, milk jugs, teaplates, pin trays, candle holders etc. appear in a variety of colours and lustres. Details of these are given in *Goss China Arms, Decorations and Their Values*. Named models appearing in lustre have thickly gilded handles and look most attractive.

Cottage Pottery Toastrack, Two section

Weston-Super-Mare Floral Clock-holder

Orange Preserve Pot and Lid

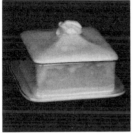

Honey Section Dish and Cover with Bee Knob

Soup Bowl, Octagonal

Cottage Pottery Cheese Dish

Cottage Pottery Pepper Pot

Cottage Tea Service Milk Jug

Cottage Tea Service Oval Dish

Cottage Pottery Four Slice Toast Rack

Cottage Pottery Beaker, 114mm

Cottage Pottery Cup and Saucer

T   W.H. Goss 'Cottage Pottery' and 'Royal Buff'

COTTAGE TEA SERVICE
All pieces are in the shape of a coloured cottage excepting cups,
saucers and plates.   £ p

Biscuit Barrel		150mm	40.00
Butter Dish and Lid	Length	107mm	25.00
Cakeplate	Dia.	240mm	25.00
Cheese Dish and Cover	Length	170mm	35.00
Cottage Mustard Pot		50mm	25.00
Cottage Pepper Shaker		50mm	25.00
Cottage Salt Shaker		50mm	25.00

The above three may be found in a rectangular tray,
for which add £30.00

Cup and Saucer		75mm	20.00
Dish, oval	Length	125mm	25.00
Milk Jug		60mm	25.00
		108mm	30.00
Sugar Basin and Lid		110mm	30.00
Sugar Basin		60mm	25.00
Teaplate	Dia.	150mm	17.50
Teapot and lid		115mm	40.00
Toast Rack	(a) To hold four slices Length	100mm	30.00
	(b) To hold two slices Length	70mm	25.00

COTTAGE POTTERY AND ROYAL BUFF

Advertising stand see **8** ADVERTISING
WARE AND LEAFLETS

Beaker. King Cole and his fiddlers **three on reverse in bas-relief**	100mm	30.00

		£ p
Beaker, Taper	85mm	11.00
with or without handle	114mm	14.00

Butter Dish in wooden surround 'Take a little butter'.
Decorated with tulips or similar — Dia. 115mm — 22.00
for *CAKEPLATE* see *PLATE*

Coffee Pot, octagonal	200mm	35.00
Cup and Saucer, octagonal	65mm	22.00
Cup and Saucer	75mm	18.50

Derringer, hand painted reproduction of, circa 1840.
Open or posy holder with two holes for hanging. Marked
Underglaze porcelain by GOSS — Length 205mm — 75.00

Duck. Coloured posy holder. Bears inscription on base:
Hand-painted underglaze porcelain by GOSS
(a) Length 100mm Height 58mm — 50.00
(b) Length 135mm Height 80mm — 65.00

Fern Pot, scallop edge	92mm	20.00
Four Egg Cups on Stand, Basket Weave	Set	40.00
Six Egg Cups on Stand. Basket Weave	Set	50.00

Honey Pot and Lid. Beehive shaped with bee as
knob on lid — 97mm — 35.00

Honey Section Dish with bee as knob [2] — Square145mm × 145mm — 30.00

Horseshoe decorative. Appears in several pastel shades — 120mm — 20.00

Jam Dish Basket weave with some
coloured fruit decoration — Dia. 100mm — 20.00

Jam Dish Two section basket weave — Length 170mm — 20.00

Jug, cylindrical or bulbous — 85mm — 15.00

Jug. Bulbous. Widdecombe Fair
decoration — 125mm — 55.00

Little Brown Jug With title or verse and
sometimes also a Black Cat transfer — 60mm–100mm — 20.00

Beehive preserve Pot and Cover

Cottage Pottery Plate 'Shakespearian Cottages'

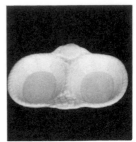

Pottery Jam Dish, Two Section

The Little Brown Jug

2 slice Toastrack and Preserve Dish

Cottage Pottery Two-handled Mug 102mm

Cottage Pottery Preserve Pot and Lid

Bulbous Jug, Widdecombe Fair Decoration

Royal Buff Tankard with Hunting Scene

Tankard, Cottage Decoration in relief

Cottage Pottery Teaplate

Cottage Pottery Basket-weave Jam Dish and Lid

		£ p
Milk Jug	70mm	22.00
Mug. Two-handled, decorated with apples, and carrying the quotation *Yaas, 'tis thirsty work – 'ave a drop o' Zomerzet Zider.*	102mm	40.00
Mug	80mm	15.00
Pepper Castor, shaped	90mm	10.00
Pin Tray, circular	Dia. 70mm	18.00
Plate	Dia. 160mm	18.50
Plate. Coloured, depicting Shakespearian cottages	Dia. 220mm	30.00
Plate. With inscription *Education is Better than Wealth*	265mm × 230mm	30.00
Preserve Pot and Lid. Poppies and *East, West, Home is Best* or similar decoration and verse Can also be found with a Pixie finial	110mm	22.50
Salt and Pepper Pots oviform, Royal Buff	Each 55mm	10.00
Salt Castor, shaped	90mm	10.00
Sugar Basin	60mm	15.00
Sugar Basin and cover, Taper	Dia. 110mm 75mm	17.50
Tankard, Widdecombe Fair decoration	125mm	55.00
Tankard, shaped, one handle	95mm	15.00
Teapot, Taper	115mm	30.00
Teapot Stand	Dia. 145mm	18.00
Toast Rack. Two section	Length 110mm	18.50
Toast Rack and Two section Marmalade Dish Basket Weave	Length 175mm	22.00
Toast Rack with coloured Pixie seated at each end	80mm	40.00

U Hand Painted Ware

As well as the normal 'W.H. GOSS ENGLAND' trade mark, there is also a 'Hand painted' mark which is usually found on domestic ware, 'Royal Buff' and 'Cottage Pottery' which covers a large range of items, varying from a cottage-shaped tea set to a pottery (as opposed to porcelain) range of 'Little Brown Jugs', beakers, cups and saucers and various other items of domestic ware. See sections S and T.

Obviously the original Goss moulds were still available during the third period, and a number of shapes were used to carry a range of floral patterns ranging from delicate pastel shades to rather garish hand-painted examples.

It is difficult to accurately list all Third Period ware as there are so many variations. If you have a similar piece to one shown than a price in the same region will apply. The reader should consult also DOMESTIC AND UTILITY WARES, ORNAMENTAL ARTICLES and the First Period after checking all the possibilities in Third Period Goss.

See *Goss China Arms, Decorations and their Values* for full details and values of all decorations on Goss china.

CRESTED CHINA

By Sandy Andrews

Collecting crested china has become one of the most interesting, rewarding and affordable hobbies enjoyed by collectors today. Over two hundred manufacturers copied W H Goss's idea of producing china replicas and applying coats of arms. The history of these manufacturers and their models is told in this large, lavishly illustrated, 304 page book which not only lists all known manufacturers of crested ware but also includes line drawings of their individual trademarks to aid identification.

A short history of each factory and its owners is given where possible including much interesting and often amusing information. The wares of one factory were often very similar to those of another and this perplexing link is explained along with other peculiarities. All of this is written in the light-hearted style of a true, enthusiastic fellow collector. It will answer many of the questions you have always wanted to ask but never knew where to look. The illustrations alone make this book a delight. Of 750 photographs of actual pieces, 90 are in full colour and are an aid to identifying models in your collection and a preview of delights yet to be found. The book can be used in conjunction with *The Price Guide to Crested China*.

303mm × 220mm. 304 pages. Cased. 753 illustrations. Colour jacket £14.95.

THE PRICE GUIDE TO CRESTED CHINA

Sandy Andrews and Nicholas Pine

This book lists and prices every known piece of crested china, and provides an update to the list of shapes given in *Crested China*, with every item priced at current ratail selling prices.

Recently gathered information including some 2,000 new pieces, 55 new manufacturers and 65 new marks makes the price guide an invaluable complement to *Crested China*.

It can, of course, be used alone as a Price Guide.

217mm × 155mm. 288 pages. Cased. Colour jacket £9.95.

Goss China Arms, Decorations and their Values

Nicholas Pine

Goss China collecting was a craze during late Victorian and Edwardian times. Tens of thousands of pieces of Goss Heraldic Porcelain were sold throughout the country as souvenirs to bring home for the family what-not or mantelpiece. This fascinating book, written by the leading authority on the subject, lists, describes and values all the different coats of arms and decorations which appear on Goss models – over 7,000 of them.

Up-to-date market values are given throughout the book showing the premium to be added to a piece for a crest or decoration.

Its 13 chapters include: U.K. and overseas arms, Royal, Nobility, Educational, Ecclesiastical, Commemorative, Transfer printed, Regimental, Flora & Fauna, Flags, Welsh, Masonic and late decorations. These are further sub-divided into 55 easy-to-use sections – with prices.

The book contains 415 illustrations in 120 packed pages and is sewn and strongly casebound with a full colour jacket.

The book has been designed for use in conjunction with **The Price Guide to Goss China** by the same author. Collectors and dealers who possess a copy of the price guide are strongly advised to acqure this book so that accurate up-to-date values may be obtained for each piece, for, as often as not, the decoration on a particular piece is worth much more than the piece itself.

245mm × 213mm. 120 pages. 415 illustrations. £9.95.

Goss & Crested China Ltd. are the leading dealers in Heraldic China

We have been buying and selling for over fifteen years and our experienced staff led by Nicholas Pine will be able to answer your questions and assist you whether you are a novice or an experienced collector.

A constantly changing attractively priced stock of some 5,000 pieces may be viewed at our Horndean showrooms which includes Goss cottages, fonts, crosses, shoes, lighthouses, models etc. and the full range of crested ware including military, animals, buildings etc. covering all the other manufacturers.

Visitors are welcome to call during business hours of 9.00–5.30 any day except Sunday. Those travelling long distances are advised to telephone for an appointment so that they may be sure of receiving personal attention upon arrival.

Most of our business is by mail order and we publish *Goss & Crested China*, a monthly 28 page illustrated catalogue containing hundreds of pieces for sale from every theme and in every price range. The catalogue is available by annual subscription; please send for details.

In addition, if you specialise, we will be pleased to offer you particular pieces or crests from time to time as suitable items become available. Please let us know your wants as with our ever-changing stock we will probably have something to suit.

Our service is personal and friendly and all orders and correspondence are dealt with by return. You will find us fair and straightforward to deal with, as we really care about crested china and we hope that this is reflected in our service.

Finally, we are just as keen to buy as we are to sell and offers of individual items or whole collections are always welcome. These will be dealt with by return and the very highest offers will be made.

Milestone Publications
Goss & Crested China Ltd,
62 Murray Road,
Horndean,
Hampshire
PO8 9JL.

Telephone: Horndean (0705) 597440

Other titles available from
Milestone Publications

Please send for full catalogue

Crested China. The History of Heraldic Souvenir Ware
Sandy Andrews

The 1985 Price Guide to Crested China including revisions to
Crested China
Nicholas Pine and Sandy Andrews

Goss China Arms, Decorations and their values
Nicholas Pine

Take Me Back To Dear Old Blighty.
The Great War through the eyes of the Heraldic China Manufacturers
Robert Southall

Arcadian Arms China Catalogue (reprinted)

The Goss Record War Edition (1916) (reprinted)

Goss for Collectors – The Literature
John Magee

Let's Collect Goss China
Alf Hedges

Goss and Other Crested China
Nicholas Pine

Goss & Crested China. Illustrated monthly catalogues listing items for sale.
Available by Annual Subscription. Details upon request from
62, Murray Road, Horndean, Hants. PO8 9JL.

In Preparation:
W H GOSS, THE MAN, THE FACTORY, THE PORCELAIN
Lynda and Nicholas Pine.